Feasting on the Father

William L Smith

A devotional walk through Song of Solomon chapter 2 verse 4.

"He has taken me to the banquet hall and His banner over me is love."

Onwards and Upwards Publications, Berkeley House,
11 Nightingale Crescent, West Horsley, Surrey KT24 6PD

www.onwardsandupwards.org

copyright © William L Smith 2012

The author chooses not to capitalise satan or related names even to the point of grammatical incorrectness. At the same time he chooses to capitalise certain references to God, such as 'Him' or 'His'.

ISBN: 978-1-907509-34-6
Cover design: Leah-Maarit

Printed in the UK

Dedication

I dedicate this work to my Father God, who has taught me to know and say, "Abba."

Also to the beautiful children of Iris Ministries, Zimpeto, Mozambique, who, having so little, possess so much. To the church on the Bocaria (city garbage dump) where joy overwhelms poverty and where thanksgiving overwhelms injustice. To Matola Rio, the place of hope, founded by my dear friends George and Jill Nuttall, whose untiring sacrifical love has produced life, hope, love and a future for the children of Mozambique.

My book began its journey among you in what seemed the most difficult of places.

Endorsements

We have known Bill for a number of years and he has captured the essence of the Fathers love and His presence among us. In a world that is desperate, even though it may not know it, for the reality of the saving grace of Jesus, Bill challenges us to live a radical Christian life, one that will overflow and announce that Jesus is Lord. We challenge you to read this book and be challenged.

Phil and Gill Hunt
Founders and Senior Pastors of Lionhunt Ministries

Feasting on the Father is a book that covers every angle of this wonderful theme. To delve into it is to begin to appreciate the sumptuous fare the Christian can enjoy with Father God. So enjoy the meal.

Bob Kilpatrick
National (UK) Co-ordinator of Partners in Harvest

I am constantly being sent manuscripts, especially by new authors. If I'm brutally honest, many of these offer only scraps of revelation. Just occasionally a book comes my way that offers far more than that - a true feast of Abba's wisdom and insight. Bill's book is a great example of this. I unreservedly encourage you to come to the table he has so meticulously and lovingly prepared. Come hungrily and you will not be disappointed. A banquet of brilliance awaits.

Dr Mark Stibbe
Founder and Leader of the Father's House Trust
Bestselling and award-winning author

Acknowledgments

I would like to thank my daughter Rebecca who, through her helplessness, has been used to teach me more than any other what unconditional love means.

I thank Jeremy & Connie Sinnott of Toronto, whose anointed ministry opened up the boxes and let the true God out into the freedom of the only place He can be.

To the people of the 'Gathering Place' in Blandford Forum, thank you. You were used to bring healing and restoration to a very hurting, broken and bleeding 'me' at the lowest time in my life.

To the wonderful fellowship at Lionhunt Ministries where I have been encouraged to fly again, thank you. You are so precious to me.

And finally, to my precious wife, Susanna. You have believed in me and in this book. You kept me going when it seemed easier to withdraw. Your love and steadfast support have been a feast to my heart through this journey.

May the Father's lavish feast be your joy and sustenance.

Contents

BANNER: Flag Waving

Imagine you are standing in front of a crowd of people in one of the poorest countries on earth. You have been asked to preach. You see the sea of faces, each one full of joy in worship - each one just a thread away from starvation. These are the blessed ones! They live in a centre where they receive food every day. They have a bed. They are safe. They are loved. Every day they receive a bowl of rice: rice and cabbage, rice and chicken... or just rice.

A bright kaleidoscope of colour: traditional 'capulanas', a wraparound skirt, threadbare second hand T-shirts, Sunday best shirts, bare feet and worn out flip-flops. This is the scene!

Almost an hour of vibrant praise and worship has just subsided. It is your first time in an overseas ministry situation, the first time preaching with a translator. A deep breath, one more quick prayer and the words begin...

You know you have the right message because on your way to the tin-roofed, well ventilated, church-cum-dining-room, you saw two boys, maybe nine or ten years old. Their heads were close together. They were both sitting on a fence, looking at a Bible. It was open at your text!

So, with renewed confidence, you launch into what is in your heart: "He brought me to the banqueting house and His banner over me is love."

Now I could easily think of many scriptures about poverty, justice, the great hope set before us for a life in heaven which lacks nothing, the comfort of His knowing what this life is really like. Oh yes, plenty of 'good sermons' there that comfortably fit into the scenario.

Instead my heart is stirred with this goodly theme: the place of Christian living, the covering of an unfurled banner called 'Love' under which we all live.

Oh, how they lapped it up - every word more precious food to them than their bowl of rice. Oh, how they raced to the front to fall on their knees before this Jesus, this God above all gods of men.

How much more can your heart be broken?

How much pain can you carry to the throne of grace as you look at your comfortable, take-it-for-granted clothes, your one of many copies of the Bible, your well satisfied body learning to cope with survival rations for a few weeks?

Even as I write this I know many people in this land exist on one bowl of rice a week. My Christian brothers and sisters! One bowl of rice a week! All the time these words hang in the air: "He brought me to the banqueting house and His banner over me is love."

I cannot reconcile such poverty, injustice and unnecessary death with the richness of my home life, the comfort of my church family.

Yet I know His word is true. Abba God is faithful. Every promise is "Yes" and "Amen" in Jesus. Your heart is broken and will always be changed, ruined, never at home in the easy, comfortable western church life.

I long to see two ten-year-olds, heads bowed over a Bible as they stroll along to church in England, to see such passion and joy in the knowledge of God's love over us, in us, upon us and toward us.

The words of Solomon are easy when your freezer is full. Now don't get me wrong - the freezer is *supposed* to be full! But in the comfort of our society such imagery is sweet and simple - and empty of reality for most of us.

Why do I say this?

I hope that by the time I have unpacked what I believe Abba God wants us to see in these words, that you too will have an ache for the reality of the 'Banqueting House' life. Also, I believe that our Christian family in Mozambique will be a little less hungry.

My premise is quite simple. In the banqueting hall is an unfurled banner with the word 'LOVE' blazoned upon it. Now, if the banqueting hall and the banner go together, then the feasting place is our 'natural habitat', because the love of God is always perfect, constant and complete toward us. Wherever we encounter this love we are faced with a feast. Being faced with a feast has implications for who we are... which determines how we live... which has an impact on all those around us, including the rest of 'the Body' - the Bride.

I love the angle Eugene Peterson brings to this scripture:

SS 2:3b, The Message

All I want is to sit in His shade to taste and savour His delicious love. He took me home with Him for a festive meal, but His eyes feasted on me.

See how much it draws out the intimacy and passion of our relationship.

"I just want to sit next to Him, and experience His love. He can't take His eyes off me."

How can I be so adorable to the most magnificent, beautiful man who has ever been? Can your heart and mind grasp this outrageous, glorious truth: "He can't take His eyes off me"?

You are the special, chosen, precious, adopted, desired, loved-from-before-time-began, joint heir with your Shepherd, King, Lover, Brother, Saviour, Friend.

How are we supposed to take this in, to grasp it, to enable our heart and mind to assimilate and receive such magnificent, beyond-words wonder and reality?

I cannot fully grasp this, but with all I am and all I have, I say, "Yes! Lord, I believe. Help me in my unbelief."

SS 2:4-5 (NLB)

He brings me to the banquet hall, so everyone can see how much He loves me. Oh, feed me with your love, your 'raisins' and your 'apples', for I am utterly lovesick!

How do you rate on the lovesick scale?

I remember as a teenager hanging around the newest object of my heart, eyes fastened on her, following her as she moved around a room, hanging about just to walk in her company part of the way home - 'wearing my heart on my sleeve', as I was told. Everyone was aware of who I loved. Oh for such a passion for Jesus, to be so taken up with Him that "I only have eyes for You."

His Banner over us is Love! We are loved by Abba God the same way Jesus is. The Poverty and Justice Bible (CEV) says:

Jn.17:23 (CEV)

They will know You love Your followers as much as You love Me.

It was this love of the Father to and in the Son, and this love from the Son to the Father, uniquely bound together in love through the Holy Spirit, that expressed itself for us on a blood-soaked cross where hung a sin-embracing, spotless, sacrificial man: the Lamb of God.

Yes, this love did not shield from suffering, pain and death. It led to it. It showed its greatness and enormity in sacrifice and death. As we learn to follow in His steps, we face death - death to our own choices - choosing rather to pursue everything that pleases the Father. As Paul says in Philippians:

Ch.3:10-12

I want to know Christ and the power of His resurrection, and fellowship of sharing in His sufferings, becoming like Him in His death, and so, somehow, to attain to the resurrection from the dead. Not that I have already obtained all this, or have already been made perfect, but I press on to take hold of that for which Christ Jesus took hold of me.

Being the beloved of God does not bring a life of ease and comfort. Ask those pioneers who live for Him and die to self in order to build that centre in Mozambique. It is those who hunger and thirst who are filled. Someone has said that "hunger is the currency of heaven".

Paul's hunger for Jesus brought him:

2 Cor.11:23-28

I have worked much harder, been in prison more frequently, been flogged more severely, and been exposed to death again and again. Five times I received from the Jews the forty lashes minus one. Three times I was beaten with rods, once I was stoned, three times I was shipwrecked; I spent a night and a day in the open sea. I have been constantly on the move. I have been in danger from rivers, in danger from bandits, in danger from my own countrymen, in danger at sea; and in danger from false brothers. I have laboured and toiled and have gone without sleep; I have been cold and naked. Beside everything else, I face daily the pressure of my concern for all the churches.

Why?

2 Cor.5:14-15

For Christ's love compels us, because we are convinced that One died for all, and therefore all died. And He died for all, that those who live should no longer live for themselves but for Him who died for them and was raised again.

Is this what took David Wilkerson to the streets of New York to have knives thrust in his face? Did Jackie Pullinger end up in Hong Kong for any other reason? Why else do Rolland and Heidi Baker keep pressing on in the poorest, dirtiest, darkest places on earth to give away this heavenly love? And how about my dear friends George and Jill, in their mid sixties, who return again and again in poor health to the poorest, weakest people they can find, sitting in the dirt of the 'bocaria' (city garbage dump) to show this same love of God; to say nothing of the millions across the world who suffer the most evil tortures for the sake of the name of Jesus, even giving up their lives to embrace "the prize for which God has called me heavenward in Christ Jesus."

I dare to suggest that these people rate highly on God's lovesick register. It is the banqueting place that is forever spread before them, and all of us, that enables and empowers, for moment by moment His unfurled banner of love hangs over us. The Hebrew word for 'banner' in this passage is 'degel'. It means 'that which is meant to be seen'. God intends for His love for us to be something that is seen. He is obviously very proud of His children. Always, in everyday events, situations and circumstances, His love banner is over us as evidence of our value to Him, and His eternal promise and commitment to us.

How conscious are you of His love being over you constantly? How conscious are you of Abba God's desire to demonstrate, moment by moment, situation by situation, experience by experience, that He loves you perfectly? And that this love is the answer, ultimately, to whatever is before you right now?

As the Psalmist says:

Ps.60:4
But for those who fear You, You have raised a banner to be unfurled against the bow.

The Lord's banner, which is a banner of love, is unfurled as His answer to the bow. Every arrow of assault, every cudgel of criticism, every dart of deception, every bullet of belittling, every rock of rejection, every missile of misunderstanding, fist of failure, hand slap of hypocrisy, is confronted with one word: love.

As Solomon's lover delights to sit in his shade (ch.2:3), so we find our security, protection and peace in the shade of His banner of love.

Ps.91:1
He who dwells in the shelter of the Most High will rest in the shadow of the Almighty. I will say of the Lord, 'He is my refuge and my fortress, my God in whom I trust.'

These are not just nice-sounding scripture verses. This is life and light to us for our daily walk into whatever is before us. We have a choice to embrace the truth Abba offers us on the banqueting table, or to struggle on our own to come through.

How are our minds renewed to see God's truth as the answer, despite what our eyes tell us or our emotions try to handle? - By giving ourselves away to Him; by rejecting our self-seeking desires to embrace His desires for us, which are always good, always better! Settle it in your heart, in your mind and with your spirit. Abba has plans for you, to prosper you, "to give you hope and a future and not to harm you" (Jer.29:11). Now, let us get this really settled. Paul says:

Rom.12:1
...offer yourself to God as a holy, pleasing, living sacrifice, which is your spiritual act of worship [or 'your reasonable service'.]

Right, let us reason this through! Here I am - a mortal - with an intellect, a will, emotions and everything else that causes me to be human.

I cannot breathe life into dust and cause it to live. I cannot command light. I cannot paint the colours of the meadows or mountains. I could certainly never have come up with the idea of a hippopotamus! The best that the best of science can do is to take of what is and, under the strictest of laboratory conditions, bring into being that which has happened naturally throughout history. Equally it can litter the heavens with tons of redundant metal or give us nuclear ambitions with which to obliterate each other.

Now, am I going to trust my own very limited and seriously flawed intellect and emotions; or trust in science that constantly re-invents its findings; or admit that the All-Loving, All-Knowing, Almighty Creator and Sustainer of all that is, who lovingly cares in every way for each of us, knows better than I how to run my life and His world?

Who should I trust most? My hopeful, limited guess? Or His loving "knowing the end from the beginning" purpose and the outcome of my trusting?

Okay, so the no-brainer is settled then - until the next time, in my experience! How easily and quickly we revert to the 'self help' struggle. Yet...

Ps.103:14

He knows how we are formed. He remembers that we are dust.

Therefore His eternal covenant of love is ever unfurled over us - reassuring, encouraging, sustaining!

He does not condemn. He does not talk down to us, nor remember our failures. God does not forget. It is wrong to speak of God as forgetting our sins. Forgetting is to do with finite, human frailty. God is God - eternally unchanging. He cannot forget. No, His love chooses not to remember. I emphasise this to show the vastness of His love. He wilfully chooses not to remember. We forget things (dates, appointments, names), but we don't forget hurts done to us. We don't forget wrongs done to us. We use them as weapons to hurt others. God is above and outside of such human emotions. In love He chooses not to remember. May we desire to emulate such love - choose not to remember wrongs.

1 Cor.13:5

Love keeps no record of wrongs.

I don't know what image of God fills your mind but I want to suggest that, above all, God is love. When Moses asked God to show him His glory, God responded by passing by, proclaiming His name: the Lord. As He passed in front of Moses, He declared who He is:

Ex.34:6-7

The Lord, the Lord, the compassionate and gracious God, slow to anger, abounding in love and faithfulness, maintaining love to thousands, and forgiving wickedness, rebellion and sin.

Primarily, He wanted Moses to understand that He is love. He is full of compassion and grace. Yes, He is holy and righteous, in equal proportion to His love, yet as He relates to us, He is saying, "Tell My children I love them. Tell them I am full of compassion and grace. Tell them I forgive seventy times seven; that I love them as I love My Son, their Saviour."

The eyes of faith will always see the unfurled banner of love. Paul prayed for the Ephesians:

Eph.1:18-19

...that the eyes of your heart may be enlightened in order that you may know the hope to which He has called you, the riches of His glorious inheritance in the saints, and His incomparably great power for us who believe.

Our hope is Jesus:

Col.1:27

Christ in you, the hope of glory.

His "glorious inheritance in the saints" is that in Jesus He has reconciled all of humanity to Himself - Jew and Gentile.

Eph.2:14-22

He has made the two one and has destroyed the barrier, the dividing wall of hostility, by abolishing in His flesh the law with its commandments and regulations. His purpose was to create in Himself one new man out of the two, thus making peace, and in this one body to reconcile both of them to God through the cross, by which He put to death their hostility. He came and preached peace to you who were far away and peace to those who were near. For through Him, we both have access to the Father by one Spirit. Consequently, you are no longer foreigners and aliens but fellow citizens with God's people and members of God's household, built on the foundation of the apostles and prophets, with Christ Jesus Himself as the chief cornerstone. In Him the whole building is joined together and rises to become a holy temple in the Lord. And in Him you too are being built together to become a dwelling in which God lives by His Spirit.

God inherits a dwelling - a place to live by His Spirit.

1 Cor.6:19

Do you not know that your body is a temple of the Holy Spirit who is in you?

1 Cor.3:16-17

Don't you know that you yourselves are God's temple, and that God's Sprit lives in you, and God's temple is holy, and you are that temple?"

2 Cor.6:16

We are the temple of the living God. As God has said: 'I will live with them and walk among them and I will be their God and they will be My people.'

God's inheritance is His people. Jesus died that He might have a bride: a body of people, a building of bodies in which to live. This Bride, this Temple, this Body, this Building is Holy. This body is you and this body is 'us together', members one of another, a place for God to call 'home'.

Since God's building and temple is made of people, He does not 'live' in buildings made of bricks and mortar.

Acts 7:48, 17:24

The Most High does not live in houses made by men.

It matters not how grand and breathtaking the building may be; God does not live there. No cathedral is God's house; no little mission hall is God's house. God's house is in the hearts of His children. The building exists to keep the weather off the church. The buildings help to facilitate the coming together of the church in corporate worship life. His banner is over you. You are His inheritance.

His incomparably great power for us who believe is that power which raised Jesus from the dead and seated Him at the right hand of the Father. This is Holy Spirit power - the same Holy Spirit who inhabits everyone who is truly a child of God.

Rom.8:9,14

If anyone does not have the Spirit of Christ, he does not belong to Christ ... Those who are led by the Spirit of God are sons of God.

So, the power that indwells us is the power exerted by the Father in the raising of the Son from the dead – an enormous 'dunamis' dynamite, dynamo expression of Abba's power indwelling the dwelling place of God. Oh, how much more we need to realise this power within us, to begin to truly believe in this reality, to take from His banqueting table the enabling grace gifts of our Lover Shepherd King!

Here then is our Father, Abba, who reveals His love to us, constantly confirming it in the ever-present abundance of His grace, the Banqueting Table. This love, which is above and beyond description, causes us to give ourselves away unashamedly to Him and to the cause of His Kingdom, desiring that His name be most highly exalted, His glory demonstrated before the eyes of all humanity. What a cause to live and die for!

Paul declared that he was not ashamed of the gospel because it is God's power to bring salvation (Rom.1:16). Further to this we have the promise that "the one who trusts in Him (Jesus) will never be put to shame." (Rom.9:33, 10:11)

Paul encourages Timothy:

2 Tim.1:8

Do not be ashamed to testify about our Lord, or ashamed of me His prisoner.

How easily we can find ourselves being ashamed of other Christians in the way they live or the things they say. I know I am guilty of this, particularly toward those whose 'Christianity' appears dubious in my eyes! Even though Paul is in a squalid prison cell, in chains, shamed in the eyes of men, he can respond:

2 Tim.1:12

I am not ashamed because I know whom I have believed, and am convinced that He is able to guard what I have entrusted to Him for that day.

From this place he encourages his young disciple to do his best "to be a workman who does not need to be ashamed." (2 Tim.2:15)

Why is this important?

2 Tim.2:15

If we disown Him, He will also disown us.

Jesus said the same thing:

Matthew 10:33

Whoever disowns me before men, I will disown him before My Father in heaven.

These are not very appealing words but straight from the heart of Jesus, who only said what His Father gave Him to say.

Why should we ever be ashamed of Jesus? Why should we ever deny Him?

Well, embarrassment before colleagues, friends and family for one thing... Strange, since our allegiance to a sports team or an entertainer causes no such shame. Every time we keep our mouths shut when He is slandered or ridiculed, we show our shame.

Why am I making something of this? Because God's unfurled banner of love, that which is meant to be seen, is always over us. God is not ashamed of us. The Bible tells us in Hebrews:

Heb.11:16

God is not ashamed to be called their God.

He has much to use to be ashamed of us in our stupidity, failure, fault-finding and everything else that we know about ourselves that makes us uncomfortable. Yet He is not. His love covers over our imperfections and transforms them. We are His holy dwelling place. We are His children, His brothers, made clean and whole through the Calvary power of His love. Abba raises His Banner over us, declaring to all, "Hey, look - My children! Aren't they wonderful? I love them so much! How awesome they are to Me."

If we desire to be like Him, to follow in His steps, we will want to glory in Him also: "Hey, look! See what Jesus has done for me! Look at how loving He is toward me today! Isn't He amazing?"

A banner also testifies to the country we belong to. The banner rallies troops around it. Ancient Rome marched with its imperial banners, striking fear into the nations it invaded and conquered. It is so with God's banner of love. It speaks of a different allegiance:

Gen.12:1

Leave your country, your people and your father's household and go to the land I will show you.

"My kingdom is not of this world," Jesus told Pilate (John 18:36). Hebrews, in telling us of the faithful, declares that "they were longing for a better country, a heavenly one." (Heb.11:16)

It is clear in scripture that as Christians, as believers in, and lovers of, God, we belong to a different country. We no longer fit in this world. Our motivation has changed. Our lifestyle has changed. Our language, attitudes, behaviour, dress, currency - all are changed. We don't fit in the kingdoms of this world.

How often do you feel uncomfortable about things you hear and see? That is because you are not part of it anymore. Peter calls us "aliens and strangers in this world." (1 Pet.2:11)

The Kingdom of God is within you. We have experienced radical heart surgery. Our old, hard, stony heart has been cut away. A new, feeling heart of flesh has been installed in its place and we will never be the same again.

Ezek.36:24-27

For I will take you out of the nations; I will gather you from all the countries and bring you back into your own land.

[How wonderful that this promise to Israel has been fulfilled in my lifetime, and He continues to gather them into their homeland.]

I will sprinkle clean water on you, and you will be clean. I will cleanse you from all your impurities and from all your idols. I will give you a new heart and put a new spirit in you. I will remove from you your heart of stone and give you a heart of flesh. And I will put My Spirit in you and move you to follow My decrees and be careful to keep My laws.

Heb.12:28

Therefore since we are receiving a kingdom that cannot be shaken, let us be thankful, and so worship God acceptably with reverence and awe.

John 17:14,16

I have given them your word and the world has hated them, for they are not of the world anymore than I am of the world... They are not of the world, even as I am not of it.

There is much in this world to enjoy, celebrate and share in: its beauty, music, laughter, creativity and so on. God has given us all things richly to enjoy (1 Tim.6:17). No, I am not suggesting that we all go and live in the desert, feasting on locusts and honey. "Where your heart is, that is where your treasure also is." We do not belong because our treasure is in heaven. His name is Jesus. We do not belong because we are of another

Kingdom: a Kingdom governed by love, not self; a Kingdom which functions out of servanthood and sacrifice, not arrogance and dominance; a Kingdom of hope not despair; of faith, not fear; of humility, not vanity.

You get the picture?

You are a brand new creation! You have died and been born anew! The old has gone; everything has become new! We really are aliens, strangers to this world's heart and ways. We have been delivered from the kingdom of darkness and brought into the kingdom of the Son of God - the kingdom of light. Ephesians tells us how we used to be strangers and outsiders to the kingdom of God, but that now, through Jesus, we are citizens of His kingdom. We now live under a new banner: the banner of Love. Everything of this kingdom operates out of love, through love, for love. Attitudes of the heart come from love. Everything about us is 'Father filtered'. Nothing gets out which has not passed through His heart.

Do I retaliate when hurt? Filter it through Father's heart: "Bless those who persecute you." No retaliation there!

Thus we live in this world, functioning in two kingdoms. We are citizens of the kingdom of heaven, living on earth among people who are not. Everything of life confronts us with a choice: do I respond from the kingdom of heaven or do I respond from my flesh nature, which is self-centred, contrary to God's kingdom and doomed to unfruitful outcomes?

Paul tells us to...

Gal.5:16-17

...live by the Spirit and you will not gratify the desires of the sinful nature. For the sinful nature desires what is contrary to the Spirit and the Spirit what is contrary to the sinful nature. They are in conflict with each other.

So, throughout our time in this body, we live in a war zone - the Spirit and the flesh - our mind being the battleground. This is where we make our choices. This is why we are told to offer our bodies...

Rom.12:1-2

...as living sacrifices, holy and pleasing to God... do not conform any longer to the pattern of this world, but be transformed by the renewing of

your mind. Then you will be able to test and approve what God's will is,
His good, pleasing and perfect will.

I grew up with the King James Version of the Bible which renders it this way: "that Good, Acceptable and Perfect will of God" (KJV). Notice, the capitals spell GAP.

Do you have such a gap which leads to constant defeat, frustration and confusion? With a mind being daily renewed we become more able to evaluate a situation.

1 Jn.4:4
Greater is He that is in you, than he that is in the world.

Jam.4:7
Resist the devil and he will flee from you.

I am behind the wheel of my car. The motorway is relatively quiet. It is 'safe' to put my foot to the floor. What do I do? Do I ignore the nagging feeling that this is displeasing Father, or do I choose to honour the law of the highway? One brings me into peace, joy and deeper intimacy with beautiful Jesus. The other may lead to a speeding fine, disqualification, an accident, maybe a ten minute earlier arrival. Is it worth the hardening of my heart as I am rationalising and excusing my actions, convincing myself futilely that God understands and doesn't really care about speed limits? I know, only too painfully, how a few moments of contrary-kingdom choices can utterly devastate lives and ministries!

Hour by hour we need to turn more toward the heart of our Lover King, to be able to walk before Him in the life of His kingdom. Oh yes, the 'not yet Christians' around us live for the moment, the excitement, danger and driven-ness of looking for life in all the wrong places. We also have a world of broken, hurting, desperate, lonely, frightened people. This is how we shine as stars in the universe, becoming blameless and pure children of God "without fault in a crooked and depraved generation" (Phil.2:15).

The banner of love signifies our kingdom - the kingdom of God - of love, but there is another 'revealing' brought by the banner. It is the banner of war. Love and war!? Yes!

Abba God loves His creation.

Ps.24:1

The earth is the Lord's and everything in it; the world and all who live in it.

Abba is not giving up His beloved without a fight. He has never for one moment given up His beloved. Not for an instant has He had any other thought than to bring to fulfilment everything that His heart has ever desired. Even before He spoke creation into being, He had chosen us in Jesus to be His holy and blameless adopted ones. All to give Him pleasure! Once again, we see His joy and delight in us! (Eph.1:4-5).

The fight was really such a one-sided affair as to be embarrassing to the enemy. There was no negotiation. There was no notice taken of enemy tactics or numbers. God took no notice of the enemy. God, the all-knowing saw that His beautiful, created children would go their own way and choose to ignore His loving directives for a happy, perfect life in His presence. So, Father, Son and Spirit made their own determination, before it all began to go wrong, in order to put things right the way they wanted to. God devised His strategy for the restoration of humanity. Jesus chose to give His life as a ransom for humanity.

Satan didn't nail Jesus to the cross. It was determined in heaven long before creation (Eph.1:4, 1 Pet.1:20). Jesus gave up His life voluntarily. Listen to His words:

Jn.10:15,17-18

I lay down My life for the sheep... The reason the Father loves Me is that I lay down My life, only to take it up again. No one takes it from Me but I lay it down of My own accord. I have authority to lay it down and authority to take it up again. This authority I received from My Father.

Throughout the gospel narratives it is apparent that Jesus is fully in control of every situation. Actually He was committed to the cross from the first day. Nothing was going to keep Him from it. I suspect that satan would have done everything possible to stop Him dying, if he had had one hint of the purpose of Calvary. But he did not. Calvary was God's plan.

Is.53:10

It was the Lord's will to crush Him and cause Him to suffer, and though the Lord makes His life a guilt offering, He will see His offspring and prolong His days and the will of the Lord will prosper in His hands.

Remember Him telling the disciples how He was to be betrayed, handed over to the leaders, to be beaten and killed? Remember His promise of resurrection? (Matt.20:17-19).

No, this 'battle' was completely from God's heart as His means of bringing reconciliation between Himself and us, us and each other, and us and ourselves. Every detail was worked out in the eternal comfort of the heavenly unity; Father, Son and Spirit (equally God, equally serving and preferring each other) fully combined in the 'becoming man', becoming obedient unto death - death on a cross – and being exalted to the highest place. Jesus, as man, fully reliant on the power of the indwelling Spirit, did only what He saw the Father do, and spoke only what He heard the Father say. Jesus said:

Jn.14:9

Anyone who has seen Me, has seen the Father.

Read John 17 again! See how inextricably the Godhead is interrelated. Salvation has always been God's idea, independent of satan, for His own purposes and glory. Impossible to fail! Yes, it was an horrendous, cruel, barbaric, bloody death. But it was the one Jesus chose to yield His heart and will to. Satan did not bring any influence to bear on the plan that Abba God designed.

God wars against that which wars against His children. Every day in every circumstance the Banner of Love prevails, bringing victory into the lives of all who yield to Him. The Psalmist declares:

Ps.20:5

We will shout for joy when You are victorious, and will lift up our banners in the name of our God.

We know that victory belongs to the Lord (1 Chron.29:11). Every victory we achieve is through the power of our Lord Jesus Christ (1 Cor.15:57). So, when we overcome and know that victory has been achieved, we raise our banners in His name. All praise, honour and glory go to Jesus! We know it is not in our own strength or will power, but in Him who is at work in us to cause us to want and to achieve His good pleasure (Phil.2:13).

How important it is to lift our banners in His name and declare that His name alone is to be honoured. To congratulate ourselves, or even each other, is shallow, empty... untrue. The more we acknowledge Him before our own eyes and before men, the greater He grows in our understanding, and the greater glory He receives.

What are these banners that we raise in His name? They are banners of love, just like His. The armies of Rome marched with banners that complemented each other - that declared the same nationhood and allegiance. So it is with our banners: love for Abba God and love for others.

The victory that overcomes the world is our faith. Not 'faith full stop' but 'faith in His faithfulness, faith in God and His covenant promises'. This faith calls us to embrace Him and all that comes with Him. This includes my love for my fellow Christians. I cannot have faith in God without loving you. Faith is born of love. I cannot love God without loving you (1 Jn.4:19-21).

See the picture: an army moving across the nation, united in worship and devotion to the Commander in Chief, united in heart, mind and purpose with each other, waging a war of love with everything and everyone they encounter. Love gives! As "God so loved... that He gave", so we give ourselves to the youth gang culture, the teen mum culture (the UK has the highest number in Europe), the alcohol and drug dependency culture, the respectable neighbour or colleague. We love them into life and freedom! We love them into Christ! Not with harsh judgmental words but acts of sacrifice, words of endorsement, and hope.

What a transformation this will bring to society. What a spectacle this will present: "terrible as an army with banners" (SS 6:4,10), striking awe and fear into all observers - awe at the amazing sight of an army of lovers healing the land, fear as in Acts 5:

Acts 5:11-14

Fear gripped the whole church and all who heard about these events. The apostles performed many miraculous signs and wonders among the people. And all the believers used to meet together in Solomon's Colonnade. No one else dared join them, even though they were highly regarded by the people. Nevertheless, more and more men and women believed in the Lord and were added to their number.

- Fear at the awesome holiness of God.
- Fear at the spectacle of ordinary people living and moving in one heart and mind demonstrating the reality of the kingdom of God on the streets. How beautiful a sight: the church, the Bride, in beautiful unity living the life of Jesus! No sight on earth can match such beauty, no 'cover girl' can compare with the Bride. See her making herself ready, clothed in the righteousness of God!
- The strange attraction of fear; scared by the undoing of every idea and prejudice against Jesus and His church.
- Fear of no longer having any sort of foundation to stand on, for Jesus has swept it away by the sight and sound of His saints.
- Fear of the lost-ness conviction brings. How can ungodliness stand when such a lovely Bride is living out love?
- Fear of becoming a part of it, yet strangely attracted, drawn by some compulsion to join this band of lovers: an ache, somewhere inside that longs to be 'home' without ever realising that this is what it has always been looking for, having spent a lifetime looking for what only Jesus can give!

Is this the evangelism Jesus had in mind when He said, 'They will know you are My disciples by the love you have for one another"? (Jn.13:35, 17:20-23)

How wonderful! Witnessing and evangelism boil down to loving each other - laying down our lives for each other's good, honouring and promoting each other. These are the strongest 'tools' for us to demonstrate the kingdom and lift up the King - the King, who said:

Jn.12:32 (KJV)
If I be lifted up from the earth will draw all men unto Me.

Yes, these words refer to Jesus on the cross, dying as the sacrifice for sin. Yet there is also another dimension to them. Whenever Jesus is exalted, lifted up in worship, words, actions, He draws people to Himself. As Isaiah said:

Isa. 11:10
In that day the Root of Jesse will stand as a banner for the peoples. The nations will rally to Him and His place of rest will be glorious.

Isa. 11:12
He will raise a banner for the nations and gather the exiles of Israel.

Isa.49:22
See I will beckon to the Gentiles. I will lift up My banner to the peoples, they will bring your sons in their arms and carry your daughters on their shoulders

God told Moses to arrange the tribes around the Tent of Meeting...

Num. 2:2
...each man under his standard, with the banner of his family.

Since the veil of the temple was torn in two from top to bottom, in Jesus we have complete access to the Throne - authority to come boldly before the King with His banner of love unfurled, carrying the banner of love allegiance in our hands, drawn by the power of love.

This is the message of the banner - the banner that unfurls at the command of the King Lover and covers us as in a 'huppar', the 'ceremonial canopy' that covers a couple who are being married within the Jewish custom.

Arise beautiful bride! Your Lover Shepherd Saviour King awaits you: Jehovah Nissi!

I refer back to Isaiah's words about the Root of Jesse. The prophet tells us that Jesus will stand as a banner planted in the ground, seen by all, drawing to Himself. It is the sign of His presence from the One who said, "I will never leave you or forsake you."

It is the sign of pledge, from the Garden of Eden to Golgotha - the pledge of God to restore His damaged, death-inflicted children. "He will crush your head" is His promise to satan - a promise fulfilled with the words "It is finished" heralded from the cross.

It is a sign of peace. "His place of rest will be glorious." Peace comes through the blood of His cross:

- Peace between Abba and me, ending my hostility toward Him.
- Peace between me and myself. I am made whole, assured of my place and standing in the heart of Father God, reconciled to who I am, knowing I am made for His glory, in His image, uniquely crafted to be 'me'.
- Peace between me and my neighbour - next door or across the world. Jesus has broken down the barrier of partition between Jew and Gentile, between Jew and Jew, Gentile and Gentile. In Jesus we become one new man. Even toward those who reject His love, I give love. I am at peace in my heart toward them.

It is the sign of power: At the defeat of the Amalakites, Moses built an altar, calling it 'Jehovah Nissi' ('the Lord is my Banner'). God had overcome their enemy. Moses held up his arms in prayer, supported by Hur and Aaron. While his arms were raised, Israel prevailed. When they lowered in fatigue, the enemy prevailed. Aaron and Hur held his arms high until victory was accomplished. Thus Moses declared God as the Banner of the Nation - a banner of victory, of power.

One glance at the banner and we are assured that all the forces of love are deployed to our benefit. It is not about our weakness or failure, not about our doubts and fears. It is about His omnipotence, His all-encompassing love and grace. This King has conquered my heart and planted His banner of love over me. He is not One who triumphs *over* but One who triumphs *in* me!

BANQUET: Party On!

SS 2:4

He brought me to the banqueting house.

He has already brought me there. It is not something waiting for the eternal future. Before we explore the banqueting house, I want to consider the glorious thought that He has brought me to this place. I didn't stumble on this feasting hall by accident. I didn't receive an invitation with an RSVP enclosing a map for me to find my own way should I choose to accept the invite. It is not something I have heard about but have no possibility of ever seeing or experiencing. It is not a place for a select few. There is no sign over the door saying 'Prophets and Preachers Only' or 'Missionaries and Musicians Only'.

My Beloved leads me! His left arm is under my head and His right arm embraces me, bringing me into the banqueting house.

The Psalmist knew this experience of God:

Ps.23:2

He leads me beside quiet waters.

The Prophet put it this way:

Isa.42:16

I will lead the blind by ways they have not known, along unfamiliar paths I will guide them. I will turn the darkness into light before them and make the rough places smooth.

Isa.47:17

I am the Lord your God who teaches you what is best for you, who directs (leads) you in the way you should go.

What confidence there is for the believer, if believe he does, in his God! We do not have a clue about the rest of this day, what will happen. Abba God knows the end from the beginning. He inhabits eternity. He upholds all things by His mighty power. Allowing Him to direct our steps into His paths of peace, means we let Him determine our destiny.

"How can I know the will of God for my life?" is a major question for so many Christians. Libraries have been written about how to discover God's will, how to know it is God's will, how to be sure it is God's will, and so on.

God doesn't seem to think it so difficult.

What makes me say this?

I don't have a simple four point step-by-step guide to knowing the will of God. Something tells me if it was as difficult as so often seems to be the case, then the Father that He is would surely have given us simple enough guidance to save us so much angst, fretfulness, fear, doubt, indecision and even paralysis. As we read the Bible, so much of His will is revealed. Everywhere He speaks of leading His children, leading His flock. As we keep our eyes on Him and follow, we walk into His will. Children happily run and play on a walk with their father, holding his hand from time to time, chatting about the incidents of the journey, or more seriously having a real heart-to-heart. In all this, where they are going is left in the care of Dad.

"Turn left here", "cross there", "down that road", and suddenly, journey's end. They have arrived at where they were going. Perhaps a cautionary "slow down; wait for me" happened en route, but otherwise, it has been a fear-free shared experience of getting from here to there. Such is the will of God. He leads; we follow. It is about choosing to give place to the desires of God.

Rom.12:1-2

I urge you brothers, in view of God's mercy, to offer your bodies as living sacrifices, holy and pleasing to God, which is your spiritual act of worship. Do not conform any longer to the pattern of this world, but be transformed by the renewing of your mind. Then you will be able to test and approve what God's will is, His good, pleasing and perfect will.

What is this saying? Because I know God's love and mercies in my life (mercies I know, and have proved, to be good for me), I choose to give myself fully in every way to belong to God. I desire every facet of my life to be for His glory, desiring to pursue only such as pleases Him. I recognise that the attitudes and mindset of the culture and society I live in are alien to God's, so I abandon them in favour of pursuing that which comes from a devoted heart to Him and His Kingdom. This means I will be living out His good pleasure and will for me.

An example could be a promotion prospect at work. Is this God's will for me? Well, there is more money - lots. That is a good thing - my offerings and gifts can increase. One up for God! I can be a witness among the business high flyers - another one for God. It would probably mean more hours, less family time and church involvement - several against God there... and so on! We can reason and rationalise everything. But, the big questions are 'what is in my heart?' and 'why do I really want this?' To prove myself successful? To have more disposable income? Bigger this, better that?

Only you know what is really in your heart. That is the place of decision. Is it all for the glory of God or to pamper yourself? At what level is the peace of God ruling in your heart?

Thessalonians tells us:

1 Thess.4:3
It is God's will that you be sanctified.

Sanctified means 'to be separated', 'to belong to'. In other words God's will for us is to be separated in heart, mind, will, attitude, lifestyle, behaviour, language, choices - to belong to Him. Our heart's real longing is to please God more than ourselves. Our minds, taken up with His truth and promises, are directed toward living in the reality of His truth, rather than the shallow ideas of a culture which is alien to His ways. This works throughout all of our being, to conform us increasingly into the likeness of Jesus. It is not a list of things we are forbidden. It is a way of life that embraces God's desires and purposes. Am I buying my new car to impress my neighbours and work colleagues, or to be more suited to my budget and need? Jesus prayed, "Your kingdom come, Your will be done on earth as in heaven."

This is obviously God's will for us all: that the Kingdom comes in reality in our living, attitudes, and will. Also His will prevails in the day-today affairs of our life. As we yield control of our hearts and affairs to Him and seek His glory, presence and power, so His life becomes greater in us, bringing in His will and Kingdom.

Then we have the big issues of 'God's will for my life'. This invariably means 'Does he want me on the mission field?'

Well the 'mission field' is wherever you are at any given time. It is not just the romantic sacrificial life in some far flung country. A missionary is God's person in God's place at God's time doing God's will. If that is you and you are a banker, you are on the mission field. If that is you and you are a bus driver, you are on the mission field. The far flung country is for those who are sent there. Surely the days are gone when someone with eyes closed sticks a pin in a map of the world to see where they believe God wants them.

Living in close communion with God in a deep, intimate, passionate love is the only safe place for proving His good will in your life, as you live out for Him the life you find yourself in.

Ps.37:4

Delight yourself in the Lord, and he will give you the desires of your heart.

You see, God's will is not essentially something hard and fast, settled in stone. It is a relationship-journey deeper into His heart. Should He want you in politics, or the police force, in painting or Peking, He is very able to let you know. His sheep hear His voice. One thing is for sure: He has not called any of us to fret about His will. Live the life you are in, seeking His face in the daily things while seeing His hand on the door of tomorrow.

So much is given us in scripture about what God's will is. Listen to Peter in his first letter:

1 Pet.2:1-3

Rid yourselves of all malice and all deceit, hypocrisy, envy and slander of every kind. As new born babes, crave pure spiritual milk, so that by it you may grow up in your salvation, now that you have tasted that the Lord is good.

1 Pet.2:11-12

Dear friends, I urge you, as aliens and strangers in the world, to abstain from sinful desires... live such good lives among the pagans that, though they accuse you of doing wrong, they may see your good deeds and glorify God...

1 Pet.3:8-9

Finally, all of you, live in harmony with one another; be sympathetic, love as brothers, be compassionate and humble. Do not repay evil with evil or insult with insult, but with blessing, because to this end you were called...

There is so much there to keep us occupied in growing in God's will. Let us endeavour to master these things in the power of the Spirit, for God's good pleasure. And whatever you are doing, do it for the glory of God!

He brought me into the place of feasting and pleasure. Surely He introduces me to all His other guests...

Could Christ be so churlish as to bring me to the party and leave me at the door to find my own place? I cannot believe that of my Saviour. "This is My favourite friend," I hear Him say as we enter. He has brought me through every discouragement, over every obstacle, confounded my feelings of inadequacy. He has opened up a new and living way that I may come boldly to the throne of grace. Through Him I have access to the Father through one Spirit (Eph.2:18). He has brought me to the place of my inheritance as His new creation. I am His brother, His blood-bought reward, the joy set before Him, and so are you. This is the New Jerusalem, adorned as a bride, presented to the Son, the Bridegroom. He gathers His treasure in His arms and brings her to the Father, for none can come to the Father except through the Son.

So, I am introduced to the guests as 'My favourite friend'. They have all heard the same words. This makes no sense to the natural mind. But, as a new creation, with a mind daily being renewed in Christ, illuminated by the Spirit, I understand that I am uniquely 'My favourite friend' as is everyone else - uniquely, perfectly loved! His delight is in me, in you. His eyes "feast on us", as it says in The Message Bible.

We enter the banqueting house. No room on earth can compare in splendour, wonder and beauty. This is none other than the place Abba has yearned for us to join Him. The hands that fashioned a squirrel and formed a rose have built this most beautiful place.

Let's look at an incident in the life of King Solomon when the queen of Sheba visited him:

1 Kng.10:1-9

When the queen of Sheba saw all the wisdom of Solomon and the palace he had built, the food on his table, the seating of his officials, the attending servants in their robes, his cupbearers, and the burnt offerings he made at the temple of the Lord, she was overwhelmed. She said to the king: 'How happy your men must be, how happy your officials who continually stand before you and hear your wisdom! Praise be to the Lord your God, who has delighted in you and placed you on the throne of Israel.'

Something similar is told in the court of Xerxes, in the time of Esther. Allow your imagination to picture the splendour and ostentation of this king.

Est.1:4-8

For a full 180 days he displayed the vast wealth of his kingdom and the splendour and glory of his majesty. When these days were over the king gave a banquet, lasting seven days in the enclosed garden of the king's palace, for all the people from the least to the greatest, who were in the citadel of Susa. The garden had hangings of white and blue linen, fastened with cords of white linen and purple material to silver rings on marble pillars. There were couches of gold and silver on a mosaic pavement of porphyry (crystals embedded in rock), marble, mother of pearl and other costly stones.

[Other versions include alabaster, turquoise, red, blue, white and black marble in their descriptions. Between them they paint a picture of dazzling opulence and staggering beauty.]

Wine was served in goblets of gold, each one different from the other, and the royal wine was abundant, in keeping with the king's liberality. By the king's command each guest was allowed to drink in his own way, for the king instructed all the wine stewards to serve each man as he wished.

However we look at these two examples, we cannot but be stunned by the wonder, beauty, richness and creativity of the scene. All this is the work of man. How much more we will be stunned by the breathtaking, captivating wonder, splendour and beauty of the banqueting house which is the handiwork of the Creator of a million galaxies, a simple flower, a majestic stag - our Abba God. Not even the collective wonders of the world can compare with the Master Craftsman. This house is splendid beyond description; awe inspiring in its size and decoration; breathtaking in the regal dressings on the walls, the adornments of its furniture, the magnificence of the utensils, goblets, platters of the purest gold and silver, the scintillating jewel decked ornaments - all reflecting the wisdom and goodness of the Host.

Xerxes spent six months displaying his greatness and splendour to his guests. Our Father will display for all eternity the riches of His grace and glory to His children. This banqueting house can be none other than the depths of the heart of God. To be 'home' is to be lost in Him. To be surrounded by such glory, beauty and wisdom, is to be where He is.

Remember the woman who pressed through the crowd to touch the hem of Jesus' garment? She had found the banqueting place. The crowd were jostling and staring, excited by the 'miracle worker', pushing and pressing to get a better sighting of what was happening, bumping against and touching Jesus, but missing the wonder of His presence. The desperate woman found the secret of the banqueting house. She knew her need. She knew the One who held the answer to that need, she pressed through to find the richest of fare spread before (and for) her, and she took of what she needed and was satisfied. She went home healed. She had met the Lord and Saviour of the world, while the crowd followed the 'entertainer'.

And so it is for us. We can be surrounded by all the 'evidences' of the faith. We can sing the songs and pray the prayers, but miss The Man. We can fulfil our religious observances and not observe the beautiful Presence, pursue His heart. Everything else is expendable. It is all no more than a means to seeking Him. They are not the goal of our worship. All these things - our fine buildings, our programmes, our rituals - are nothing more than aids to bring us to His Banqueting House - His very heart. Should they ever become more than that, we are serving idols. Should our way of 'doing church' ever become something we cling to, our denomination something we honour; should inflexibility ever grip our heart; then we are losing sight of His heart and pursuing empty forms of religion.

I recall incidents where people left a church because they changed the colour of the carpet. I recall painful experiences over months trying to change seating arrangements and the way the offering was taken up. Such things were not change for the sake of change. It was recognition that something more of the reality of Jesus could be found. Yes, even down to how the chairs are set. You see, at that time the chairs were set so that a large central aisle prevailed. The pastor faced this wide emptiness as he looked down the sanctuary. He saw the doorway and the clock above it, which constantly reminded him of how close 'Sunday lunch syndrome' was. Not a very positive outlook! He had to play tennis with his congregation to engage their attention, first to the left, then the right and back again. I have sat in meetings where a group of people with responsibility for the vision of the church have argued half an evening away over responsibility for coffee utensils - this group or that group not giving up long cherished 'ownership'. God help us!!

Everything is about God, Abba Father. Jesus came to bring us to Father. He said:

Jn.14:6
I am the Way, the Truth and the Life. No one comes to the Father except through Me.

Through Jeremiah He cries to His beloved children:

Jer.3:19
I thought you would call Me 'Father' and not turn away from following Me.

God's heart has always been to be Father to us. Jesus brings many sons to glory. He is not ashamed to call us brothers. We share the same Father. Before the world was spoken into being, we were chosen and adopted as sons - sons of the Father. In Abba is a Father who is perfect in all His fathering. Even the pain we experience is evidence of His Father heart; for those the Lord loves, He disciples. Look at Hebrews 12:5-13. These verses assure us of the true nature of a father's heart. In His love He disciples His children. Without that they are as illegitimate, knowing no father.

Never equate discipline with punishment. Discipline is a form of teaching in order that we may learn more of Him. Punishment has to do with judgment. Abba Father looks out daily, searching the horizon for a sight of His wayward child. Then, ignoring dignity, He runs out to embrace His precious child. Throwing Himself on the neck of one who fears for his existence, all dignity is gone. His child has come home. This is overwhelming passion and joy. "My son was lost and is found, was dead and is alive." This is the picture of the heart of God. His child has come home; that is all that matters. Amazing grace!!

Paul puts it this way:

Phil.3:7-8

I count everything a loss compared to the surpassing greatness of knowing Christ Jesus my Lord, for whose sake I have lost all things. I consider them rubbish that I may gain Christ, and be found in Him.

All things, no matter how legitimate, how positive, how honourable, how long I have worked for them, how religious, are ultimately worthless compared to knowing Jesus. Nothing is worth holding on to if it interferes with my pursuit of His heart. He brings us, under His banner, right into the heart of His heart - the very place of His being. This is His banqueting house, the place of feasting and celebration.

The literal translation of 'banqueting house' is 'house of wine'. Add to this the fullest meaning of 'banquet' which is the after meal 'drinking of wine' and we have a picture of an abundance of wine flowing in celebration within the house of wine.

Now, I have visited more than one 'house of wine' as I have holidayed. One of my mild interests is wine. I enjoy what I enjoy and I like untried vineyards. So, I may plan my route to take in a 'cave' or two, for some 'degustation'. At such places I will see row on row of rack on rack of wines - some great and world renowned, others less noble.

One of the joys is that of having the opportunity to taste a vintage I cannot normally afford. I am spoilt for choice. Where to begin? What fits the budget? Do I go for red, rose or white; sparkling, AOC or Grand Cru? Add to this the wonder of the quantity: more bottles than could be drunk in a lifetime. Add to this the deep, dark, cavernous, slightly musty-smelling depths of the earth where the age-old oak barrels and dusty bottles live, and the picture is complete - a wine lover's delight! "Oh taste and see, that the Lord is good!"

This is it - His abundant grace arrayed in magnificent splendour, lining the walls of the banqueting house. Every grace here is 'Grand Cru'. There are no cheap, budget graces in the heart of Abba. Every grace fully expresses who He is: the Lord of Lords and King of Kings, the Master and Creator of all that is, the Love that will not let me go. Thus every grace equally flows with this love - the love which is the answer to that for which the grace is needed. The grace to be free from gossip or anger is as excellent as the grace to walk through the deepest, darkest sickness or valley of death, the agonies of divorce or failure.

Sheba was overwhelmed by the magnificence of Solomon. Xerxes' guests were awed by his greatness. How much more will it be so of us as we come into the banqueting house and view the awesome splendid abundance of all-sufficient grace! This grace of God is so much more than I was taught in my youth. Back then I was taught that grace was the 'unmerited favour of God', or God giving me what I did not deserve: salvation. Mercy was *not* getting what I *did* deserve: judgment and punishment for my sin.

Yes, this is a part of grace. But, remember, Jesus came "full of grace and truth" (Jn.1:14). Now how can Jesus be the carrier of undeserved or unmerited favour? This grace is the very presence of the Holy Spirit, to glorify the Saviour who brings us to the Father and to empower and enable us to live through any and every moment of life, as Jesus did. This is how Jesus lived - every moment in total reliance on the Spirit - for He emptied Himself, taking the very nature of a servant, being made in human likeness. As such He declared:

Jn.5:19,30; 8:28
I can do nothing of Myself.

He lived a life of sinless obedience in a relationship of unbroken intimacy, such that He spoke what the Father said and did what He saw the Father doing. His desire is for us to live such a life, so that we have abundant, available grace flowing from an endless depth of love.

In His amazing love for us, Jesus brings us in the new birth into new creation life: life in the Spirit, living in the depths of His love, embraced in His everlasting arms. This is the inheritance of the saints of God!

Now, don't go all religious on me and tell me you are not a saint. God says differently.

"But I don't feel like a saint."

Well, what is a saint supposed to feel like?

"I don't look like a saint".

You mean you are not wearing sandals, with a mystical glaze on your face and a halo hovering above your head?

"But you don't know how sinful I am, how often I fail and feel defeated."

Ok, you mean you are telling me that a saint is someone who has successfully qualified by completing the requisite number of religious tests or acts of kindness and has succeeded in overcoming every temptation, so that when they die they become saints and have a special place in heaven? I cannot find that picture anywhere in scripture.

The words used in the Bible for saint are:

1. 'chasid' meaning 'pious, kind', as in Ps.37:28
2. 'qadosh' meaning 'set apart, separate, holy', as in Zech.14:5
3. 'qaddish' meaning the same, as found in Dan.7:22
4. 'qodesh', 'separation, holiness', as in Deut.33:2

These are all Hebrew terms.

The New Testament word is 'hagios', a Greek word meaning 'set apart, separate, holy'. It is used over sixty times and always carries this meaning. 'Holy' means 'set apart, separate'.

A 'saint', in God's eyes, is someone set apart to be His, belonging to Him, living for Him, loving and worshipping Him. Any superficial reading of the NT reveals that saints are ordinary people who have received Jesus as Saviour and Lord and have been made new in Christ.

He brought me into the house of wine to the wine-flowing celebration with His glorious love filling all. In the passages referred to earlier, Sheba declares that the half had not been told her. In our Father's banqueting hall, the half has not yet been told.

1 Cor.2:9

Eye has not seen, nor ear has heard, no mind can conceive what God has prepared for those who love Him.

Your relationship with Abba and your experiences of Him are only the beginning. This is not all there is. The half has not yet been told. You think you know God? Think again! There is always more. He cannot be contained in any box or file system. Our theology at best falls short. He is beyond human knowing and understanding.

Isa.55:8-9

"My thoughts are not your thoughts, neither are your ways My ways," declares the Lord. "As the heavens are higher than the earth, so are My ways higher than your ways, and My thoughts than your thoughts."

I believe that all I believe is true, but I know that I don't know all the truth. God will do what God will do, whether it fits my box or not. He does not need my opinion or approval. As Guy Chevreau says, "God, I give You permission to change my mind about anything You and I disagree on."

The half has not yet been told.

I grew up in a church tradition where alcohol was frowned upon. I was told that the wine at the wedding in Cana was non-alcoholic, despite the textual evidence to the contrary. I grew up knowing nothing of the baptism of the Holy Spirit. We believed in the Holy Spirit, in a quiet, well-ordered, under control, gentle-inner-sense-of-God sort of way. We had the Bible. We didn't need all that 'Pentecostal stuff'! These are just two very sad examples of religion confining God to man's comfort and fear!

It is wrong to have your religious life so organised that its predictability is boring. There are, sadly, thousands of churches where the local rituals are observed, programmes followed, and God is not needed! In fact if the Holy Spirit showed up, He probably would not be welcome. He would cause so much disruption and disturb the gentle, friendly, inoffensive, spiritually empty religion. There is so much more!

At the other end of the scale I have witnessed church where without various dramatic noisy happenings 'we have not really had church'. I have witnessed the whipping up of greater emotion and noise - more manifestations! Some of it reminds me of Elijah on Mt. Carmel witnessing the prophets of Baal becoming more frenzied in their efforts to awaken their god. Let's get out of the box!

There is so much more than our vision sees, so much more than our denominational parameters, so much more... Are you hungering and thirsting for 'so much more'? Does your heart and flesh cry out for the Living God? Would you rather be a doorkeeper in the house of the Lord than live in the tents of the wicked?

To know that the half has not yet been told is to be a part of the most exciting experience you can ever know: the pursuit of Jesus - what Tommy Tenney terms 'The God Chasers'.

I remember an old saying: 'A man chases a woman till she catches him'. It is a little like that with God. We have been caught by Him, apprehended, arrested. And we spend the rest of our lives pursuing Him, longing for His heart, aching to live in His sweet presence, to be in His banqueting house.

The imagery of this expression 'the banqueting house' is a picture of great celebration - the abundance of free-flowing wine in a house of wine. God purposes our lives to be lived in celebration. As we drink of His abundance, proving His grace sufficient for every need, helping ourselves from His lavish provision set out in breathtaking beauty and richness, so we celebrate His love, uniquely displayed in each of our lives. As we think about this 'banqueting house', let me ask a simple question: "If you *are*, what are you doing *under* the circumstances?"

Sheba's testimony to Solomon says:

2 Chron.9:7-8

How happy your men must be! How happy your officials who constantly stand before you and hear your wisdom! Praise be to the Lord your God who has delighted in you and placed you on His throne to rule for the Lord your God.

How happy your men must be!

Joy is a basic characteristic of the child of God. "Joy unspeakable and full of glory", as Peter puts it (1Pet.1:8).

Ps.16:11

In Your Presence is fullness of joy, at Your right hand pleasures for evermore.

Neh.8:10

The joy of the Lord is your strength.

Jn.15:11

I have spoken this to you that My joy may be in you and your joy may be full.

Isa.61:10

My soul shall be joyful in my God.

Hab.3:18

Yet will I rejoice in the Lord, I will be joyful in God my Saviour.

Ps.51:12

Restore to me the joy of Thy salvation.

1 Pet.1:8

You rejoice with joy unspeakable and full of glory.

Gal.5:22

The fruit of the Spirit is love, joy, peace...

Isa. 51:11

Everlasting joy shall be upon their heads, they shall obtain gladness and joy.

There are many more scriptures expressing joy in the heart of the believer.

The Psalmist said, "In Your presence is fullness of joy." Living close to Jesus is living in the presence of joy. We are surrounded by joy. I am not speaking of a false happiness, but a lifelong experience of joyfulness. This may well be punctuated with sorrow, indeed, "weeping may last for a night, but joy comes with the morning." (Ps.30:5)

David cried out to God, "Restore to me the joy of Your salvation." He obviously knew that joy was the norm for his life. Joy should be a significant expression of our walk with God. Habakkuk had an insight into living in faith before God. He knew something significant.

Hab.3:17-18

Though the fig tree does not bud, and there are no grapes on the vine; though the olive crop fails, and the fields produce no food; though there are no sheep in the pen, and no cattle in the stalls, yet I will rejoice in the Lord, I will be joyful in God my Saviour. The Sovereign Lord is my strength.

I have seen this joy in the midst of the abject poverty of the church in Mozambique but not much of it in the luxury and affluence of the western church. Beyond the basic needs for this life, there is a heart's place of trust in the strength of the Sovereign Lord.

Nehemiah, during the stresses and demands of rebuilding the walls of Jerusalem, calls the people to a celebration, declaring that their strength is in the joy they have in God and His joy in them. As we draw all our life source and support from Jesus there is joy. As Isaiah says:

Isa.12:3

Therefore with joy shall you draw water out of the wells of salvation.

Turning every experience and situation into God's hand, allowing the Holy Spirit to bring God's fullness in that situation, is for us His joy.

James goes even further, calling us to "consider it pure joy whenever you face trials of many kinds." (Jam.1:2)

Why? Because they bring us into greater Christ-likeness!

Are you able to trust Abba in every situation to work good for us, as He promises? Do we trust His love to enable us to come out the other side still intact?

Jesus has brought His truth to us so that "My joy may be in you, and your joy may be complete." His words bring great joy to us - not judgment, hardship or fear - only joy. Remind yourself: "The fruit of the Spirit is... joy."

This tells us that the natural outflow of living in Jesus is joy. This joy is an image of the celebration of life at the banqueting table in the banqueting house. It appears to me that according to the scriptures, Abba God is inviting us to a lifestyle of joy - a very clear testament to the wonderful reality of being His beloved. If people claim that church is dull and boring, then something has gone very wrong between the supply and the expression.

John tells us that the commands of God are not a burden, or irksome, oppressive, or grievous, as the Amplified version adds. If your obedience to God relates to any of these words then I suggest the possibility that you have invited and expected God to bless your efforts for Him rather than walking in His best purposes for you. "My yoke is easy and My burden is light," said Jesus. He calls to the weary and heavy laden, "Come to Me. I will give you rest."

He calls us to "take My yoke upon you and learn from Me." He wants us to put down our yokes and pick up His. "You will find rest for your souls."

Find rest?

We find rest when we cease from our own labours and efforts and embrace God's rest as Hebrews chapter 4 points out. We are urged to make every effort to enter this rest. We have to work at abandoning our own ways and ideas and picking up what God shows us in the Spirit.

The godly 'disciplines' of prayer and Bible study, a life of worship and submission, empower us to say 'yes' and come into co-operation with God in the Spirit.

Phil.2:13

It is God who is at work in you to both will and to do of His good pleasure.

The text of the NIV puts it this way:

Phil.2:13 (NIV)

To will and to act according to His good purpose.

So we see that the Holy Spirit within us wills us to say 'yes' and empowers us to act as pleases the Father. He wants us to know this rest.

Ps.37:7 (Amplified)

Be still and rest in the Lord, wait for Him and patiently lean yourself upon Him.

Do you see it?
"...lean yourself upon Him..." Let God take the strain. You may be carrying the box, but God is carrying you.

Jer.6:16

Ask where the good way is and walk in it, and you will find rest for your souls.

The good way is always God's way.

- What is the good way to conduct myself in this situation?
- What is the good way to behave at this moment?
- What is the good way to speak about this?

Learning to have the attitude of Jesus at any given moment of choice is the good way. That is the way of rest for your souls. There is never any guilt in God's good way. There is never any confusion or doubt. There is no uncertainty in following in His steps. My heart and mind can be at peace when I ask for and walk through His good way. I know it is His way. I know it gives Him pleasure that I have chosen Him above the challenges and conflicts of this body of flesh in which I live. When we get it wrong (as get it wrong we do) there is still a place of rest.

Isa.30:15

In repentance and rest is your salvation; in quietness and trust is your strength.

Everything is found in Father God!

Now I know there are many children of God who are weary and burdened. There are many in leadership who are running on empty. There are many in overseas mission situations who regularly feel exhausted, overwhelmed, stretched to breaking. This is the challenge of walking humbly before Him, confessing our weaknesses and mistakes while taking no notice of our reputations, not fearing failure. This is His rest. We believe Father's good pleasure is in us - not in what we do, but in who we are. We do not, and cannot, earn His approval. We call on Him. We take from the banqueting house the grace we need right now. This is the joy of serving. The easy life of self-centred Christianity holds no attraction to the one who has tasted and knows that the Lord is good.

The latter years of my life as a teacher were spent in supply teaching. This meant I was called to a school when the regular teacher was absent. What this meant for me was to be ready for work early in the morning without knowing if there was any work. I would wait by the phone for the call which meant another day's pay. I chose to say, "Thank You, Lord" when the phone rang and "Thank You, Lord" when it didn't. This was not a form of fatalism. It was about trusting my loving Father who knows everything I need. It was about believing that in every situation He is always working for my good. It was about praising Him rather than grumbling or fretting. Our times are in His hands. We can choose to thank Him, whatever is happening. He is Love. When I begin to question that, I fall into unbelief. This opens my mind to the lies of the enemy which will compound my unbelief, which will probably lead me into my own pity party. This in turn leads me to doubt Abba's love and care for me. Before I know it I am right down in the pit, lost in a mire of deception, self-pity and unbelief. How far that is from the banqueting house! Beloved, we do not need to live like this. Jesus promised:

Jn.16:33

In this world you will have trouble, but take heart, I have overcome the world.

Earlier in this same chapter Jesus tells His disciples that it is good for them that He is leaving them so that the Holy Spirit may come - the Holy Spirit who will fill them, be with them and in them; the Comforter, the Paraclete; One who walks alongside to support; He who leads into all truth, who brings glory to Jesus and conviction to the world. This is good for the followers of Jesus.

I love how the Amplified reads:

Jn.16:33 (Amplified)

I have told you these things so that in Me you may have (perfect) peace and confidence. In the world you have tribulation and trials and distress and frustration; be of good cheer (take courage, be confident, certain, undaunted) for I have overcome the world (I have deprived it of power to harm you and have conquered it for you.)

Jesus always sets Himself up as the answer to whatever is going on in our lives. The call to be cheerful is centred in this truth. He is the answer. He has deprived everything in this life of its power to harm us and He has conquered it. He promised us a tough ride. We get hurt in our bodies, minds, emotions and spirits, but whenever we apply the balm of His love to our pain and hold on in faith to His truth, our spirit is healed. We are empowered to keep going, to come through, to live in the midst of seemingly impossible pressures with a heart that has a foundation of joy, of cheer, in the knowledge of God's love and grace.

The banquet constantly reminds us that He has already provided the answer to every question we realise. He has already provided the means of our deliverance. His grace answers every need, whatever situation or circumstance. This becomes increasingly real for us as we set our hearts less on the life in the natural and more on our life in the Spirit in Him.

Col.3:1-2

Since you have been raised with Christ, set your hearts on things above where Christ is seated at the right hand of God. Set your minds on things above, not on earthly things.

"It's alright for you," I hear you say. "You try living in my shoes! You try living in this wheelchair, living with this terminal condition, living with a disabled child, being unemployed, struggling to pay bills, being a lone parent, being the only Christian in my workplace..."

You are right of course. I am not living in your shoes. But I know someone who is. He said, "I am with you always" and "I will never leave you or forsake you."

I recall a most beautiful couple who have been through some of the most challenging and faith-destroying situations in their life. They wake every morning and declare, "Thank You Father that I woke up alive today. You obviously still have work for me to do."

They should both have died years ago, medically speaking. Abba God has need of us still, despite our situation. His mercies are new each morning, for all of us. He desires today's events to conform us more to the likeness of Jesus. Here is cause for thankfulness. God wants to make me like Jesus. Remember Paul's words: "I count everything as loss for the sake of knowing Christ."

It seems to me that we have two options.

1. We can bemoan our condition, feel sorry for ourselves, and give satan opportunity to play destructive mind games with us. Result: Falling away from the banquet.
2. We can declare the Lordship of Christ over our lives and recognise that "you died and your life is now hidden with Christ in God." (Col.3:3)

Gal.2:20

I have been crucified with Christ and I no longer live, but Christ lives in me. The life I live in the body I live by faith in the Son of God, who loves me and gave Himself for me.

In the enabling of the Holy Spirit, we can choose to respond in faith at every challenge. We can choose to focus on Him, seeking to know the attitude Jesus would bring to that challenge. As Paul tells us:

Phil.4:11-13

I have learned to be content whatever the circumstances. I know what it is to be in need and I know what it is to have plenty. I have learned the secret of being content in any and every situation, whether well fed or hungry, whether living in plenty or in want. I can do everything through Him who gives me strength.

"I have learned the secret." What secret?

- The secret of contentment in Christ, of being secure in His love and care.
- The secret of drawing, moment by moment, on the all-sufficient grace that is abundantly available at the Banquet.

You see, it does not begin with us and our problems. It is not based on our challenging situations. It all begins in the heart of Abba God. He opens His heart and says:

Matt.11:28

Come to Me, all you who are weary and burdened, and I will give you rest.

I love the way this is spelt out in The Message:

Matt.11:28 (The Message)

Walk with Me and work with Me... watch how I do it. Learn the unforced rhythms of grace. I won't lay anything heavy or ill fitting on you. Keep company with Me and you'll learn to live freely and lightly.

This is the banquet - the place of awe, of wonder, of beauty and abundance, the place of joy, contentment, security and celebration. This place is the very heart of the heart of the Father.

HOUSE: You, Me and Us

Depending on which version of the Bible you are reading, it will have either 'house' or 'hall'. A popular song speaks of the banqueting table, which we will consider in the next chapter. Right now I want to explore the 'house', the 'house of God'. God does not live in buildings. The nations of the earth are littered with some amazing, beautiful buildings built in honour of God or gods. Millions of people pay homage to buildings. The very buildings are held in awe and honour. There are very strict codes of dress. The shape and positioning of buildings speak of the tenets of the faith. Many of these edifices are magnificent in structure and invoke a sense of wonder at their size and grandeur. Many are constructed using the most costly materials: gold, silver and precious stones.

I have visited some of this nation's cathedrals: Canterbury, Exeter, Salisbury and Liverpool among them. What can compare with Gaudí's magnificent 'Sagrada Família' in Barcelona?! As I look at them I marvel at the architecture, the supreme chiselling and shaping which covers these places. I confess I see that first, before any sense of God hits me. I gasp at arches, windows, pillars and ceilings - incredible detail, much portraying history or Biblical stories. Such skilfulness! Yes, they are truly amazing buildings. I recognise that for hundreds of years peoples' voices have been raised in praise! Sermons and ceremony in the name of Jesus have filled the place, as in many less striking buildings. There is something truly wonderful about that. I pause to thank God for such a rich heritage. Yet sadness tinges the experience. Where is the dynamic, vibrant life of God?

Many such places seem to survive more as museum pieces than witnesses to the gospel. So many historic, beautiful buildings have become little more than incredibly expensive handicaps to local Christian communities which use them while unable to afford their upkeep.

Government agencies determine the future of 'God's house'. What a strange and distant idea from all that the scriptures teach. There are many buildings owning the name of God, where the community who gather there claim allegiance to the God of creation and all glory - the God who doesn't need our money, who owns the cattle on a thousand hills, who promises to supply all our need - yet who urge the 'not yet Christian' community around it to finance repairs to churches deemed too historical or beautiful to bulldoze to the ground. We have a very strange anomaly on our hands!

How to see this scenario as an expression of God living among His people is difficult. I remember as a young Christian, in my teens, spending much of my lunch break reading and praying in an old small church, or occasionally in the cathedral. I worked quite close to these buildings. They are precious memories of a haven of stillness amidst the bustle of city life. I would not wish to deprive anyone of such a time. I also know that I can be walking down the street and enjoying sweet moments with Father God. I hear of people, usually older ones, slipping into churches to be alone with their thoughts. It appears to be quite a common practice, so it must be helpful. How much this brings people into communion with God, I do not know. God is always seeking His precious children and delights to meet with us, in whatever circumstances make that possible.

I am convinced that there is much superstition in the UK attached to church buildings. In my childhood I was under strict orders as to my behaviour in the 'house of the Lord'. Talking had to be in subdued tones; walking, careful and respectful. We were not allowed to run or play, particularly around the pulpit area, while waiting for our parents. This was 'holy ground' as we understood it. What puzzles me is the idea that God finds children's laughter in the sanctuary 'offensive', while in the garden He loves it. Sentimentality tells us that 'we are nearer God's heart in the garden than anywhere else on earth'. It seems that 'being in God's Presence', i.e. 'in church', demands some rather unnatural behaviour. Whilst I am not an advocate of various forms of 'fashionable' dress, I ask this question: Who or what is being respected when people are told to cover up arms, legs, shoulders, heads, when entering many religious places, particularly during summer months?

I remember as a new, young pastor standing before my people. I was wearing a suit and 'dog collar'. It was summer and very warm. My body was becoming uncomfortable. Some young people who dressed very casually, with bare arms, legs, shoulders, caused a measure of envy to rise up. They were able to worship God in shorts and T-shirts. Why did I need such a uniform? It seems to me that we carry history and ancient culture with us into our day as if it has been 'deified'. Buildings and rituals (every denomination has them) seem to carry a force of the 'sacred'.

I remember being in a particular church for the first time. I was being shown round and the gentleman guiding me stooped and kissed a tiny inset glass box which apparently contained a piece of bone of one of the disciples or else a saint from the church's earliest days. My Bible tells me that "Elijah was man just like us" (James 5:17). In Acts, Paul shouts to the crowd, "We too are only men, human, like you," when the mob began to worship them on account of a healing (Acts 14:15). We carry a tradition of veneration of men when the scriptures categorically show that only Jesus is to be worshiped. There is so much attached to the Christian faith that is really irrelevant.

I am thankful for buildings. They keep the weather off the church. They can facilitate the ministry of the local body into acts of love and grace among the community. Yet God said to Moses, "Take off your sandals. You are standing on holy ground."

He was in the middle of the desert - not even in a tent (Ex.3). Jacob stopped for the night on his journey, set a stone for his pillow and slept under the stars. As a consequence of his dream he exclaims:

Gen.28:16-17
The Lord is in this place and I am not aware of it. How awesome is this place! This is none other than the house of God; this is the gate of heaven.

He was out in the open countryside. I do not believe that God lives in buildings, although I recognise that a sense of His presence can remain in a place. As Jesus said to His disciples:

Matt.10:13
When you enter the house, give it your greeting. If the house is deserving let your peace rest on it; if it is not, let your peace return to you.

Luke takes a slightly different angle:

Lk.10:5-6
When you enter a house, first say, 'Peace to this house'. If a man of peace is there, your peace will rest on him. If not it will return to you.

These scriptures show us that in the spirit world there is a reality that often we may ignore in the natural world. Many people testify to the feeling they have on entering a building, both positive and negative. I have been called to homes to pray through them with the owners, to call down the peace and presence of God, also to clean out in Jesus' name residual spirits of evil associated with former owners. I have seen spirits sliding under doors - even trying to hide behind furniture. The presence of God remains as His people have worshipped, honoured and loved Him. Church buildings reverberate with His name and His presence remains, something beautiful to recognise. Yet He does not 'live' in buildings.

I have never visited a megachurch. I have seen some on TV, and I struggle with the concept - so many seem to be across the road from poverty and deprivation. How much of Jesus' teaching was about the needs of the poor? Is it possible that Abba God happily 'lives' in 'megachurch' while the poor squat across the street? Maybe they do run food programmes and welfare classes, yet the contrast is blatant.

The scriptures declare:

2 Chron.2:5-6

The temple I am going to build will be great; because our God is greater than all other gods. But who is able to build a temple for Him, since the heavens, even the highest heavens, cannot contain Him? Who then am I to build a temple for Him, except as a place to burn sacrifices before Him?

This Temple Solomon was to build was the heart desire of his father David. David was grieved that he lived in a palace while the meeting place with God was a tent. God was really happy with David's desire - more, I believe, with what was in his heart than for a building itself. God had never sought a building as a monument to Himself. He was happy to meet with Israel's leaders in a tent throughout all their wanderings across the desert and settling in the land. God demanded no permanent structure. It came from the heart of a man. Is it too bold to think that God says, "Ok, David, since this is what is in your heart I will go along with it and give you your heart's desire"?

It was the Psalmist who declared:

Ps.37:4

Delight yourself in the Lord, and He will give you the desires of your heart.

What an exciting prospect this could open up for us: delighting ourselves in Abba; finding Him to be the absolute desire of our heart; finding His company the most satisfying experience, knowing that nothing equals that precious intimate closeness (which we gain by choosing to press in to a closer, deeper, place with Him); preferring His presence, His voice, His touch to anything else. Such delight brings us into the experience of our hearts' desires. Wow! Listen to God:

2 Sam.7:6-7

I have not dwelt in a house from the day I brought the Israelites up out of Egypt, to this day. I have been moving from place to place with a tent as My dwelling. Whenever I have moved with all the Israelites, did I ever say to any of their rulers whom I commanded to shepherd My people Israel, 'Why have you not built Me a house of cedar?'

It was never God's idea to have a permanent building as a meeting place. It came from David, and God said:

2 Chron.6:8

Because it was in your heart to build a temple for My name, you did well to have this in your heart.

God always looks on the heart. It is our heart which is the standard of our delight in Him. Jeremiah tells us:

Jer. 17:10, 24:7

I the Lord search the heart and examine the mind... I will give you a heart to know Me that I am the Lord.

Eph.1:18

I pray that the eyes of your heart may be enlightened.

Ezekiel says:

Ezek.11:19, 36:26-27

I will give them an undivided heart and put a new spirit in them. I will remove from them their heart of stone and give them a heart of flesh.

As God looks into our hearts He sees that which pleases Him or that which causes us pain. It is not primarily our actions that express our devotion and true obedience. All our actions need to spring from the heart. Actions without love are empty, meaningless, noisy things   (1 Cor.13). Actions springing from love carry the blessing and fruit that Abba desires to see. Only Jesus has walked in perfect fellowship with the Father. Only He has known the words and actions of the Father so as to live in them completely.

Us? We get it wrong sometimes!

I dare to suggest that Abba prefers us to do the wrong thing from the right heart than to do nothing. God initially instituted the *tent of meeting*, or *tabernacle*, as the physical place of meeting with His people. This tabernacle was to represent something. This is why God instructed Moses to make everything "according to the pattern shown you on the mountain" (Num.8:4).

This is because this tent of meeting is a pattern of Jesus. Jesus has come - therefore the tabernacle is now redundant, superfluous to requirements. The tabernacle was the forerunner of the temple, so that makes the temple redundant also.

Jn.2:19-20

[Jesus said,] 'Destroy this temple and I will raise it again in three days.' The Jews replied, 'It has taken forty six years to build this temple, and You are going to raise it in three days?' But the temple He had spoken of was His body.

Jesus chooses to turn the peoples' thoughts away from the stones of the walls of the temple to the "living stone, rejected by men, but chosen by God and precious to Him" (1 Pet.2:4). Jesus also prophesied that the stones of the temple would lie in ruins, not one atop another (Mk.13:2).

This had happened before when the nation had been taken into captivity and Jerusalem all but destroyed.

2 Kings 25:8-9

And in the fifth month, on the seventh day of the month, which was the first year of king Nebuchadnezzar, king of Babylon, Nebuzzaradan, the captain of the guard, a servant of the king of Babylon, came to Jerusalem. He burned the house of the Lord and the king's house, all the houses of Jerusalem that is all the houses of the great, he burned with fire.

This was in 587 BC. God was prepared to let His 'home' be destroyed because of the sin that pervaded its use in the sacrificial system, the priesthood, and the building.

The Tabernacle was a special tent representing the place of God's presence and meeting with His people. Exodus chapters 35-38 give us a very detailed outline of this structure. All the items used in it by the priests for the sacrifices came with precise directions for their construction and use. God's command to Moses was that everything had to be done exactly as He outlined. Hebrews 8 tells us why:

Hebrews 8:5

They (the priests) serve at a sanctuary that is a copy and shadow of what is in heaven. That is why Moses was warned when he was about to build the tabernacle 'see to it that you make everything according to the pattern shown you on the mountain'.

The Tabernacle was to be the focal point of relationship. It was not possible for the people to offer sacrifices anywhere else. God concentrated their hearts and minds on this place of meeting. Every aspect of their relationship was affected through the Tabernacle. It was portable, so that in all their journeying the people had this place of meeting. Solomon's temple was a permanent structure within the settled kingdom. It represented the place in Jerusalem where God dwelt among His people.

Wherever the people lived from Dan in the north to Beersheba in the south, they were secure in knowing that God was among them. There was a temple in Jerusalem. Following its destruction in 587 BC, and the return from exile about 536 BC, the rebuilding began. This second temple was much less grand than the original, causing great distress to those with long memories of former glory. Herod began restoration of it about twenty years before Jesus' birth; then, in AD 70, Jesus' words were fulfilled when it was destroyed. I want to highlight just a few of the characteristics which show Jesus as the perfect fulfilment of that temple.

It will be noted that the tribe of Judah camped on the eastern side of the Tent. This is the side on which was the entrance. The entrance to the Tabernacle was through Judah. The tribal banner displayed a lion on a scarlet background.

Rev.5:5-6

'Do not weep. See the Lion of the tribe of Judah, the root of David, has triumphed. He is able to open the scroll and its seven seals'. Then I saw a lamb looking as if it had been slain standing in the centre of the throne.

What a graphic picture of Jesus, the Lion and the Lamb. No one comes to the Father but by Him. The Tabernacle housed the *Brazen Altar* - the first thing you see as you approach through the gateway toward the Tent. The altar is where the priest receives your sacrifice, where the blood is shed and the altar consumes the offering. The sacrificial animal takes your place, to cover over your sin so you can continue to walk with God. The cross of Jesus became the altar on which He offered Himself as the One and Only all time sacrifice for all the sin of all humanity. Corinthians tells us that Jesus "who knew no sin became sin for us, so that, in Him, we might become the righteousness of God" (2 Cor.5:21). Paul refers to Jesus as our 'Passover Lamb', who was sacrificed on our behalf (1 Cor.5:7).

Next we come to the *Laver*: a highly polished wash basin. This was where the priests washed to be clean in order to enter the Temple. Remember that when the spear pierced Jesus' side, out flowed blood and water. John tells us that Jesus came by water and blood.

1 Jn.5:6-8

He did not come by water only, but by water and blood. It is the Spirit who testifies, because the Spirit is the Truth. For there are three that testify, the Spirit, the water and the blood, and the three are in agreement.

Hebrews speaks of us "having our bodies washed with pure water" (Heb.10:22). Peter uses the story of Noah to symbolise the waters of baptism which, he declares, save us, not by removing dirt from our bodies, but of the pledge, or response, of a good conscience toward God (1 Pet.3:20-22). I am not talking of baptismal regeneration.

Eph.2:8

By grace we are saved through faith, and that not of your selves; it is the gift of God.

What I would say is that baptism is the inevitable consequence of becoming a Christian. On the day of Pentecost, when the people under deep spiritual conviction cried out, "What shall we do?" the answer came back, "Repent and be baptised," not "Repent and go to church" or "Repent and be good neighbours." It was clear and sure:

Acts 2:37-38

Repent and be baptised.

This was lived out throughout the book of Acts: three thousand on the day of Pentecost, Philip in Samaria, Philip and the Ethiopian, Saul's conversion, Cornelius, Lydia, the believers in Ephesus. These examples show the practice of the early Christians. Yes, we are saved by God's grace alone. There are no 'add-ons'. Yet, as James says:

Jam.2:17

Faith without works in dead.

Abraham was counted righteous by his acts of obedience as when offering Isaac (Jam.2:20-24). So it is with all true believers. There is no biblical provision for un-baptised believers. "Repent and be baptised" means just that. It does not say, "Be baptised, and maybe someday repent." Baptism is the initial evidence of loving obedience to Jesus. Show me an un-baptised believer and it raises questions in my mind.

Okay, enough of a diversion; back to the Tabernacle. We come to the Holy Place. The Tent is divided into two parts. The first part is the Holy Place, and beyond that, behind a floor-to-ceiling veil, the Holy of

Holies. This outer part has the Candlestick, the Table with Shewbread and the Altar of Incense.

The *Candlestick*, made of gold, had seven branches - a central one which fed the others. The candlestick was always burning. It provided the only light in the Tabernacle. There was no natural light. Oil was constantly provided to flow and fuel the candlestick.

The *Table* displayed the bread of the covenant meal. Twelve loaves were provided by the tribes week by week showing the nation's covenant relationship with God. This was the sacred bread which David ate. (1 Sam 21:6).

The *Incense Altar* was where fire was placed morning and evening and incense sprinkled on the flames. This created a thick cloud of fragrant smoke. Once a year, on the Day of Atonement, the priest would put blood on the horns of the altar and move into the Holy of Holies through a cloud of thick incense smoke. This veiled the glory of God from the priest as he fulfilled his duties. Within this section was the *Ark of the Covenant*: a box, covered in gold, containing a pot of manna, Aaron's rod which budded, and the two slabs with the Ten Commandments written on them. The lid was called the *Mercy Seat*. Blood was poured onto the Mercy Seat, so that God would see it and know that the suitable sacrifice had been made. Thus His mercy is extended from His throne to the people as His justice and wrath are satisfied.

This is the deepest, closest place of God's presence. Jesus is the Light! There is no need of sun in the New Jerusalem for the Lamb is the Lamp and the Glory of God gives light. The nations will walk by its light. (Rev.21:23-24). Jesus is the Light of the World; without Him there is only spiritual darkness. It is only He who gives light to His word - the lamp for our path. Jesus is the Bread of Life. He is our daily bread. All our sustenance comes from Him. Our unity is expressed in the one loaf we all share (1 Cor.10:16-17).

Of course the blood of the sacrifice speaks of the blood of Jesus, the spotless Lamb of God who takes away the sin of the world. The Incense Altar gives evidence that the sacrifice has been made. Blood sits on the horns; incense, representing the prayers of the saints and of Jesus Himself, our constant intercessor.

Ps.141:2

May My prayers be set before You like incense.

Rev.5:8

The four living creatures and the twenty four elders fell down before the Lamb. Each one had a harp and they were holding golden bowls full of incense, which are the prayers of the saints.

Another thought on the Tabernacle...

It was covered with badger skins with an inner red-dyed ram skin covering. It did not look particularly appealing. The beauty and glory were hidden in the inner Holy Place. Jesus looked just like any other Jewish man. Isaiah tells us that:

Isa. 53:2

He had no beauty or majesty to attract us to Him, nothing in His appearance that we should desire Him.

Yet...

Col.2:9

...in Him dwells all the fullness of Godhead bodily.

Jn.1:14

The Word was made flesh and dwelt [tabernacled] among us, full of grace and truth.

All the glory of God was hidden behind the veil in the Holy of Holies. When this was torn from top to bottom as Jesus died, the glory of the Father burst out. Jesus has made the way for us to come to the Father, to live in His glorious Presence. Jesus is "the radiance of God's glory and the exact representation of His Being" (Heb.1:3).

Now we see Him glorified, but only dimly. When His *Kingdom* is fully come we shall see Him face to face and the knowledge of the glory of the Lord will cover the earth as the water covers the sea. Thus this building to 'house' God was always to be a temporary, portable structure. It constantly pointed to a greater, the perfect, Jesus - the only One in whom we can come to God. Only through the complete once-for-all-time sacrificial offering upon the altar of Calvary can any person know the joy and peace of sins forgiven and fellowship with God.

Are we still locked into a building mentality and focus? It has never been God's purpose for us to box Him into a building. Jesus' words to the woman at the well vividly illustrate this.

Jn.4:21-24

A time is coming when you will worship the Father neither on this mountain nor in Jerusalem... a time has now come when the true worshippers will worship the Father in Spirit and Truth, for they are the kind of worshippers the Father seeks. God is Spirit, and His worshipers must worship in Spirit and in Truth.

Not here or there, not your holy place or mine, but in Spirit and in Truth. Jesus is saying you do not have to go somewhere particular to worship God. We can worship Him from the life of the Spirit in us. The Holy Spirit leads us to Jesus who points us to the Father. We are in the 'Holy of Holies', not because we are in a building, but because our life is hidden with Christ in God (Col.3:3).

There is not one New Testament or New Covenant example or story to turn to for a sermon suitable for dedicating a church building. We have to go back to the Old Covenant, Old Testament literature for that. Hebrews tells us that the Old Covenant is obsolete (Heb.8:13). In Acts Paul tells us that "the Most High does not live in houses made by men" (Acts 7:48-48, 17:24).

So, where does He live?

Isaiah 66:1

Heaven is My throne, and the earth is My footstool. Where is the house you will build for Me? Where will My resting place be?

God is asking the question. Is it possible to build a house for Him? Let's see what the scriptures actually say:

Zech.2:10

'Shout and be glad, O daughter of Zion. For I am coming, and I will live among you,' declares the Lord. 'Many nations will be joined with the Lord in that day and will become My people. I will live among you and you will know that the Lord Almighty has sent Me to you.'

God will live among His people.

Zech.8:3

I will return to Zion and dwell in Jerusalem.

God will dwell in Jerusalem.

Ezek.43:7

Son of man, this is the place of My throne and the place for the soles of My feet. This is where I will live among the Israelites forever.

God has chosen to live in His temple.

Isa.8:18

Here I am and the children the Lord has given me. We are signs and symbols in Israel from the Lord Almighty who dwells on Mt. Zion.

God dwells on Mt. Zion. The Psalmist tells us the Lord chooses to reign on His mountain where he will dwell forever (Ps. 68:16). The Lord is exalted for He dwells on high (Isa.33:5).

Ps.74:2

Remember the people You purchased of old, the tribe of Your inheritance whom You redeemed, Mt Zion, where You dwell.

These words clearly reveal that Mt. Zion is God's redeemed people, and God has chosen to live there, in among His people. Now, listen again to Isaiah:

Isa.57:15

This is what the High and Lofty One says, He who lives forever, whose name is Holy, 'I live in a high and holy place, but also with him who is contrite and lowly in spirit, to revive the spirit of the lowly and to revive the heart of the contrite.'

These scriptures clearly show that God lives in and among people, in Jerusalem, in His temple, on Mt. Zion, in a high and holy place and with the contrite and lowly in spirit. For me this is still not definitive enough. It still sounds too 'mystical'. It somehow has yet to be grounded in what we know in our spirits.

What does it all mean?

- Does God live in Jerusalem in the land of Israel, the land inhabited by Jews, Christians, Muslims and others?
- Does God live in a city which has a huge mosque in honour of Allah?
- Does God live in the temple?

There is no temple, only a ruin. The only other dwelling place left for us is 'people'.

Heb.3:5

Moses was faithful as a servant in all God's house, testifying to what would be said in the future.

But Moses did not serve in the tabernacle. That was reserved for the priests. What else could it mean, other than the house representing the people of Israel, the nation God called to Himself, of whom He said, "Out of all the nations you will be My treasured possession"?

Heb.3:5

But, Christ is faithful as a Son over God's house. And we are that house if we hold on to our courage and the hope of which we boast.

There we have it! Moses testified by his servanthood among God's people, the house, of that which would come and is now here: Jesus, the Son over the house of God, you, me and every blood-bought child of God on this earth past, present and future. I said there is no temple, and that is true as far as bricks and mortar are concerned, but listen to Paul:

1 Cor.3:16-17

Don't you know that you yourselves are God's temple and that God's Spirit lives in you? If anyone destroys God's temple, God will destroy him, for God's temple is sacred and you are that temple.

We are God's temple. God lives in us. The word used here for live or dwell is 'oikeo' which means 'to use as' or 'have a house'. God uses me, you and us as a house to call 'home'. Ephesians speaks of this same 'living' when it says:

Eph. 3:17

That Christ may dwell, or settle down, in your hearts through faith.

2 Corinthians carries the same emphasis as it states:

2 Cor.6:16

We are the temple of the Living God. As God has said, 'I will live, (dwell, be in a house,) with them and walk among them and I will be their God and they will be My people'.

We have become the place where God has chosen to live by the Holy Spirit. We are His temple. Peter saw this when he wrote:

1 Pet.2:4-5

As we come to Christ, the Living Stone... we also like living stones are being built into a spiritual house to be a holy priesthood, offering spiritual sacrifices acceptable to God through Jesus Christ.

We are the spiritual house in which God dwells. As His priests we offer Him spiritual sacrifices from within this living temple. Through His amazing love we have been changed, transformed, made new creations. No longer dead in trespasses and sins, no longer strangers, without hope and without God in the world. No! Now we have been brought near. We have been made into pure temples in which God is pleased to dwell. We are united with Christ. We are a chosen people, a royal priesthood, a holy nation, a people belonging to God. (1 Pet.2:9)

Jn.17:11,20-23

Holy father, protect them by the power of Your name, the name You gave Me... so that they may be one as We are One... My prayer is not for them alone, I pray also for those who will believe in Me through their message, that all of them may be one, Father, just as You are in Me and I am in You. May they also be in us so that the world may believe that You have sent Me. I have given them the glory that You gave Me, that they may be one as We are One. I in them and You in Me. May they be brought to complete unity to let the world know that You sent Me and have loved them even as You have loved Me.

Wow! Peter reminds us that we are the living house of God.

1 Pet.4:17

For it is time for judgment to begin with the family of God.

For 'family' also read 'house' or 'household'. To Timothy, Paul uses the same idiom.

1 Tim.3:14-15

I am writing you these instructions so that... you will know how people ought to conduct themselves in God's household, which is the church of the Living God, the pillar and foundation of the truth.

Eph.2:19-22

Consequently, you are no longer and aliens, but fellow citizens with God's people and members of God's household, built on the foundation of the apostles and prophets, with Christ Jesus Himself as the chief cornerstone. In Him the whole building is joined together and rises to become a holy temple in the Lord. And in Him, you too are being built together to become a dwelling in which God lives by His Spirit.

Father God has chosen us as His dwelling place.

1 Jn.4:12

No one has seen God at any time. If we love one another, God abides in us (rests, remains, lives) and His love has been perfected in us.

Ps.132:13-14

The Lord has chosen Zion. He has desired it for His dwelling. This is My resting place forever and ever, here will I sit enthroned, for I have desired it.

God has desired and chosen a dwelling for Himself. He has chosen and desired you and me as His home. The outcome of this is so amazing. Listen to the Psalmist:

Ps.84:1,2,4,10

How lovely is Your dwelling place, O Lord Almighty. My soul yearns, even faints for the courts of the Lord. Blessed are those who dwell in Your house. They are ever praising You… Better is one day in Your courts than a thousand elsewhere. I would rather be a doorkeeper in the house of my God than swell in the tents of the wicked.

"How lovely is Your dwelling place, O Lord Almighty." That refers to you. It refers to me. It refers to every Christian everywhere. When you look in a mirror, say to yourself, "How lovely is Your dwelling place, O Lord." This is you through the eyes of God. Not through your own eyes, not through the eyes of the world, but through the eyes of everlasting love. "You are beautiful" is Father God's testimony about each one of us.

Ps.27:4-6

One thing I ask of the Lord, this is what I seek, that I may dwell in the house of the Lord all the days of my life, to gaze upon the beauty of the Lord and to seek Him in His temple. For in the day of trouble He will keep me safe in His dwelling, He will hide me in His tabernacle and set me high upon a rock. Then my head will be exalted above the enemies who surround me. At His tabernacle will I sacrifice with shouts of joy, I will sing and make music to the Lord.

There is an old saying; I don't know where it comes from, but it says this:

To dwell above with saints we love, ah yes, that will be glory.
To dwell below with saints we know, well, that's another story!

The miracle work of the Holy Spirit is to make a lie of those words - a wonderful witness to the world of our loving, living Father God!

What am I talking about?

I am talking about me and you looking at the people in the church we attend, or the home group we belong to, and the ones we don't; then saying, "Wow, that's lovely! There is nothing I long for more than to be in worshipful company with these people" - to eagerly anticipate seeing Jesus in our beloved friends!

Read these scriptures again and ask yourself, "Is this my heart toward the church?"

"How lovely you are! I yearn, I faint just to be around the family. I would rather spend a day among my Christian family than a thousand anywhere else. What I most seek, ask for, is to spend all my life among my Christian family. I seek Jesus and gaze upon Him in my fellow Christians."

Wow! That is something different to our regular attitude and experience!

Christ loved the church and gave Himself up for her, we read in Ephesians. Jesus died for His church. The joy set before Him when He endured the cross is this: you, me and all the church living in captivated love and servanthood, oozing grace and peace in every encounter with each other, because He is presenting us to Himself as a radiant church. (Those who look to Him are radiant; their faces are never covered with shame - Ps.34:5. They are without stain or wrinkle or any other blemish, but holy and blameless - Eph.5:25-27.)

This is the reason Jesus died. He saw before Him the reward of His suffering: countless millions of people from every tribe, tongue, people and nation, of every race and colour on earth, throughout every generation, made as one new man, flowing in love toward each other, joining with the Father, Son and Spirit in the great eternal dance of the celebration of Trinitarian love and honour.

I believe it is the will of the Father that we live in this awesome place here and now. By it all men will know that we are His disciples, brought into this unity in order that the world will know that Father sent Jesus and that He loves us as He loves Jesus. He has given us His glory that this may become so.

Jn.1:14

The Word became flesh and made His dwelling among us. We have seen His glory, the glory of the One and only, who came from the Father, full of grace and truth.

Jesus said, "I have given them the glory You gave Me" (Jn.17:22). This is the glory John testified to, the glory of being the eternal Son of the Father, glorious in holiness. We are inheritors of the glory that is upon and in Jesus.

Remember the words of the father in the story of the two sons?

Lk.15:31

My son, you are always with me, and everything I have is yours.

Jesus sees us not as servants, but as friends (Jn.15:15). He goes further and recognises us as brothers...

Heb.2:10-12

In bringing many sons to glory, it was fitting that God, for whom and through whom everything exists, should make the Author of their salvation perfect through suffering. Both the One who makes men holy and those who are made holy are of the same family. So Jesus is not ashamed to call them brothers. He says, 'I will declare Your name to My brothers, in the presence of the congregation I will sing Your praises.'

Rom.8:15-17

You received the Spirit of Sonship and by Him we cry 'Abba [Daddy] Father'. The Spirit Himself testifies with our spirit that we are God's children. Now if we are children, then we are heirs, heirs of God and co-heirs with Christ, if, indeed we share in His sufferings in order that we may also share in His glory.

These truths are for all of us. There is no elite group of Christians who alone receive such blessings.

Gal.3:26-29

You are all sons of God through faith in Christ Jesus. For all of you who were baptised into Christ have clothed yourselves with Christ. There is neither Jew nor Greek, slave or free, male or female, for you are all one in Christ Jesus. If you belong to Christ, then are you Abraham's seed and heirs according to the promise.

What is this promise?

That Abraham would be heir of the world (Rom.4:13). We are heirs of the world. It belongs to us!

Ps.24:1

The earth is the Lord's and everything in it, the world and all who live in it.

We are inheritors of Jesus' Kingdom along with Him. We are heirs of God and co-heirs with Jesus. Jesus said:

Jn.16:15

All that belongs to the Father is mine.

We are co-heirs with Him. All that belongs to the Father is ours. We need to grasp this amazing truth: the Father in Jesus, Jesus in us, us in Jesus. There is no separation. We are all one in Christ. Unity is the heart of the Father. Unity is the witness of the Trinity. Unity is the goal of the Bride. To be perfectly united with the Father in and through Jesus and to be perfectly united with each other through the abiding, indwelling Holy Spirit is the life Father God has given us. Please don't scoff and say it cannot happen. Please don't say how wonderful that sounds and that you can't wait for heaven to experience it. We are all part of it now. Christ is in me, in you, the hope of glory. As we choose to submit to the Spirit so we live in this place with each other. I believe this reality is as real as our willingness to embrace it. It means daily laying down our lives for each other, preferring one another, choosing not to be judgmental or critical, choosing to see the good in others and ignoring the rest "for love covers over a multitude of sins."

Do you remember Jesus washing the feet of His disciples? He knew that He had come from the Father and was returning to God. His identity, security and worth were all here. It was in who He was in the Father. He did not have to prove He was number one. He was able to choose to serve in the most servile ways those who were proud, self-seeking, doubting, fearful, disloyal: the disciples whom He loved. The more we choose to embrace this heart attitude, the more beauty we see in all those people who last week "needed to hear some truth from me!!"

"This is My command," said Jesus. "Love one another!"

I sometimes think how good it would be for us all to read and read again the 13th chapter of 1 Corinthians, at least once a week, until the words are written so deeply on our hearts that we begin to live them.

Are you able to imagine the impact in your church, your community, your town, if all the Christians, from every denomination and none, learned to love one another like this and lived it out? We are speaking of the dwelling place of God, who is love. This will be such an amazing witness to the revolutionary power of love, the greatest power in the world. It must be for this time. Why else would Jesus say:

Jn.13:35
By this all men will know that you are My disciples, if you love one another.

It has a 'now' application.

Heaven is too late for 'all men to know'. This is the glory of our inheritance: that we grow together to mirror the unity of the Godhead.

Jn17:20-23
You in Me, Me in them, them in Us.

Matt.5:5
Blessed are the meek, for they will inherit the earth.

This meekness of servanthood, humbling ourselves to become Christ to one another, brings us the world as our inheritance. God's wisdom turns man's arrogance on its head. Humans use force, strength and fear to overwhelm one another and take what they want. God, in love, gives so that all may be made whole.

Eph.3:10-13

This is His glorious intent, that now, through the church the manifold wisdom of God should be made known to the rulers and authorities in the heavenly realms according to His eternal purpose which He accomplished in Christ Jesus our Lord. In Him and through faith in Him we may approach God with freedom and confidence.

The spiritual forces are at enmity with the kingdom of God. Their goal is to steal, kill and destroy; to rob humanity of its God-centred purpose; to turn brother against brother, nation against nation; to destroy God's kingdom and build their own kingdom of darkness and fear. How can it be that fallen humanity, dead in trespasses and sins, can rise up into its eternal inheritance and reign in glory in Christ Jesus, with everything placed in subjection under His feet, to the praise and glory of the Father; living in perfect oneness; joyfully, fearlessly, freely, confidently, approaching the Father through the everlasting new and living way, the blood-stained Lamb of God, into the very throne room of heaven; sons of the Living God, transformed from one degree of glory to another; no longer in fear, no longer in shame, no longer covered in the filth of a sinful nature; now clean, new-made; in full confidence of knowing they are in the Father and His grace and love fill and surround them? Only through the gift of grace in Jesus can this be real. So, we too, can take that towel and wash one another's feet. This is the glory: humanity living in the Godhead, all things restored by the wisdom of humility and sacrifice - life through death. The principalities and powers are speechless. Their working of death seeks hopelessness. Father God gives life and hope.

Our attitude should be the same as that of Christ Jesus...

Phil.2:6-11

...who being in very nature God, did not consider equality with God something to be grasped, but made Himself nothing, taking the very nature of a servant, being made in human likeness, and being found in appearance as a man He humbled Himself and became obedient to death,

even death on a cross. Therefore God exalted Him to the highest place and gave Him the name that is above every name: that at the name of Jesus every knee should bow in heaven and on earth and under the earth and every tongue confess that Jesus Christ is Lord to the glory of the Father.

Living in this attitude, having this heart and mind, exalts servanthood to the highest place.

Matt.23:11
The greatest among you will be your servant.

Mk.9:31
Whoever humbles himself like this child is the greatest in the Kingdom of heaven.

Serving one another and serving the world by laying down our lives brings great glory to the Father. For by serving we bring men everywhere to confess that Jesus is Lord. The glory is in serving, not in lording it over others. This is the manifestation of the heart of the Father. Our glory is not in our cathedrals, megachurch or mission hall. Our glory is in serving as a living building, held together by love (Col.3:14); growing into a breathtakingly beautiful building, drawing gasps of wonder from all who see, bringing glory to the Father, through the Son, for this can only happen through Jesus.

Eph.3:20-21
Now to Him who is able to do immeasurably more than all we ask or imagine, according to His power that is at work within us, to Him be glory in the church and in Christ Jesus throughout all generations, forever and ever, amen.

Did you see that? Glory in the church! Glory in the church, glory in us. The scriptures teach that:

Isa.42:5

I am the Lord, that is My name. I will not give My glory to another or My praise to idols.

How can we carry and display God's glory? He does not share it. He does not give it to another.

The answer is that we are not 'another'. We are in Christ, in God. We are the body of which Christ is the head. We are the same in the life of the Holy Spirit. We walk in our heavenly Father. We come boldly into His very presence. Jesus is the door through whom we come in and go out and find pasture (1 Jn.10:9). I see in these words children who come into their daddy's presence, then go off to enjoy themselves in the consciousness that their father is there. They know the parameters and live within them so that there is only openness between them and their father - living carefree in the covering of Father's love and commitment. "Unless you become as little children..."

God has determined that His Bride will carry His glory.

Isa.62:1-2

For Zion's sake I will not keep silent. For Jerusalem's sake I will not remain quiet, till her righteousness shines out like the dawn, her salvation like a blazing torch. The nations will see your righteousness and all kings your glory.

Isa.60:12

Arise, shine, for your light has come and the glory of the Lord rises upon you.

We read in Isaiah 48 God's argument with His 'treasured possession'. He reveals their stubborn disobedience, their rebellion and idolatry. Then He concludes by saying:

> *For My own name's sake I delay My wrath... so as not to cut you off...*
> *See, I have refined you, though not as silver; I have tested you in the*
> *furnace of affliction... For My own sake I do this. How can I let Myself*
> *be defamed? I will not yield My glory to another."*

The chastisement we undergo in love brings glory into our lives.

Jam.1:2-4

Consider it pure joy, my brothers, whenever you face trials of many kinds, because you know that the testing of your faith develops perseverance. Perseverance must finish its work so that you may be mature and complete, not lacking anything.

This is how we all "with unveiled face, behold as in a mirror the glory of the Lord are being transformed into the same image from glory to glory, just as by the Spirit of God" (2 Cor.3:18, NKJV).

When our wonderful, beautiful Lover King brings us into His banqueting house, this is the house we are brought into: his amazing creation of fellow lovers, transformed by His love in the blood of the Lamb; made into a completely new creation of God in the Spirit; empowered to serve and manifesting King Jesus as we do it. We see Him in each other as we lay down our lives, His glory indwelling us and radiating from us to witness to the world that we are sons of the living God, the dwelling place of Almighty God.

One other thought before we move on: I hear far too frequently the term 'dead church'. To my mind that phrase is oxymoronic. How can the living organic creation of Jesus be dead? What is there that can overpower the purposes of God?

Matt.16:18

I will build My church and the gates of hell will not overcome it.

I cannot accept that can happen.

Obviously there are many church buildings which lie empty and, sadly, many congregations which lack true spiritual life and power. Right across the land there are former church buildings changed into sophisticated contemporary homes, carpet outlets, restaurants, supermarkets, and worst of all, temples to the false gods of our 'multi-faith' society. Obviously the gospel has ceased to be proclaimed from such places. The 'faithful' have failed to follow their Shepherd, and the King of

Kings has come and removed His lampstand. The cities set on the hills have failed to let the light shine, thus allowing the darkness to continue.

These same points, I believe, can also be questions to all those places without any obvious signs of Spirit life that still masquerade as the 'church of the Living God'. Across the land there are buildings of many traditions and denominations where a small handful of people gather together, go through the form of service that they are familiar with. Nothing new ever happens; every word is predictable. And as age takes over, the numbers diminish until there is no one left.

Why?

I can only surmise that God has left the building.

Why?

Probably because He is not particularly welcome! What I mean by that is that God disturbs. Where we reject change and new things, where we refuse to give up control and long cherished ways, there is little room remaining for God. It is something all of us need to be constantly aware of. Should we become so slick, so entertaining, so power-point confined, so time conscious, so well organised and planned for months ahead, we live in danger of God saying, "Ok, you have this down to a fine art; you don't need Me. You do your thing happily enough. I am out of here! I am building My church, not yours!"

You see, God's church is His people. It is never buildings! It is never religious forms or institutions! It is never traditions! It is always people, joined in His love and Spirit who serve and glorify Him through love and service to one another and a dying fear-filled world. As Erwin McManus says in his challenging book 'The Barbarian Way', "Jesus is being lost in a religion bearing His name" (pg. 17).

So - dead church?

No - not really!

Dead religion?

Definitely!

We desperately need to recognise the difference, so that we become such a dwelling place of the Father, Son and Spirit, that their celebration dance of mutual absolute love will be something we become caught up in and live the dance in and with them. Thus the difference between His dwelling place and man-encrusted religions that dare to carry His name will be as obvious as a lighthouse beam and a single candle.

We are His house, His dwelling place, His place of rest and pleasure!

TABLE: Always Available

Every banquet needs a table.

Where else can the platters, dishes, goblets and sweet meats be made available?

In Luke 22, Jesus asks:

Luke 22:27-30

Who is greater, the one who is at table or the one who serves? Is it not the one who is at the table? But I am among you as one who serves. You are those who have stood by Me in My trials, and I confer on you a kingdom, just as My Father conferred one on Me, so that you may eat and drink at My table in My kingdom and sit on thrones…

Obviously the one sat at the table is acknowledged as the greater. In this context, we who have inherited *the kingdom* sit at the table with Jesus, being waited on. What a wonderful scenario.

Solomon's wisdom was demonstrated in the food on his table (1 Kings 10:5). How much more the heavenly banqueting table! David, the man after God's own heart, sought out Mephibosheth because of the covenant that existed between himself and Jonathan. This ended with Mephibosheth eating daily at the king's table for the rest of his days. The covenant David was living by overwhelmed all the enmity between his family and the family of Saul, who had sought his life.

Mephibosheth was the crippled son of David's covenant partner. He was therefore the undeserving recipient of all the blessings, benefits and responsibilities of covenant. He chose to embrace these covenant blessings and enjoyed them in abundance until his life ended. He lived in the palace, sharing the feasts and every benefit of royalty as a covenant companion of the king. I have glossed over the deeper wonders of covenant, but I am sure you get the picture.

The *Table* demonstrates the covenant commitment of the King. Being brought to this banqueting table by our Lover Shepherd King of the New Covenant reminds us that we are the undeserving recipients of all the blessings of covenant. At the construction of the tabernacle, as already alluded to, Israel had to furnish the table with the 'shewbread'. This *Bread* represented the covenant with God - a visual reminder that "I will be your God; you will be My people."

Now, a simple loaf of bread on a table reminds us of the covenant made and sealed in the blood and body of our Sacrificial Lamb. This table is not an altar. The altar was a place of sacrifice. This table is the *Table of Provision*. The altar has been used, the sacrifice recognised. We have no need of an altar now, except the daily dying to self, carrying the cross and following the Saviour. Jesus died once for all. The work of the altar is over. There is no place any more for such an altar on earth. The bloody bleeding Lamb before the eyes of the Father in heaven is all that is left of the altar (Rev.5:6).

Whatever term is used in your church for the table that is used in whatever way the tradition dictates, 'altar' is not the correct word. Ultimately it is no more than a table - pieces of wood crafted into shape. It holds no divine power or presence. Take it out of the building and the table could end up in a shed, holding tools and garden implements. It is imperative we lift our eyes to Jesus only, the Lamb upon the throne. The table is a means to an end, never an end in itself. Remember that King David, before he was king, 'abused' the table by taking the bread from it to feed his hungry soldiers. If the 'man after God's own heart' was free to violate the traditions of his religion and still enjoy God's favour, it reveals something bigger than our ideas.

Wake up, church! It is never the utilitarian items that are important. It is always what they are pointing to and the state of the heart of the worshippers.

We began with the table in the context of covenant. I am constantly amazed at the wonderful faithfulness of God in His provision for our every need. This table is always full of everything to gladden our hearts, heal our pain, refresh our weary souls, encourage our spirits and strengthen our will to pursue God's heart and truly know Him. No matter how often you take from the table, it is always full. It never runs low. There is never anything lacking that you need.

I thank You Lord, and I am ever thankful
To know my flour barrel never shall empty be
And I am grateful that my cruse of oil

Shall ne'er run dry for 'tis supplied by Thee.
Grant me assurance Lord, that when supplies are lowest
When in my heart I need so much to know
That every time I go into my barrel
There'll be enough, even though it may be low.
And when I lift my little cruse of oil
But fear to tip it o'er lest it be dry
Teach me to trust and simply turn it over
To see once more Thy bountiful supply.
Help me, O Lord to never, never doubt Thee
For thou dost graciously supply my need
And every day my barrel is replenished
And I have flour and oil enough, indeed.

This poem, relating to the truth of Elijah's words to the widow at Zarephath has been in my possession since my childhood. I came across it in a book of daily devotions. The book is long gone, yet somehow these words have remained with me. I do not know the author.

God is a covenant-keeping God. He has committed Himself to us. His love will not countenance anything harmful to us. It is the thief who comes to kill, steal and destroy. Jesus came to give us abundant life in Him. As the Psalmist says:

Ps.63:5
My soul will be satisfied as with the richest of fair with singing lips my mouth will praise You.

I know some of this sounds so far removed from much of our daily experience. I can almost hear the catalogue of circumstances and experiences that seem to deny the reality of these words. I know God is truth and in Him is no deceit. It is impossible for God to lie. If God were a liar, He would not be God. So, His table is ever present in every situation, at every turn, whenever that letter demanding "money, or else..." lands on the hall floor. God's love is everlasting! He never withdraws love! His unfurled banner hovers above us in the divorce, through the trauma of death, in unemployment, in being overlooked for promotion, in sickness, in a split in the church fellowship, in every painful disappointment, He is always speaking love to us. The Psalmist caught something of this when he said:

Ps. 23:5
You prepare a table before me in the presence of my enemies.

This is it, in words which are so familiar and popular among Christians and non-Christians alike. Our covenant God prepares a table of abundance right in the face of our enemies. Beloved, once we come into relationship with God in Jesus through the indwelling Holy Spirit, we sign up to a lifelong battle. We are involved in war. Even a superficial reading of the bible reveals that warfare is a major thrust of its writers. God is a warring God. He wages war on everything that wars against His children. Jesus encouraged His disciples with words such as:

Jn.16:33
In the world you will have trouble, but, take heart, I have overcome the world.

A few verses earlier we read:

Jn.16:2
A time is coming when anyone who kills you will think he is offering a service to God.

Jn.15:18-19
If the world hates you, keep in mind that it hated Me first. If you belonged to the world it would love you as its own. As it is, you do not belong to the world, but I have chosen you out of the world. That is why the world hates you.

Back in the *Garden* at the beginning of life, God spoke these words to the tempter:

Gen.3:16

I will put enmity between you and the woman and between your offspring and hers. He will crush your head and you will bruise his heel.

There has been war in the human arena since our first parents. The battleground is your heart and mind, the places of choice and passion. The battle is not about 'Who is right here?' It is about 'How do I behave in this situation?' It is about 'Is my heart pure before God?

- Are my feelings under control?
- Am I seeing things in a true light or through the lens of my messed up emotions?

At such times Abba God lovingly invites us to feast at His table, to take to ourselves everything we need to empower and enable us to come through intact, in faith and in the secure knowledge of His love. He doesn't sweep these enemies away, necessarily. We still have to confront them. We do this in the knowledge that "He that is in you is greater than the one in the world." (1 Jn.4:4)

The church might split, the marriage end, the unemployment become a reality. In and through it all, the battle is for your heart and mind.

Matt.5:44-45

Love your enemies, pray for those who persecute you, that you may be sons of your Father in heaven.

Everyone loves those who love and flatter them. Everyone hates those who hate them. The sons of the Father in heaven demonstrate the heart of the Father in heaven. We choose to take from the table of grace the grace, healing, peace and love we need to bless the one who has brought us to pain.

- Without the bullies, how do we grow?
- How do we know His love casts out all fear if we never encounter a situation which brings fear? How do we prove the sufficiency of His grace?
- How do we grow more like Jesus?

He learned obedience by the things He suffered.

Why do you think this table is spread out in the face of the enemy?

Ps. 8:2

From the lips of children and infants You have ordained praise because of Your enemies to silence the foe and the avenger.

"Has God said?" is the challenge of the enemy. Praise God, He is my shield and my fortress! He is my glory and the lifter of my head. He is my faithful friend and deliverer. He always loves and keeps me as the apple of His eye. This is our response. The enemy goes apoplectic!

- How can this be?
- Who are these puny humans to overcome adversity in joy and faith?
- Why are they not grovelling in self-pity?
- Why aren't they lashing out with fists and cursing?
- Why aren't they drunk?
- Why are they staying with their spouses and loving their leaders?

And the enemy is silenced.

Also the child of God, surrounded by the enemy, who is only interested in stealing your heart, killing your hope and destroying your life, stands. We know in whom we have believed and are convinced that He is able to guard what has been entrusted to Him for that day. We are learning that "I can do all things through Him who gives me strength" (Phil.4:13).

We are facing opposition and standing in the grace of God. What a powerful demonstration of the wisdom of God in filling His new creations with Holy Spirit, that all the forces of darkness must acknowledge we have been redeemed and are the inheritors of His eternal kingdom. What a slap in the face *that* turns out to be for his satanic majesty!

It is the purpose of Father that we live and move and have our being in Him among the millions who unwittingly live in the deception that there is no devil, no hell, or heaven, among whom we shine as stars, spreading the light of the truth of Jesus before those whose hearts are blinded. This is how it works. And every time we come through victorious, because we have turned to the *Table Prepared,* so the light grows and the darkness diminishes.

Anyone who has met Dennis and Melanie Morgan-Dohner[1], know how they live out this life of victory and joy, despite living in the face of the 'last enemy', which is death. Medically speaking they should both have been in heaven years ago. Naturally speaking they should be full of bitterness, despair and loss of faith. The truth is they have learned to rejoice in their adversity - to celebrate life as God's daily gift - and they glow with His glory. Their song is of His goodness all the time; of His perfect love; of how He is always working good in every situation and how the 'worst' that can happen is that they die, then they are face to face with Jesus (so it is a win-win scenario.) They live in the truth of this song, an inspiration to everyone who moves within their shadow.

"In this world," said Jesus, "you will have trouble." Paul tells Timothy that those who will live a godly life in Christ Jesus will be persecuted (2 Tim.3:12). Get it settled! We live in the presence of our enemies in that they are always about, ever ready to pounce on our fears.

The answer?

Heb.12:2
Let us fix our eyes on Jesus.

As we set our hearts and affections on Jesus we are not enticed away. The table is always laid, heavy with provision for every need, every eventuality. Jesus constantly says, "Come to Me."

Let us look at the example of the chosen ones, living in slavery in Egypt. Such were you and I - slaves to our sinful nature, always choosing our own way, oblivious to His healing love, amusing ourselves with the empty trinkets of this life's enticements.

We drink deeply of what is offered: the glitz and glamour, the sex, drugs and rock and roll of our time. We drink in the lies of our culture, the empty promises of satisfaction: the great flashy car, the show home with all mod cons, the lavish vacations, the fashion, the messages of easy love from the entertainment business. We drink deeply of it all! And we are

---

[1] Since the time of writing, Melanie has gone to be with the Lord. Fireworks were displayed at her funeral in celebration of her life.

unsatisfied. So we throw ourselves in deeper - more of all of it! And still the taste it leaves behind, when the music stops and the lights go out, is like poison in our hearts. Don't misunderstand me. Some of this stuff is not harmful of itself. The emptiness comes when such is used as an answer to what only God can give. We are slaves to our passions, desires and habits "without hope and without God in the world" (Eph.2:12).

God hears the cry of our hearts. He hears the despairing cry of crushed and broken hearts, cries of hopelessness and helplessness, cries of anguish and desperation, and He comes to our aid:

Ex.3:7-10

I have indeed seen the misery of My people in Egypt. I have heard them crying out because of their slave drivers, and I am concerned about their suffering. So I have come down to rescue them from the hand of the Egyptians and to bring them up out of that land into a good and spacious land, a land flowing with milk and honey... the cry of the Israelites has reached Me... so, go now, I am sending you to Pharaoh to bring My people... out of Egypt.

As Moses was sent to bring deliverance to the Hebrews and lead them out into the place God had prepared for them, so Jesus has come, smashed down the gates of hell and brought us out in triumphal procession, to bring us home to the Father and the glory and joy of His kingdom. But, before they could enter into the experience and possession of their *Promised Land* inheritance, they had to go through the desert. Yes, forty years of it because of their rebellion and lack of faith.

Again the whispers of the enemy came to their ears.

"There are giants in the land. They are too big and numerous for you. You will fail. You will die. You would be better off going back to Egypt."

And they believed it.

In the wilderness experience they learned the blessing and provision of God as well as His protection. In the wilderness they experienced 'Jehovah Nissi' ('the Lord is my Banner'). Day by day God sent manna to feed them; year by year, for forty years, "your clothes didn't wear out, nor did your sandals on your feet" (Deut.29:5). Yet they were typical of humanity. Even with a cloud of glory leading them before their very eyes, even though a pillar of fire guards them by night, they were still filled with fear and doubt. They stumbled from crisis to crisis, from victory to crisis, from worship to idolatry, from obedience to rebellion.

Sounds familiar doesn't it?

Paul understood this. He uses this history to warn and encourage his readers and listeners.

1 Cor.10:1-10

Our forefathers were all under the cloud and they all passed through the sea. They were all baptised into Moses in the cloud and in the sea. They all ate the same spiritual food and drank the same spiritual drink, for they drank from the spiritual rock that accompanied them and that rock was Christ." Yet, "do not be idolaters, as some of them were… we should not test the Lord as some of them did, and were killed by snakes. Do not grumble, as some of them did and were killed by the destroying angel…

"These things", he said, "happened to them as examples and were written down as warnings for us, on whom the fulfilment of the ages has come." (1 Cor.10:11) "Learn from history," he says. Read your Bible; learn from what God has said and done before. Realise that "He will not let you be tempted beyond what you can bear. But, when you are tempted, He will also provide a way out so that you can stand under it" (1 Cor.10:13).

"He will provide a way out." This way out is the table. "Can God spread a table in the desert?" is the cry (Ps.78:19). The answer from heaven thunders out.

Ps.78:20,23-27

When He struck the rock, water gushed out and streams flowed abundantly… He gave a command to the skies above and opened the doors of the heavens. He rained down manna for the people to eat. He gave them the grain of heaven. Men ate the bread of angels. He sent them all the food they could eat…. He rained meat down on them like dust, flying birds like sand on the seashore.

"Yes!" is the emphatic word from heaven, a word supported by action. God is not an idle deity. He has not filled the Bible with richness and variety of promise to excite then disappoint us. He has not promised what He cannot deliver. For forty years He faithfully fed, watered, clothed, protected, fought for, 'presenced' Himself among, healed and led this mass of grumbling, unbelieving, fickle, failing treasures of His heart. For forty years angels carried the table of abundance, constantly replenishing every delicious and painful delicacy from the heart of the Father. Day by day, moment by moment, challenge by challenge, the table carried the answer. As Jesus says, in Luke 10:

Luke 10:19

I have given you authority to trample on snakes and scorpions and to overcome all the power of the enemy; nothing will harm you.

A dishful of authority! A bowlful of protection!

In the desert place the table is always spread. The desert is not always a bad place. It is certainly not the place to live, but it can be a place of incredible grace. Jesus was led by the Spirit into the desert and endured the temptations of satan. Returning victorious in the power of the Spirit, He began His ministry of making the Kingdom known. We read in Hosea:

Hos.2:14-17,19-20

'I am now going to allure her. I will lead her into the desert and speak tenderly to her. There I will give her back her vineyards, and will make the valley of Achor (trouble) a door of hope. There she will sing as in the days of her youth, as in the day she came out of Egypt. In that day,' declares the Lord, 'you will call Me, "My Husband". You will no longer call Me, "My Master". I will remove the names of the Baals from her lips... I will betroth you to Me forever... I will betroth you in righteousness and justice, in love and compassion. I will betroth you in faithfulness and you will acknowledge the Lord.'

A table of grace, healing, restoration and marriage - all found in the desert. This desert time was love-led. "I will lead her into the desert" - a harsh place, a place of deprivation, a place of dependence, a place of aloneness. Here, freed from every trapping of the heart, His healing, restoring balm is freely applied to our pain, disillusionment, disobedience, busyness, indifference, and we are loved back to life. Do not always be desperate to leave a desert place. They are scary experiences, difficult to embrace, but often love-led.

I remember a time when the 'felt presence' of God suddenly lifted off my life. You know about the 'felt presence'...

Yes, He is always with us. Whatever we are doing or experiencing, He is near. He is in us. No matter how painful, hard, strange, unjust our experience, the Spirit of God is with us. He has given us His precious promises: "I will never leave you. I am always with you." All of us have this truth before us, written on our hearts, yet how often we question this.

Remember Martha and Mary, Jesus' friends, sisters of Lazarus?

"If You had been here, my brother would not have died," they declared.

They believed that Jesus' presence would have meant their brother would have still been alive. His absence was almost seen as the reason Lazarus died. Is there a hint of "It's Your fault, Jesus; you weren't here when we needed You"? They are expressing the belief that when Jesus is present there is life. The strangling tentacles of death are kept away.

Jesus has promised to be with us forever. Jesus declared that Lazarus' sickness would not end in death even though He knew Lazarus would die. What would happen to Lazarus would be for "God's glory so that God's Son may be glorified" (Jn.11:4). Of course we know the end of the story. Lazarus was restored to life. Three words from the 'Resurrection and the Life' and death was subdued. The man walked out into life and health.

"Lazarus, come out!"

A consequence was that many put their faith in Him (Jn.11:45). At Bethany we read:

Jn.12:9-11

A large crowd of Jews found out that Jesus was there, and came, not only because of Him (Jesus) but also to see Lazarus whom He had raised from the dead... on account of him many of the Jews were going over to Jesus and putting their faith in Him.

Now, this is an extreme 'desert place'. Not one I would welcome. Yet it does illustrate that in everything God works for the good of those who love Him. How often, how easily, we turn against love, because of the pain or pressure of a circumstance.

- Where were You God?
- If You love me, why?
- If You had been here...

These desert times are difficult. We need the table spread before us. We need to know it is there - the place to run to and find everything needed for the challenge. Pick from the table the 'knowing'.

Zeph.3:17

The Lord your God is with you, He is mighty to save. He will take great delight in you, he will quiet you with His love, he will rejoice over you with singing.

Isa.43:1-3

Fear not, for I have redeemed you. I have summoned you by name, you are Mine. When you pass through the waters, I will be with you. When you pass through the rivers, they will not sweep over you. When you walk through the fire, you will not be burned; the flame will not set you ablaze, for I am the Lord your God.

Pick up this 'knowing'. Grasp it close, rehearse it often and draw strength from such truth. "Jesus my Lord is with me. He delights in me, even in the middle of this when my heart is bursting and I am frightened, angry, frustrated, hurt, feeling deserted, confused..." Apply the balm of love. "I will speak tenderly to her... and will make the valley of Achor a door of hope."

During this time when the 'felt presence' was not upon me, I was confused.

- What has happened?

- What sin has brought this veil?
- What have I done wrong?

These are the questions which crowd in, attempting to drown out the voice of love singing over us melodies of hope, rejoicing, sheer joy in our being His. You know, as well as the 'still small voice', He also thunders.

Ps.29:3-9

The voice of the Lord is powerful, majestic, it breaks the cedars, it strikes with flashes of lightning, it shakes the desert.

Did you see that 'it shakes the desert'?

It is important that we don't only listen for the 'still small voice'. Sometimes amid the clamour and violence of deceitful venomous voices assaulting our mind, His lightning word breaks through, His thunder shatters the demons, His majestic sound hushes everything to silence.

This experience was upon me for some time. Once I was fully aware that His 'feltness' had lifted, I resolved in my spirit to believe Him. I deliberately spoke out the truth that 'I will never leave you'. Many times a day I spoke to my heart and mind this glorious truth. Then suddenly, one evening, months later, during a worship service as I was on my knees before Him, He 'whooshed' down on me afresh - such an overwhelming sense of His 'felt presence'. It was wonderful. Eating daily bread for weeks sustained me in truth and kept my heart secure. I lived off the 'knowing'. The table was groaning under the weight of provision - something for every need - and I chose to grab some.

1 Kings 18:21

How long will you waver between two opinions? If the Lord is God, follow Him, but if Baal is god, follow Him.

Deut.30:15-20

See, I have set before you today life and prosperity, death and destruction. For I command you today to love the Lord your God. To walk in His ways and to keep His commands, decrees and laws; then you will live and increase and the Lord your God will bless you in the land you are entering to possess. But, if your heart turns away and you are not obedient and if you are drawn away to bow down to other gods and worship them, I declare to you this day that you will certainly be destroyed. You will not live long in the land you are crossing the Jordan to enter and possess. This day I call heaven and earth as witnesses against you that I set before you life and death, blessings and curses. Now choose life so that you and your children may live and that you may love the Lord your God, listen to His voice and hold fast to Him. For the Lord is your life.

That is it; choose life. Take from the table. It is always spread for you in the presence of your enemies and in the desert places.

1 Cor.10:13 (Amplified)

For no temptation (no trial regarded as enticing to sin) [no matter how it comes or where it leads] has overtaken you and laid hold on you that is not common to man (that is no temptation or trial has come to you that is beyond human resistance and that is not adjusted and adapted and belonging to human experience, and such as man can bear). But God is faithful (to His word and to His compassionate nature) and He (can be trusted) not to let you be tempted and tried and assayed beyond your ability and strength of resistance and power to endure, but with the temptation He will (always) also provide the way out (the means of escape to a landing place) that you may be capable and strong and powerful to bear up under it patiently.

We are never under pressure greater than we can endure. We can never use our weakness as an excuse. His strength is perfected in our weakness. It is Christ in me, the hope of glory. It is "greater is He that is in you that he that is in the world". Yes, we do fail and fall; and thank God, we have our advocate, the "One who speaks to the Father in our defence, Jesus Christ, the righteous One. He is the atoning sacrifice for our sins" (1 Jn.2:1-2).

Even when we are drowning under a flood of temptation and trial, His love perfectly calls us to life. By His Spirit in us we are enabled to choose life. His banner of love is always over us and His table gives evidence of that. We are never left alone. All that we need and the desire to find it and use it come from His Spirit within us. It is God who works in you to will and to act according to His good purpose (Phil.2:13). Every way we turn we are hedged in by Love - Love that cares, supports, upholds, encourages and provides. It is as if heaven is watching us, saying, "Come on, you can do this! Come on, you can come through and overcome that trial!" As parents we know the pride and joy of shouting encouragement to our children as they attempt a fresh challenge.

"My grace is sufficient"? It is laid out on the table in dazzling glory. We feast on the abundance of His house (Ps.36:8). When we choose to listen to the pain, or doubt, fear, anger, frustration, elation even, we are despising His grace. We are choosing to make it on our own which means we give in to fear, instead of laying hold of Life. We choose death; we give way to unbelief. We end up making God in our image. We end up listening to the voice in the Garden: "Has God said?"

Yes, He has said and His words are words of life.

"Come and eat," said Jesus to the disillusioned disciples after a night of fishing. "Come to Me and I will give you rest," He said to the weary and burdened. The table, shaded by His unfurled banner of love, is a constant reminder of who God is.

Faithful One, so unchanging.
Ageless One, You're my rock of peace.
Lord of All, I depend on You
I call out to You again and again.
You are my Rock in times of trouble
You lift me up when I fall down
All through the storm, Your love is the anchor
My hope is in You alone.

The table: a testimony to who God is!

The table is laid out on the finest, pure white linen, with the most lavish, exquisite, luxurious settings: goblets of wine, dishes of fruit, plates of breads, bowls of oil and meat, all of the finest, sparkling gold, wonderfully crafted with delightful filigree fineness, of amazing patterns and decoration; no two objects the same, yet so restful and re-assuring to the gaze, while provoking awe and wonder; breathtakingly displaying the handiwork of the Master Craftsman Designer. This table is endless to our eyes, stretching into eternity, the colours so startling - many never seen on earth - the array of choice beyond imagination. Our beautiful Bridegroom, Lover, King stands over it all, arms open wide, love shining from His eyes, and calling:

"Come!"

"Take these scriptures to strengthen your heart."

"Take this oil to heal your pain."

"Take this fruit of peace."

"Don't struggle and suffer without Me. Be of good cheer, I have overcome the world."

As the writer of Hebrews says:

Heb.4:14-16

Therefore since we have a great High Priest who has gone through the heavens, Jesus, the Son of God, let us hold firmly to the faith we profess. For we do not have a High priest who is unable to sympathise with our weaknesses, but we have one who is tempted in every way, just as we are, yet was without sin. Let us then approach the throne of grace with confidence, so that we may receive mercy and find grace to help us in our time of need.

'Who God is' is essential to our relationship with this table. We can grasp that 'God is love' because Jesus died for us. We know that much. What that love really means, I believe, is beyond the understanding and experience of many of us. Therefore 'who God is' is difficult to lay hold of, because the magnitude of Love is so beyond our embraced knowing. And God is love. Thus, if love is not fully taken hold of, God becomes to us other than He is, which diminishes Him in our hearts and minds. That leads us to fear and out of faith. Doubt is fear. It is the fear of not really trusting that what God has said He will do. When we doubt we hesitate. Hesitation leads to consideration of alternatives. Because we have moved into doubt, trusting God now seems to be a lesser option and the devices of our minds appear to be far more reasonable. Let's face it - who is going to jump without seeing the safety net? It is possible because Love says, "Underneath are the everlasting arms" (Deut.33:27).

When we see God as other than He is, He becomes too much like us. This is idolatry. We make God into someone He is not. When He has become too much like us, we struggle to trust His word, His love. We begin to reject His truth as 'unreasonable' and turn to our own devices. This always leads to failure, futility, pain, anxiety and disillusionment. Now we have in the bank of our experience all those negatives. So, next time we need to write a cheque to get us out of trouble, all we have are negatives. We have nothing in our credit or benefit account. All because we are not sure who God is.

The Israelites celebrated Passover year after year. This was a constant reminder of the God who delivered them and brought them into the land 'flowing with milk and honey'. They had something real, tangible, to hold on to. Yes, we know they messed up regularly, but they had this reminder that God was their deliverer. As generation gives way to generation, so the memory grows dimmer, and faith gives way to doubt. As time passes, our memory of Father's goodness grows dim, unless it is regularly celebrated and experienced.

- When was the last time you had the courage to trust God?
- Is He the daily source of all that is?
- Is God your provider? Or is it the monthly pay cheque?
- Is God your source of joy? Or is it the TV, the bottle, the friends?

The table prepared in the sight of every enemy and spread in the desert of our hardest times will only hold appeal to us as we trust the provider.

When we know that He is altogether Perfect Love who always has plans for good in our lives; who always promises to work good in everything; who always is committed to completing the beautiful work He has begun in us; who can be depended on because He is God; who makes sense when nothing else seems to; who never lets us down, despite our perceptions; a God who cannot fail; then we can approach the table in confidence, with a security in who He is. I have used the word 'always' because God is unchangeable. He is the same today as He has always been and ever will be. He never changes His mood. He is in a good mood today, tomorrow, the day after, right into eternity. He does not favour one above another. From everlasting to everlasting, He is God. It is impossible for Him to lie. He inhabits eternity. He is far above even the best we can grasp of Him.

My wife and I share a wonderful deep love. We trust each other fully. I know she would never cheat on me. She believes the same of me. We have no secrets; everything is always brought to the 'light', into the open, no matter how painful. We have a great security in each other. She trusts my care and provision. She has no doubts about my love. We don't have private messages on the phone or mobile. We don't keep separate accounts at the bank. We believe we are meant to be one in God and that is our commitment. If we can find this level of trust with each other, how much more may we trust our heavenly husband - Jesus, the bridegroom?

Do you know, I mean *really* know, not just accept in a creedal way, that "My grace is sufficient for you"; that "I will never leave you or forsake you"; that "nothing can separate us from the love of God that is in Christ Jesus our Lord"; that "I am God, I change not"?

If so, come quickly, confidently and help yourself. Should you admit your belief is more in the mind than the heart then come to this table anyway, for here you will find gifts of life to answer everything within you, and move your knowledge of God from your head to your heart and enrich your experience and heart knowledge of Father God.

There is a story in the gospels about a Canaanite woman who implored Jesus for her daughter's deliverance. Jesus appeared to reject her request telling her she was not 'fitted' to receive His blessing. She refused to give up and pressed in.

Matt.15:27

Even the dogs eat the crumbs that fall under their master's table.

Here, she doesn't argue her case. She doesn't defend her status. She only has one desire, to touch the heart of the Saviour. Jesus responds to her passionate declaration affirming that He is the answer, and her daughter is healed. It matters not how many times you have failed. It matters not how important and deserving you think you are. Even the crumbs from the table, the careless discarding, are meat to a hungry soul.

He that comes to God must believe that He is, and that He is the Rewarder of those who seek Him.

God keeps no record of wrongs. Your slate is wiped clean because of the blood of the Lamb. This woman is like the sinner in the temple who beat on his breast and said, "Lord be merciful to me, a sinner."

She too knew she had need. She was not proud. She came and asked, yes, implored, refusing to go away empty.

Matt.5:6
Blessed are those who hunger and thirst after righteousness, for they will be filled.

Isa.55:1-2
Come, all you who are thirsty, come to the waters and you who have no money, come buy and eat. Come buy wine and milk without money and without cost. Listen, listen to Me, and eat what is good, and your soul will delight in the richest of fare.

If you have a need, the Father says, "Come." Come and receive what you cannot buy. Consume what is good, not the bread of affliction, but the Bread of Life.

Isa.41:17-18
The poor and needy search for water, but there is none; their tongues are parched with thirst. But I the Lord will answer them; I, the God of Israel, will not forsake them. I will make rivers flow on barren heights, and springs within the valleys. I will turn the desert into pools of water, and the parched ground into springs.

Come, for the feast is ready!

ROYALTY: Who do you think you are?

Parties are for people, banquets are for royalty!

From all my years as a Christian, I know that there are many people within what is broadly called 'the church' who have no concept of being anything other than 'a vile sinner'- having an attitude of grovelling, of embracing the words of the Psalmist:

Ps. 22:6
But I am a worm and not a man.

...words also echoed by the prophet Isaiah:

Isa.4:14
Do not be afraid, O worm Jacob, O little Israel.

There are people who are always living in guilt, feeling unworthy; always needing to make retribution to God for their sins and perceived wrongs; people never coming into the truth of the gospel. What great sadness! What a travesty of the glorious gospel of our Lord Jesus Christ!

1 Jn.1:7
The blood of Jesus, His Son, purifies us from all sin.

My next statement may surprise you or even offend. But before you throw this book away, bear with me - all will be explained.

I am not a sinner!

I was a sinner, but since Jesus brought me to the Father as a cleansed, restored, made-new Christian, I ceased to be a sinner and became a saint - a saint who sins. Even the most casual of readers of the New Testament cannot help but see the legitimacy of this statement. Note, I have not said, "I don't sin." I am emphasizing the cosmic shift in who I am, and therefore who you are, as a child of God. There is no sin in God's kingdom. There is no sin in Christ. There is no sin stronger than the blood of Jesus.

Col.1:13

For He has rescued us from the dominion of darkness and brought us into the kingdom of the Son He loves, in whom we have redemption, the forgiveness of sins.

Col.1:17

I am in Christ and Christ is in me.

Col.1:21-22, emphasis added

Once you were alienated from God and were enemies in your minds because of your evil behaviour. But now He has reconciled you by Christ's physical body, through death, to present you <u>holy in his sight</u>, without blemish and <u>free</u> from accusation.

Notice Paul's greetings to the churches: "To all the saints in Christ Jesus", "to the saints", "together with all the saints", "called to be saints." Yes, once you are a Christian you are no longer a sinner. You are now a saint, who fails and sins.

2 Cor.5:17

If anyone is in Christ he is a new creation; the old has gone, the new has come.

Why have I brought this up?

Because to not embrace the full reality of the gospel is to despise the love and grace which Abba has shown us in Jesus; also we remain in bondage rather than the freedom for which Christ has set us free.

You are a *Prince*, not a pauper!

As Kris Valloton says, "Identity does not come from education but from impartation" (Supernatural ways of Royalty, Pg.64). God has imparted His life into us. It defies all human logic. It defies our consciousness of ourselves. It defies our experiences. But, God has made us His new creation.

1 Pt.2:9

You are a chosen people, a royal priesthood, a holy nation, a people belonging to God.

There we have it: "you are a royal priesthood".
You are royalty!

James.2:5

Has not God chosen those who are poor in the eyes of the world to be rich in faith and to inherit the Kingdom He promised those who love Him?

God has chosen you to inherit the kingdom. Those who inherit a kingdom are royal sons of the king. Jesus is our Prince of Peace. God has exalted Jesus as Prince and Saviour (Acts 5:31).

Now, if Jesus is Prince, so are you!

Why?

Because Jesus "is not ashamed to call them brothers" (Heb.2:11).

If your brother is a prince, what does that make you?

Rev. 19:16

On His robe and on His thigh He has this name written, 'King of Kings and Lord of Lords.'

Jesus is the King (and we are His brothers - the children of God), who is King forever, therefore *we* must be royalty.

Why do I see this as important?

We are ambassadors of Christ and His kingdom. We represent Him on earth. As in the natural an ambassador is seen as representing his nation and speaks and conducts business on behalf of his nation, so we stand as Jesus' representatives on earth, manifesting the affairs of His kingdom and government. Our lives, in every way, are a little piece of heaven on earth. Thus, as familial representatives of God the King, we must be seen as royalty and own it for ourselves. We are not paupers; we are princes. Royalty! To evidence our elevation from the pit to the palace, our wonderful King and Father dresses us with the most suitable attire for our high calling.

Isa.61:10

For He has clothed me with garments of salvation and arrayed me in a robe of righteousness.

In salvation Jesus has removed our shame and guilt. I love the beautiful picture Zechariah gives us of Joshua the high priest in the third chapter of his book.

Zech.3:3-5

Now, Joshua was dressed in filthy clothes, as he stood before the angel. The angel said to those who were standing before him: 'Take off his filthy clothes.' Then he said to Joshua, 'See I have taken away your sin and I will put rich garments on you.' Then I said: 'Put a clean turban on his head'. So they put a clean turban on his head and clothed him, while the Angel of the Lord stood by.

Isaiah's pen almost seems to run away from him as he exults in the work of Christ on our behalf.

Isa.61:3

To bestow on them a crown of beauty, instead of ashes: the oil of gladness instead of mourning: a garment of praise instead of a spirit of despair.

Isa.62:3

You will be a crown of splendour in the Lord's hand, a royal diadem in the hand of your God.

We are a royal priesthood, not by any merit on our part but completely by the love gift of our Father in heaven. It behoves us to embrace the gifts of God, even while we struggle to understand how it can be so. "Lord give me the grace of faith to be able to grasp and embrace that You have made me a royal son in Your Kingdom."

What does it mean to be 'royal'?

It means we live in a way that displays our royal standing. It means we acknowledge what God has brought us into. We take it on board, not only intellectually but experientially. Realising what royalty means brings us to a way of living and behaving. Every aspect of living speaks of being royal.

As brothers and disciples of our great high priest, brother, lover, king Jesus, we should find ourselves being imitators of Him and His example. Paul had the audacity to say to the Corinthians:

1 Cor.4:16

I urge you to imitate me. [i.e 'be followers of me.']

Again he says:

1 Cor.11:1 (Amplified)

Pattern yourselves after me [follow my example] as I imitate and follow Christ [the Messiah].

Is this not what each of us deeply desires - that our whole life will be a reflection of following Jesus - to be a reflection of Him?

One thing I know: where God calls and commands us in scripture to embrace certain attributes and attitudes, it is plain that we are able, through the indwelling Holy Spirit, who is in us to will (cause us to want to) and to act (follow through in our actions) according to His good pleasure, to come into the reality of His call. If it is His pleasure that we be holy, humble, not afraid, then it truly is real for us to enter into such living experiences by the power that works in us, which is as the working of His mighty strength, which He exerted in Christ when He raised Him from the dead and seated Him at His right hand in the heavenly realms (Eph.1:19-20).

It is not about human effort, trying with all our might to clean up our minds and mouths. It is in reliance upon the indwelling Spirit and choosing to respond to His promptings that we will change our language and library, our looking and listening. Thus as we look into living royally as Jesus did, does, and ever will, we can confidently will to bring our lives into agreement, because on the banqueting table is the provision of will and enabling to become more like Jesus. Some of the best-known and loved words in the New Testament open up the way to living royally.

Phil.2:5-11

Your attitude should be the same as that of Christ Jesus, who being in very nature, God, did not consider equality with God something to be grasped, but made Himself nothing, taking the very nature of a servant, being made in human likeness. And being found in appearance as a man, He humbled Himself and became obedient unto death, even death on a cross. Therefore God exalted Him to the highest place and gave Him the name that is above every name; that at the name of Jesus every knee should bow in heaven and on earth and under the earth and every tongue confess that Jesus Christ is Lord, to the glory of God the Father.

Jesus' attitude was to make Himself nothing, of no reputation, to strip Himself of all privileges and rightful dignity, so as to assume the guise of a servant, a slave. He was not even content to embrace this level of humility but sought to humble Himself even further.

Ch.2:8 (Amplified)

He abased and humbled Himself (still further) and carried His obedience to the extreme of death, even the death of the cross.

Oh, how far we have to go in becoming like Jesus! How easily we become offended should someone sit in 'our seat' in church, or be preferred to *us* for a particular task we believed we were best suited for. How difficult many of us find it to assist with the dusting of the furniture and preparing the sanctuary for public worship.

How many church leaders never conceive of putting out chairs or not having a parking place marked out for them?

Being royal in God's kingdom is the complete reverse of royalty in the natural world of men. Being royalty is evidenced by humble service. Of the religious leaders of His day Jesus said:

Matt.15:8-9

These people honour Me with their lips but their hearts are far from Me. They worship Me in vain, their teachings are but rules taught by men.

Matt 6:16

When you fast, do not look sombre as the hypocrites do, for they disfigure their faces to show men they are fasting.

Lk.11:43

Woe to you Pharisees because you love the most important seats in the synagogue and greetings in the marketplace.

Living in humble servanthood will probably bring similar reactions to what Jesus experienced. Religion is always affronted by humility and righteousness. Yet, in all His teaching, Jesus emphasises this cornerstone of royal character!

Matt.5:3 (Amplified)

Blessed (happy, to be envied and spiritually prosperous with the life, joy and satisfaction in God's favour and salvation, regardless of their outward conditions) are the poor in spirit (the humble, who rate themselves insignificant) for theirs is the kingdom of heaven.

Mk.9:35

If anyone wants to be first, he must be the very last, and the servant of all.

On one occasion an argument broke out among the disciples over who would be the greatest. Jesus took a young child, stood him in front of the arguing disciples and said:

Lk.9:46-48

Whoever welcomes this little child in My name, welcomes Me. And whoever welcomes Me welcomes the One who sent Me. For he who is least among you all, he is the greatest.

Choosing to serve is so dear to the heart of the Father. Jesus demonstrated it throughout His earthly life. On one occasion a leper came and asked Jesus to heal Him. We read that Jesus "reached out His hand and touched the man." Not only did He command healing and set the man free, He associated Himself with the man and his condition. Touching a leper was tantamount to inviting leprosy to take over your body. Lepers were isolated: separate, unclean. Jesus touched a man who probably had not known a human touch for years and gave him respect and dignity through that act of humility and coming alongside.

On hearing the news of the death of John the Baptist, Jesus took a boat ride to get away from the crowds and busyness. On landing He found a large crowd of hungry, expectant, needy, hurting people. He had compassion on them, and healed the sick - no excuses like being tired, having a busy schedule, being hungry, needing a break and some peace and quiet. He was overwhelmed with compassion and gave Himself in service to give life to the needy. He gained a reputation as a friend of drunks and undesirables. He was not known for mixing with the 'movers and shakers'. He did not court favour with the rich, famous and influential. Somehow I doubt He would have had a photograph of Himself enjoying lunch with the Prime Minister or President hanging on his study wall. Our attitude should be the same as that of Christ Jesus!

Alongside humility and compassion, Jesus showed mercy.

Matt.9:10-13

While Jesus was having dinner at Matthew's house many tax collectors and 'sinners' came and ate with Him and His disciples. When the Pharisees saw this they asked His disciples, 'Why does your teacher eat with tax collectors and sinners?' On hearing this, Jesus said, 'It is not the healthy who need a doctor, but the sick. But go and learn what this means, "I desire mercy, not sacrifice" for I have not come to call the righteous, but sinners.'

- How many of us have sat in a doorway with an unwashed, unshaven, destitute person?
- How many have welcomed in to our home someone in need of a bath and a bed?

I have heard alarm bells warning about such actions, but I am constantly faced with the question: is my stuff of greater worth than this person Jesus loves and died for? How easy it is to look down on others. We quickly put on a 'cloak of righteousness' that crosses over to the other side of the road.

Remember Paul's words to the Corinthians?

1 Cor.6:9-11

Do you not know that the wicked will not inherit the kingdom of God? Do not be deceived, neither the sexually immoral nor idolaters, nor adulterers nor male prostitutes, nor homosexual offenders, nor thieves nor the greedy, nor drunkards nor slanderers will inherit the kingdom of God. And, that is what some of you were. But you were washed, you were sanctified, you were justified in the name of the Lord Jesus Christ and by the Spirit of our God.

"That is what some of you were"... It is easy to forget how far from God we used to be. How easily we can lose sight of who and what we were before the grace of God invaded our lives. But for the grace of God, I am that drunk, that thief, that prostitute, that child molester, that spouse beater. Oh yes – "Mercy there was great and grace was free, pardon there was multiplied to me. There my burdened soul found liberty, at Calvary."

Placing our tithe in the basket while shutting up our hearts to the needy draws this response from God:

Mal.1:6-8

'A son honours his father and a servant his master. If I am a father, where is the honour due Me? If I am a master, where is the respect due Me?' says the Lord Almighty. 'It is you, O priests, who show contempt for My name. But you ask, "How have we shown contempt for Your name?" You place defiled food on My altar. But you ask, "How have we defiled You?" By saying that the Lord's table is contemptible! When you bring blind animals for sacrifice, is that not wrong? When you sacrifice crippled or diseased animals is that wrong?'

Isa. 58:6-7

Is not this the kind of fasting I have chosen, 'To loose the chains of injustice and untie the cords of their yoke, to set the oppressed free and break every yoke?' Is it not to share your food with the hungry and to provide the poor wanderer with shelter, when you see the naked to clothe him, and not turn away from your own flesh and blood?

Matt.5:7

Blessed are the merciful, for they will be shown mercy.

Matt.10:8

Freely you have received, freely give.

You know, there are more than two thousand verses of scripture which speak about poverty and justice. Mercy is in God's heart. It is shown in those who are His royal sons. Sacrifice finds its place in the royal heart. Jesus said to His disciples:

Matt.16: 24-25

If anyone would come after Me, he must deny himself and take up his cross and follow Me. For whoever wants to save his life will lose it, but whoever loses his life for Me will find it.

Denying yourself is part of taking up the cross. In this denial we choose not to please ourselves. We choose not to give in to the easy way, the comfortable path, saying 'no' to our natural desires. We do this not for its own sake but to enable us to follow Jesus. Of course this can also mean we have to hang in there in the difficult place and not abandon such responsibility for an easier way. Denying ourselves is an act of the will, as is taking up the cross. The cross is a place of death. It means execution. It means:

Gal.2:20

I have been crucified with Christ and I no longer live, but Christ lives in me. The life I live in the body, I live by faith in the Son of God, who loved me and gave Himself for me.

Gal.5:24

Those who belong to Christ Jesus have crucified the sinful nature with its passions and desires.

Gal.6:14

May I never boast except in the cross of our Lord Jesus Christ through which the world has been crucified to me and I to the world.

If we are dead we cannot make choices to please ourselves. We cannot be offended or insulted. Coming to this understanding releases us from so much of the sinful nature. It is this natural nature which reacts when it is hurt or mocked or its throne is challenged. So we can make choices when someone offends us, insults us, despises us. We can choose not to receive that which is directed at us and to react to it in an ungodly way. It is by faith in Jesus, believing His love, His truth, His good desires toward us that we will respond to every situation according to His example. We can look at the world we live in, the culture that presses in on us, and see that in Jesus we have something better. Therefore we are not subject to the pressures and mindset of society. We fix our eyes and will on Jesus, holding the things of this life loosely, that He may have our hearts. We either give in to the words and enticements of our culture, or we step out and live in a Christ-like culture, where others matter more than our status symbols.

"We all have our cross to bear"... I have heard this cry all my life. That is not what these scriptures are saying. We do not bear a cross; we die on it. The stuff that comes to us in life is just that - the stuff of life. In Father's hands it produces *kingdom fruit* as the character of Jesus is more perfectly formed in us. It is not about feeling sorry for ourselves in our situation - enduring the difficulties while telling God all the things we have given up for Him.

1 Pet.5:7

Cast all your care on Him, for He cares for you.

No, that is not being crucified; taking up the cross is a daily act of the will to choose to please God with everything of our life that day, by living as Jesus did. It is not putting up with the stuff of life. This is demonstrated by Jesus in Gethsemane:

Matt.26:39,53-54

My Father, if it is possible, may this cup be taken away from Me. Yet, not as I will, but as You will... Do you think I cannot call on My Father and He will at once put at My disposal more than twelve legions of angels? But how then, would the scriptures be fulfilled that say it must happen in this way?

Jesus, out of His love and devotion to His Father, chooses to please the Father, to submit to His ways, not pleasing Himself. This is the springboard for all 'taking up the Cross'. It comes from love - love for the One who has brought us to the banqueting house and draped a love banner over our head. This love so captivates and compels us that we have no other choice than to agree with Love.

How was Jesus able to live like this?

Jn.13:3

Jesus knew that the Father had put all things under His power and that He had come from God and was returning to God.

Jesus' identity and security was completely found in His Father. He never needed the applause of people. He never had to prove Himself, show people how clever He was. He lived in the 'shalom' of being known and perfectly loved by the Father. You are known and perfectly loved by the Father. He has made you His sons and daughters, raised you to glory.

Therefore we can follow Jesus and wash the feet of the saints. I don't mean in a religious ritual! I mean in a life given away to God, to humbly serve those around us. Sacrifice is royal character. Some time ago, while I was meditating on the story of Abraham and Isaac, I was held captive to this tale. I could not get away from it as I allowed the Spirit to speak into me. One day He so startled me with, what was to me, a revelation of seismic proportions. He showed me that sacrifice is not following Him into whatever He opens up. Sacrifice is staying put. Sacrifice is in not saying 'yes' to Him. He showed me how those who take the easy life, doing their religious duty Sunday by Sunday, but living for themselves, have chosen to sacrifice all the wonders of knowing His heart, His power. They have chosen to sacrifice; to give up experiencing His revelations, hearing His voice, being anointed to accomplish *kingdom* things.

'Giving up' everything of this life, its security, comforts, ease, is not a sacrifice in kingdom terms because it opens us up to all the fullness of His heart, His grace, the excitement of partnering with Him in kingdom adventures, of seeing the lame walk, the deaf hear, the prisoners released, the lost coming into salvation relationship with Him.

"What sacrifice is that?" He asked me.

I was blown away. It still affects me. Sacrifice boils down to choosing not to enter into the deeper, more wondrous things of the heart of the Father. Yes, sacrifice of my heart to His will, choosing to die to me to live to Him, is royal character. The power and desire to walk in it is a finger-length away, waiting on the table of endless provision of grace.

Further to this is the reflection of royalty in our words. Speech often reflects the social class we were born into. Something which should define the children of God is that which comes out of our mouths. James states that which seems to be so obvious when he declares that "no man can tame the tongue" (Jam.3:8).

He likens the tongue to a fire, something that consumes and spreads destruction wherever it goes. A person is corrupted by what comes out of the mouth. We can praise God and curse men. Our tongues destroy or build up. Fresh and bitter water cannot both come from the same spring, yet the same mouth praises and curses at will. How true it is that no man can tame the tongue. We are not capable because it is always out the abundance of the heart that the mouth speaks (Matt.12:34).

Therefore until our hearts are changed, our speech will not alter. It is only God who creates in us a clean heart, a new heart of flesh that feels with His compassion. When our heart is made new, so are our words. With a new heart filled with the abundance of the Father's love, we can speak love to everyone we meet.

Prov.18:21

The tongue has the power of life and death and those who love it will eat its fruit.

This shows the importance of everything we say and how we say it. I am either speaking life to people or my words speak death. If I tell my child it is stupid, I am speaking death to the heart and spirit of that child. To tell yourself, "I'll never be any good," is to speak death to your heart. To speak words of hope, encouragement and affirmation speaks life to the heart and spirit in a man.

Prov.15:4

The tongue that brings healing is a tree of life, but a deceitful tongue crushes the spirit.

On this basis Paul instructs the church at Colossae:

Col.4:6

Let your conversation be always full of grace, seasoned with salt, so that you may know how to answer everyone.

"Always full of grace"... not only among the faithful in a Christian gathering but equally in a social gathering or work environment. You see, "the lips of the righteous nourish many" and "the tongue of the righteous is choice silver."

Prov.10:20-21,20:15

Lips that speak knowledge are a rare jewel.

Jeremiah makes this challenging revelation:

Jer.17:16

What passes my lip is open before You.

Every word we utter is known to God. As the Psalmist says:

Ps.139:4

Before a word is on my tongue, You know it completely O Lord.

That joke, comment, observation, that bit of gossip, every word is known to Father God. Every word we use witnesses that we are sons of the *King*, or denies it! As *royal* sons we seek to emulate the King and His Kingdom. Of the King we read:

1 Pet.2:22-23

He committed no sin, and no deceit was found in His mouth. When they hurled their insults at Him, He did not retaliate. When He suffered He made no threats.

This is part of the example Jesus gave that we should follow in His steps!

You know, we can say, "God bless you," when unkind and untrue words are hurled at us. It works life in us, and life in the person to whom they are addressed. The confusion of not receiving a hot, nasty, angry retort leaves a person wondering about the life, power and grace at work in you.

What do I mean?

Col.3:8-10

But now you must rid yourselves of all such things as these; anger, rage, malice, slander, and filthy language from your lips. Do not lie to each other, since you have taken off your old self with its practices and have put on the new self which is being renewed in knowledge in the image of its creator.

Eph.4:29

Do not let any unwholesome talk come out of your mouths, but only what is helpful for building others up according to their needs, that it may benefit those who listen.

And again in chapter 5:

Eph.5:4

Nor should there be obscenity, foolish talk or coarse joking which is out of place, but rather thanksgiving.

These words are very specific: "Clean up your mouths, church!" And, we can do it! We can make that choice, because at our side at all times is the supply of grace on the banqueting table: pleasures forevermore, containing every good thing of kingdom wholeness and wholesomeness. Remember Isaiah as he has a wonderful vision of God in His glory:

Isa.6:5-7

'Woe to me,' I cried, 'I am ruined! For I am a man of unclean lips and I live among a people of unclean lips and my eyes have seen the King, the Lord Almighty'. Then one of the seraphs flew to me with a live coal in his hand, which he had taken with tongs from the altar. With it he touched my mouth and said, 'See, this has touched your lips, your guilt is taken away and your sins atoned for.'

God is ready to clean up our language and speech. The fire of His refining Spirit is waiting for a heart that yearns for a holy life which mirrors and reflects His glory. God is not impressed with our excuses. We have to make up our mind that we are choosing for God, choosing life.

Heb.13:15

Through Jesus, therefore, let us continually offer to God a sacrifice of praise, the fruit of lips that confess His name.

The fruit of confessing Jesus is that we offer praise to God. Praise is the inevitable product of relationship with God. We cannot have experience of God, know Him as Lord and Saviour, without offering Him praise. He is God. Drink that in afresh right now. Does not praise, adoration, worship, awe well up deep within? God the Almighty, Holy, Majestic, Awesome Creator King of my life and all that is within the universe has revealed His love to us. He has made us His children, His sons, royal sons of the King of all kings. What can I do but praise?

Ps.63:3-4

Because Your love is better than life, my lips will glorify You. I will praise Your name as long as I live. In Your name I will lift up my hands.

Ps.51:15

O Lord, open my lips and my mouth will declare Your praise.

To which our heavenly Bridegroom replies:

SS 4:11

Your lips drop sweetness as the honeycomb, My Bride, milk and honey is under your tongue.

The pleasure dear Jesus finds in our words of grace and blessing, of encouragement and wisdom, of praise and exaltation, far outweighs the momentary satisfaction of telling someone what we think, whether they like it or not.

"Do everything without complaining," says Paul.

Why?

So that we become more fully children of God, faultless in a crooked and depraved generation, shining like stars in the universe, as we hold out the word of life (Phil.2:15-16). What we say causes us to shine in the darkness as we speak the words of life.

Col.3:15-17

Be thankful, let the word of Christ dwell in you richly, as you teach and admonish one another with all wisdom, and as you sing psalms, hymns and spiritual songs with gratitude in your hearts to God. And whatever you do, whether in word or deed, do it all in the name of the Lord Jesus, giving thanks to God the Father, through Him.

Phil.4:4

Rejoice in the Lord, always, and again I say rejoice.

Eph.5:20

...always giving thanks to God the Father for everything in the name of the Lord Jesus.

No complaining, always thankful - this is the call of God to the church. Remember, He is not impressed by our excuses, but is always at work in us, for us, to accomplish His purposes in us. As His royal representatives in this world, we exhibit attitudes of humility, compassion, servanthood, matching our hearts with our words, and all for the glory of the King and Father of us all.

Rom.15:5-6

May the God, who gives endurance and encouragement, give you a spirit of unity among yourselves as you follow Christ Jesus so that with one heart and mouth you may glorify the God and Father of our Lord Jesus Christ.

CLOTHING: The Great Fashion Designer

We saw in the last chapter how God has clothed us in garments of royalty. He clothed our first parents to cover their shame and nakedness. The blood of Jesus makes us clean from every sin. Joshua the priest was stripped of his filthy clothing as a sign that his sin had been taken from him (Zech.3:1-3). God has taken from us all the filthiness of our sinful life, stripped us clean and free of it - in the Spirit, separated.

Now he comes to give us the clothes of our new life and relationship: robes of beauty to replace the ashes of a dead life, garments of praise to take the place of the burdensome weight of a life struggling without knowing the power of His love. Now thankfulness fills our hearts. He has lifted us from the pit, from the mire of sucking mud that drags us down. We are free to be thankful and give Him praise for all He has done. He has given us the garments of salvation. It is our uniform. As a policeman is recognised by his uniform, so the garments of salvation make us recognisable as royal sons and daughters, kingdom servants, the army of God. As Ezekiel says:

Ezek.16:14

'Your fame spread among the nations on account of your beauty, because the splendour I had given you made your beauty perfect,' declares the Sovereign Lord.

The gracious works of Abba God in us and upon us make us a breathtakingly beautiful bride, whose beauty will fill the earth with His fame. Before this can happen, as with Joshua the priest, the filthy garments, the rags of sinful pride and self, have to be stripped away.

Jesus tells us that those who wear fine clothes are in king's palaces (Matt.11:8). He is drawing the analogy between John the Baptist, the hermit-like great prophet who went about in skins, a sort of spectacle to the people, yet the greatest born of woman. Closely allied to this comparison of extremes is the style of the Pharisees, the religious leaders and influencers of His day.

Lk.20:46-47

Beware of the teachers of the law. They like to walk around in flowing robes and love to be greeted in the market places and have the most important seats in the synagogues, and the places of honour at banquets. They devour widows' homes and for show make lengthy prayers. Such men will be punished most severely.

Wearing long robes and flowing garments may signify earthly position and wealth, but that is all it signifies! Our British culture is riddled with many forms of costume that represent authority, position, power and importance. Any newsreel of the law courts or opening of Parliament show such costume and colourful pageant.

- Is it really important?
- Does justice triumph because the lawyer is wearing a wig?
- Are compassionate and moral laws on the statute books as a consequence of men parading in dark suits and 'pantomime' outfits?
- Is it anything other than pomp and circumstance?

Our British mindset sees a businessman dressed in a city suit as someone efficient, skilled and trustworthy because of the clothes he wears. We see a teenager wearing a 'hoodie' as a thug! Is this why so many religious leaders and clergymen feel a need to wear a 'human costume' to distinguish them in their role? I certainly did in the early days of my time as a pastor. I felt the need to be recognised as 'the pastor', hence my very uncomfortable dog collar. Well, uncomfortable when sitting on a hot morning with your head deep in a book and the collar digging into your neck!

- What is the spiritual value of all the robes, mitres, dog collars, different coloured robes for different seasons and occasions?
- Is this what God wants?
- Is it anything other than age old power trophies paraded as vital symbols of spiritual leadership?

Priestly robes can never cover a sinful heart, any more than a pinstriped suit can cover a clever, crafty thief in the business world. The recent banking collapse clearly illustrates this! What we are is known to God. Nothing can ever cover that up - no amount of charitable work or generous giving or even attendance at a church building. Only the precious blood of Jesus can take away sin.

"Watch out for false prophets," said Jesus. "They come to you in sheep's clothing, but inwardly they are ferocious wolves. By their fruit you will recognise them." (Matt.7:15-16)

James warns us against seeing people from the outside only. He tells us:

Jam.2:2-4

My brothers, as believers in our glorious Lord Jesus Christ, don't show favouritism. Suppose a man comes into your meeting wearing a gold ring and fine clothes and a poor man in shabby clothes also comes in. If you show special attention to the man wearing fine clothes and say 'here's a good seat for you', but say to the poor man 'you stand there', or 'sit on the floor by my feet', have you not discriminated among yourselves and become judges with evil thoughts?

Impressed by outward show, we display the inclinations of the heart. A phrase came into the language some years ago as part of the feminist package: 'power dressing'. It represented women 'getting on' in the business world, assisted by the cut of their clothes - the female equivalent of the 'pinstriped suit'. Ability had to cover itself in a certain way to gain credibility. How shallow the heart can be.

Which is worse: the age-old practice of dressing in a sexually provocative way to get 'noticed' or this contemporary style of power dressing? Both are demeaning of personhood and ability.

- Does the sermon carry greater authority because the preacher is wearing robes or a dog collar or both?
- Is bread and wine more enriching because it is presented and offered by a person in a uniform?

God cuts to the quick so often. He is never impressed with our performance. It is unction He desires, not uniform!

Joel 2:12-13

Return to Me with all your hearts, with fasting, weeping and mourning. Rend your hearts and not your garments. Return to the Lord for He is gracious and compassionate; slow to anger and abounding in love.

Tearing of garments was a sign of mourning in Israel. When someone died, the relatives would put a cut in their clothes as a sign of deep sorrow and mourning. God cuts through the outward formal religious demonstration and looks for the heart. It is never our outward exhibition which reaches His heart. It is what is real in ours.

Matt.7:21-23

Not everyone who says to Me 'Lord, Lord' will enter the kingdom of heaven, but only he who does the will of My Father who is in heaven. Many will say to Me on that day 'Lord, Lord, did we not prophecy in Your name, and in Your name drive out demons and perform many miracles?' Then I will tell them plainly, 'I never knew you. Away from Me, you evildoers.'

Even performers of miracles can find themselves on the outside, because, when it comes to the reality of things, "the Lord does not look at the things man looks at. Man looks at the outward appearance, but the Lord looks at the heart" (1 Sam.16:7).

Paul picks this up in Romans when he addresses the topic of rituals and laws. A real Jew, he says, is not one who only keeps the law or attempts to, including circumcision, the mark in the flesh of belonging to God in covenant. No, he says, a real Jew is one who inwardly embraces the way of God and the cutting he undergoes is the cutting of his heart to make it new - a work of the Holy Spirit, not a set of rules (Rom.2:28-29).

It is the same with being a Christian. A true disciple is not one who wears his best suit on Sundays and follows the rules of his church. A real Christian is one who has a new heart, a new life, is a new creation of God in the Spirit and has the knowledge and experience of the washing away of their sin. Wearing your best suit does not impress God. I grew up with 'Sunday best'. I enjoyed it. It made me feel good, important, special - I was wearing my best clothes! They felt so much nicer, did wonders for my ego, coming from relative poverty in Liverpool. I continued like this into adulthood. As a new, young pastor I put on my dog collar and sat studying with it pressing most uncomfortably into my neck. But I was a pastor, and pastors wore dog collars!

As God revealed more of Himself, and more of myself, He brought me to realise that uniforms count for nothing in His kingdom. It is the life laid down to Him that counts - the heart of passion for Him, His church and those who are strangers to His love and grace. Never mind that age-old argument which goes like this: "You wouldn't dress like that for the Queen, would you? Well, isn't God more important than the Queen? Doesn't He deserve better than jeans and a T-shirt?"

I believe that is looking through the eyes of the kingdoms of men, imposing human regulations on spiritual issues. We have to see everything from the principles Father God gives us in the scriptures. That is the truth, the highest standard and most to be desired way to live. If we wear Sunday best because we are meeting with God in a church meeting, what do we wear the rest of the week when we meet Him in every event and situation of every day? When I go swimming or skiing, walking or gardening, dancing or driving, God does not take a break from being in me and with me. He is intimately part of everything. He is to be at the centre of everything of our lives. He has made a commitment to never leave or forsake me. I don't put on my 'best' for these activities, yet they are all spiritual, all in fellowship with God.

God calls us to divest ourselves of everything of self and the flesh nature, everything that is alien to the pure life of the Spirit of God, since at Calvary this is exactly what Jesus did. Then we embrace what God has prepared for us to wear instead.

Isa.61:10

For He has clothed me with garments of salvation; and arrayed me in a robe of righteousness.

My clothing now is of the heart. God covers the nakedness of my exposed heart with the precious cleansing blood of Jesus, through whom I have been made right with God. As His royal son, I have royal garments waiting for me to dress myself in. And these garments are forever.

Neh.9:21

For forty years You sustained them in the desert; they lacked nothing, their clothes did not wear out nor did their feet become swollen.

Deut.29:5

During the forty years that I led you through the desert your clothes did not wear out, nor did your sandals on your feet.

God's salvation, righteousness and kingdom are eternal; nothing can separate us from Him. The story of the Prodigal shows us something of the extent of the joy the father has in the return of his son.

Lk.15:22

Quick! Bring the best robe and put it on him. Put a ring on his finger and sandals on his feet.

Bring the best robe, not just any robe - the best most costly luxurious robe I own - the robe that speaks of rank, of standing, of family honour. The father was in a hurry to dress his son in appropriate clothes. The slave clothes were no longer suitable. He was home, in his father's house, at his father's banqueting table. He was restored to his rightful place. As soon as the words of repentance and recognition were uttered, he was restored.

Rev.7:9-10

After this I looked and there before me was a great multitude that no one could count, from every nation, tribe, people and language, standing before the throne and in front of the Lamb. They were wearing white robes and were holding palm branches in their hands. And they cried out in a loud voice, 'Salvation belongs to our God, who sits on the throne, and to the Lamb.'

At Sardis, we read of a great church, fallen into disrepute, somewhat like the city itself which had been great, powerful and important. Both were in a state of having seen better days. The church had a reputation for life, yet was dead. God's words are strong: "I will come as a thief." They had fallen far short of God's calling. Yet in the middle of this we find:

Rev.3:1-6

...you have a few people in Sardis who have not soiled their clothes. They will walk with Me, dressed in white, for they are worthy. He who overcomes will, like them, be dressed in white. I will never blot out his name from the Book of Life but will acknowledge his name before My Father and His angels.

These people, free from compromise, pure in heart and living, were rewarded with garments of glory and eternal security and intimacy - known by name.

Do you sometimes feel like just one among a mass of believers?

Jesus has assured us that even the hairs on our head are numbered. Jesus calls out His sheep by name. He acknowledges our name before the Father. You are so much more than a faceless blob within the mass of redeemed humanity. You are an individual, uniquely crafted by Father to be 'you', a vital member of His beloved Bride and Body. Out of every tribe, people, nation and language, Abba God knows you by name. Without you there is a lack within the Christian family. You are essential as a life joint, as the fitting stone in the building, as the living body part which means we are all healthy because you are there.

"Put a ring on his finger," says the Father. This ring is closest in thought to the signet ring which speaks of several important aspects of our life in God. Firstly it represents the testimony of ownership. The ring was commonly used as a seal in days of limited literacy. The stamp of the ring spoke of ownership and validated the contents of any package bearing it. It carried the same strength that Paul picks up on when he states:

1 Cor.9:2, emphasis added

Even though I may not be an apostle to others, surely I am to you. For you are the <u>seal</u> of my apostleship in the Lord."

He uses the same idea when addressing Timothy:

2 Tim.2:19, emphasis added

God's solid foundation stands firm <u>sealed</u> with this inscription: 'the Lord knows those who are His,' and 'everyone who confesses the name of the Lord must turn from wickedness.'

God's seal, carrying all the authority of heaven, is likened to the ring placed on the finger of the repentant son. This grants him authority as the son of his father to be that son again. He knows he has been restored into the life, intimacy and responsibility of 'sonship'. When the seal was stamped upon the end of a document, it spoke of finality, of completion. The seal marked the conclusion of the transaction. The son sees that in wearing the ring his welcome home, forgiveness and restoration to full sonship is an irrevocable act. It is completed, done, finished.

The seal on a document meant it could not be broken open. It was inviolable. Nothing can ever again strip the son of his place and recognition within the family. To have broken the seal would have meant all the forces of its owner coming against the perpetrator to their destruction. The son knows in his heart that he is safe, forever. In Haggai, we read this of Zerubbabel, God's appointed one:

Hag.2:23

I will make you like My signet ring for I have chosen you.

"And sandals on his feet." Sandals are a novelty for this son. He has returned barefooted to his home, as a slave. Any dignity he may have left home with has certainly been left behind in the bitterness of his experiences and the pig swill. He returns in shame and poverty, humbled. As his feet are fitted with new sandals he receives dignity. There is great dignity in being a child of God.

The last chapter helped us to see that we are royalty because our Father is the King of all kings. Though unrecognised in this world, we stand in honour and dignity bearing the face and name of God Almighty.

In Ephesians Paul speaks of our feet "fitted with the readiness that comes from the gospel of peace" (Eph.6:15).

Are you wearing the correct footwear?

When walking on the beach it is flip flops; in the hills, walking boots; at a function, dress shoes. Daily as God's children we wear the readiness of the gospel of peace. It is said of us:

Isa.52:7

How beautiful on the mountains are the feet of those who bring good tidings, who proclaim salvation, who say to Zion, 'Your God reigns.'

Do you hear Father God tell you that you have beautiful feet?

In Revelation we read that the Bride makes herself ready for her Bridegroom.

Rev.19:6-8

Hallelujah, for the Lord God Almighty reigns. Let us rejoice and be glad and give Him glory. For the wedding of the Lamb has come, and His Bride has made herself ready; fine linen, bright and clean was given her to wear. (Fine linen stands for the righteous acts of the saints.)

How does a bride make herself ready?

By putting on her wedding dress! For us the dress is bought and paid for. Fine linen, bright and clean was *given* her to wear. We do not even have to find, choose and pay for the wedding dress. Abba God has provided it! At the banqueting table where He leads us in delight is, strangely, the place where our garment is provided. We wear the righteous acts of our obedient service.

Ep.2:10

[For] we are God's workmanship, created in Christ Jesus to do good works, which God prepared in advance for us to do.

Everything is provided - a perfect fit, a perfect representation of all that reflects the bride of the glorious Son of God, crafted to fit each individual.

Col.3:12

Therefore, as God's chosen people, holy and dearly loved, clothe yourselves with compassion, kindness, humility, gentleness and patience.

Can you see a reflection of the Spirit's fruit in these words?

As we live in Jesus, His life begins to shine out of us and we choose to clothe ourselves in the garments of the Kingdom.

What do I mean?

A vagrant asks for money as you pass him on the street. You ignore his needs. You are choosing not to clothe yourself with compassion. You sing a beautiful song in worship and are thanked afterwards. You receive the appreciation and give all the glory to God. You have chosen to clothe yourself in humility. Peter calls us to:

1 Pet.5:5-6

Clothe yourselves with humility toward one another, because God opposes the proud, but gives grace to the humble. Humble yourselves therefore, under God's mighty hand, that He may lift you up in due time.

Remember the testimony of Jesus who humbled Himself as the lowest of servants, even to the point of death.

- How much of 'me' reigns in my heart?
- How much of 'me' occupies my thinking and waking hours?
- How easily am I hurt and offended if I don't secure the credit and gratitude I believe I am due?

Humility is the garment of a son of the King. Clothe yourselves with godliness.

Col.3:8-10, emphasis added

But now you must rid yourselves of all such things as these: anger, rage, malice, slander, and filthy language from your lips. Do not lie to each other, since you have <u>taken off</u> your old self with its practices, and have <u>put on</u> the new self, which is being renewed in knowledge in the image of its Creator.

Paul reiterates this in his letter to the Ephesians:

Eph.4:22-24, emphasis added

You were taught with regards to your former way of life, to <u>put off</u> your old self, which is being corrupted by its deceitfulness, to be made new in the *attitude of your minds, and to put on the new self, created to be like God in true righteousness and holiness.*

Paul's image is one of taking off and putting on different clothes. It reflects our hearts. If we are looking for credit, appreciation, thanks, promotion, reward then our hearts are full of ourselves. If we are looking for Jesus to be exalted, praised, for His church to be encouraged, served, built up, for the lost to be found, then our hearts are motivated by godliness. It boils down to the questions:

- Why do I do what I do?
- Why do I say what I say?

Even our praying, giving, preaching, fasting can be in the wearing of garments that are not of the kingdom, clothes that do not belong on the backs of His royal offspring. Jesus spoke strongly to the religious leaders of His day because He knew the heart all their words and actions sprang from. People saw them praying; Jesus saw them saying, "I thank You God that I am not like other men." When they fasted the people saw dishevelled, gaunt looks and admired them. Jesus saw the emptiness of their actions for they were all about self (Lk.18:11, Matt.6:16-18).

By the indwelling Holy Spirit we are empowered to live with a heart that longs for God more than for ourselves. Peter has some exquisite words about this when addressing the way Christian women should dress. I know his words have a particular application, but I believe they portray God's heart about everything of life.

1 Pet.3:3-4
Your beauty should not come from outward adornment such as braided hair and the wearing of gold jewellery and fine clothes. Instead it should be that of your inner self, the unfading beauty of a gentle and quiet spirit, which is of great worth in God's sight.

What is of great worth in God's sight?
- Is it how I look when I go to church on a Sunday morning?
- Is it what I place in the offering?

- Is it what I do in greeting people, or making coffee, or managing the sound system, or playing an instrument, or preaching, or overseeing communion?

All of these are important. They are integral aspects of our corporate times of worship. But what God values is "the unfading beauty of a gentle and quiet spirit". It is our heart. All of the above can be done from selfish motives, thus carrying no worship value to God. Notice it is the "unfading beauty". We can become disillusioned in the things we do. "No one said, 'thank you', so that's me finished with making coffee!!" But, when our spirit is settled in God and vibrates with His love, is nurtured in worship and intimacy, so it remains beautiful, whether there are thanks or not. Our service is always to God before it is to people.

Do I spend more time and thought on what I will wear to church than I do preparing my heart?

In Romans Paul strongly attacks the externality of religious observance. He challenges those who 'glory' in the outward show and observance of religion.

Rom.2:28-29

A man is not a Jew if he is only one outwardly, nor is circumcision merely outward and physical. No, a man is a Jew if he is one inwardly, and circumcision is circumcision of the heart, by the Spirit, not by the written code. Such a man's praise is not from man, but from God.

Externals of themselves are meaningless. Indeed we need to take care lest they become a snare to us and our religion is evaluated by the faithfulness and intensity of our actions. Surely the most beautiful, glorious clothing, the most powerful, transforming garment is a towel. It is what Jesus wore when He showed His disciples the extent of His love, when He demonstrated the heart of God and the foundation of Christian attitude and behaviour. John tells us that Jesus took off His outer clothing and wrapped a towel around His waist and proceeded to wash the feet of His disciples, including Judas, whom He knew would betray Him.

Jn.13:1-17

I am your teacher, I am your Lord, yet I have washed your feet. This is the example I have set you. Now, live in 'foot washing' humility toward one another. There is such blessing to those who live like this.

So says our Master, King, Saviour and Friend. To move from our external observations to the inward spirit of life in Christ demands much more than just a couple of add-on ideas. We have to go through radical transformation. We need heart surgery. Failure to allow this will result in us being destroyed! Listen to Jesus:

Matt.9:14-17

No one sews a patch of unshrunk cloth on an old garment, for the patch will pull away from the garment, making the tear worse. Neither do men pour new wine into old wineskins. If they do the skins will burst, the wine will run out and the wineskins will be ruined. No they pour new wine into new wineskins, and both are preserved.

Trying to fill a rigid religious Christian with the new wine of the Holy Spirit will bring ruin. We have to become malleable first in the things of the Spirit to become a fit receiver of the life in the Spirit. So it is no use trying to make the old better. There is no permanent blessing in changing one or two things. Worn out worshippers won't be revived by changing the organ for the guitar, or song books for PowerPoint. My heart will not be changed by removing my tie or undoing a button. Something much more radical is needed. We must be made new. Every day we need to be renewed in the Spirit. There is fresh bread, every day.

Matt.6:11

Give us this day our daily bread.

Yesterday's 'manna' will be mouldy by today. Yesterday's grace is history, stored in our spiritual memory bank, that we "forget not all His benefits". But, we cannot live yesterday again. It is now 'today'. That demands the new wine of sweet fellowship, healing, restoration, grace and power for today's walk. We must discard how we were, who we were, so that He can make us new in Him today. Made new, with renewed hearts and spirits, we can receive the new wine of the Spirit.

Another aspect of externals is the cause of 'head covering' for women in public worship. What a contentious issue! Almost everywhere you turn within Christendom, you will find conflicting views. I am not going to claim any new ground, but I believe it should be mentioned. Obviously these verses suggest that womankind has a subordinate role to man-kind. The need to illustrate this is seen in head covering. Of course, in Paul's day, women did not wear hats. They wore veils covering their head and face! Nobody is going to advocate that today, are they?

Women in Corinth in the first century would never be seen bare-headed. It symbolised women of loose morals and went completely against all normal social conventions. Thus Paul endorses the continuing use of head covering (1 Cor.11:1-16). Paul discusses the authority of Christ as head and source of man, and of man as head and source of woman. Notice that nowhere does Paul declare that a man is more important than a woman. In fact, in Christ gender becomes unimportant as Galatians points out:

Gal.3:28

There is neither male nor female... you are all one in Christ Jesus.

Tell me:

- Is your pastor more important than you?
- Is your teacher more important than your cleaner?

Paul breaks with Jewish convention when he states that for a man to pray whilst wearing a hat is dishonouring to God. Jews always wear a head covering when they worship. I suggest this has to do with the words about 'glory'. Man reflects the glory of God because he was first made in God's image. Woman was made from man, thereby reflecting the glory of man or humanity. Worship is to glorify God alone.

I grew up in a church where every woman wore a hat. They would never be seen without one. I think it was a combination of the culture of the day mingled with spiritual ideas. One thing I do know: wearing a hat does not prove a heart of submission to God, nor does *not* wearing a hat show lack of submission. People look at the externals. God looks at the heart.

In cultures where wearing a head covering is a natural part of life, it is not demonstrating greater spiritual observance than in cultures that do not. This same passage speaks of the disgrace of men having long hair.

- How long is long?
- What determines this?
- Is it possible we can degenerate to the point of using measuring tapes to determine the depth of true spirituality?

In the 1970's it was very fashionable for men to wear long hair. I have photographic evidence of myself sporting long curly hair on my shoulders. I could use some of it now! With this long hair I was pastoring a church and seeing God graciously bless us in amazing ways, bringing many to salvation, healing and freedom. Obviously my fashionable long hair did not offend God as His blessing flowed over my life.

- So, whether you wear a hat or not, have long hair or not, what heart is God seeing?
- Where a form of head covering is demanded, what heart is God seeing? A submissive one or a resentful or angry one?

If I were to replace your head covering with a crown, we would be in territory where no one could disagree. If I were to cover your uncovered head with a crown, it would be a reflection of His glory, for crowns are the symbolic head covering of royalty, and that is what we are. Proverbs tells us the prudent are crowned with knowledge (Prov.14:18).

Using good sense, being careful in considering issues and consequences, brings us knowledge. Jesus gave an illustration of this when He spoke about the king who sat down to consider whether his army was strong enough to go to war. If not, he would seek peace. That is the prudence Proverbs speaks of. In the same way we, by careful consideration, can arrive at only one conclusion: that is, to give up everything to follow Jesus.

Why?

Because He crowns our life with love and compassion (Ps.103:4).

Where else can we know such love - such life-transforming, ever complete, unconditional, all-embracing love - this love, this *depth* of love that reached into the deepest pit to draw us out; this love, so broad that it reaches from east to west to find us; this love, so high it lifts us into the heavenlies where He has seated us in Christ?

Such is the love that ever pursues the human heart, that ever forgives and restores, that ever hopes in its own grand purposes to present us perfect and whole in Christ Jesus. It is no wonder that the prophet declares:

Isa.62:3
You will be a crown of splendour in the Lord's hand.

Such will be the radiance and beauty of the work of God's grace that we will be as a glorious coronation crown to present to Jesus, our awesome Bridegroom King. We are the reward of His faithfulness.

Heb. 12:2
Jesus... who for the joy set before Him endured the cross, scorning its shame, and sat down at the right hand of the throne of God.

The Father presents this glorious crown to the Son for His pleasure. It signifies His victory over sin, death and hell. It is His reward, His prize for His achievement. How amazing is this! Jesus values us so highly as to desire us as His reward from the Father for the sacrifice He undertook. You are of inestimable worth in the eyes of God!

We are privileged to be offered a crown for our faithful endurance even unto death, as Revelation 2:10 tells us.

Rev.3:11
I am coming soon. Hold on to what you have, so that no one will take your crown.

A crown, the symbol of victory and reward, awaits those who faithfully follow the Master right into His Kingdom.

Jam.1:12

Blessed is the man who perseveres under trial, because when he has stood the test, he will receive the crown of life that God has promised to those who love Him.

Paul testified:

2Tim.4:7-8

I have fought the good fight, I have finished the race, I have kept the faith. Now there is in store for me the crown of righteousness, which the Lord, the Righteous Judge, will award me on that day. And not only to me, but also to all who have longed for His appearing.

In these words we see the way for the Christian. It is a way of faithfulness, whatever the cost; the way of endurance, knowing the enabling of the Holy Spirit to empower our standing firm; it is the way of holding tightly to all that God has graced us with through our life. Let us never be guilty of despising His grace by our careless handling of anything that He places before us. Every good and perfect gift comes down from the Father of Light. Let us never be guilty of praising ourselves for the acquisition of all that we see around us in our homes, possessions, bank accounts. It is all of His grace. We are stewards of all, the owners of none.

It is the way of successive trials. Jesus promised in this world we will have trouble. But "take heart! I have overcome the world" (Jn.16:33). We cannot be Christians and not know difficulties. I am not speaking of struggles that are common to all men - there is no uniqueness in that. Why would Jesus speak these words to men who lived under Roman occupation - whose families knew illness; who were used to being robbed by tax collectors; who, more than once, had worked all night for no reward? No, these words speak of the struggles which are faced because we faithfully follow the way of the Saviour.

James.1:2

Consider it pure joy, my brothers, whenever you face trials of many kinds, because you know that the testing of your faith develops perseverance.

Perseverance must finish its work so that you may be mature and complete, not lacking anything.

1 Pet.4:12-16

Dear friends, do not be surprised at the painful trial that you are suffering, as though something strange were happening to you. But, rejoice that you participate in the sufferings of Christ, so that you may be overjoyed when His glory is revealed. If you are insulted because of the name of Christ, you are blessed, for the Spirit of glory and of God rests on you... if you suffer as a Christian, do not be ashamed, but praise God that you bear the name.

The table is there, present and spread for us to avail ourselves of its provision to equip us, sustain us and enrich us as we keep our eyes fixed on the beautiful face of Jesus, who will not allow us to be tested beyond our ability to endure. For this... a crown! A crown crafted by the loving hands of the Father, uniquely to fit your head, reflecting His love, His joy in His child and the heart that longs after Him. Paul urges us to set ourselves to win such a crown. It is not seen as an optional extra! The crown is seen as a worthwhile reward for all the training and discipline of seeking that prize. Olympians train for years, endure the loss of ease and comfort, pay the price, go through the pain, to win a medal. In Paul's day it was to win a wreath or garland, which would last only a short time. Our crown is an eternal one. For Olympians there is one gold medal winner; for us, a crown for all who have longed for His appearing. Do not fear failure. There are no failures in God's economy. You cannot let God down.

God is sovereignly, eternally, immutably, perfectly, gloriously God. Before anything became, God has always been all that He is. He has never needed anything. He is eternally, perfectly complete in Himself. You cannot let Him down. It is for our sakes that He made us and called us, making us His children. Yes, it gives Him great joy and pleasure to receive our worship, our love. Yes, His joy and pleasure have from eternity been complete. The pleasure that fills His heart is the pleasure that has *forever* filled His heart, for we have been in His heart from everlasting. What an amazing God!

Paul expands these thoughts of crowns when he calls the church at Philippi his crown.

Phil.4:1

You whom I love and long for, my joy and crown.

He said the same thing to the Thessalonian believers. Paul had won so many of these people to Christ. All he endured on his missionary trips was for this purpose: to present to Jesus the joy He anticipated at His crucifixion. The converts were Paul's joy; they were his crown, his victory symbol and reward for all his faithful endurance to the end, that some may be saved and found in Christ.

There is a real pleasure found in bringing to Jesus those snatched from the darkness. I know that feeling. There is hardly anything on earth like it - all as an offering to Jesus!

To those whom God has appointed as shepherds among His flock there is a crown of glory that will never fade. Ministering God to His children brings this reward. You are set apart for this unique calling. There is always a banqueting table at your fingertips to feed you everything you need for your wellbeing and to feed to others. It is a crown reserved for those who are "shepherds of God's flock that is under [their] care, serving as overseers, not because [they] must, but because [they] are willing, as God wants [them] to be, not greedy for money, but eager to serve, not lording it over those entrusted to [them], but being examples to the flock" (1 Pet.5:2-3).

These are those who serve by leading and lead by serving. To such is given this crown whose glory will never fade away. God remembers and sets aside His reward for those who take up this responsibility to shepherd His people. You are never alone, even when the way is a lonely one. You are never forsaken, even when men turn from you because they will not embrace the truth and grace you bring. His banner of love still hangs above your head, His banqueting table, your constant supply and joy.

I see this crown in its making, the purest gold, its jewels not yet in place. When you take up this task, a jewel of delight is fitted. As you graciously teach and urge His people into deeper intimacy, other jewels are added. Each time you bless those whose criticism is false and hurtful, fresh jewels are placed in prominent positions. Each time you stand in His truth with humility and tears as the flock struggle with their fears, then deeply-embedded, sparkling, dazzling colours encrust the crown. It is a crown of testimony to the faithful fulfilling of your calling. The glory brought to His name by your life is reflected in this crown of glory. Such is what I saw as I reflected on this.

A vital outfit for us all is the "full armour of God" as outlined in Ephesians 6:10-17. The purpose of the divinely designed and created outfit is that we may take our stand against the devil's schemes, to enable us to stand, fully equipped, holding our ground when evil times come at us. One thing this clearly tells us is that Christians are vulnerable.

Our eternal security is guaranteed - for nothing can snatch us from His hand; nothing in all creation can separate us from God's love in Christ Jesus our Lord (Jn.10:28-29, Rom.8:39). The vulnerability comes in our daily walk of faithful obedience and fruitfulness. Satan is obviously able to mess with our walk; to mess with our joy and sense of worth, our effectiveness as light and salt; mess with our worship and prayer life, our relationships and pleasures. We are vulnerable. Therefore God offers us garments of security and warfare. They are available on the banqueting table, handmade, uniquely fitted to each one of us, comfortable, flattering even, for we are always glorious in His sight. His yoke is easy and His burden is light. This outfit fits perfectly.

Where do I find this armour?

Not at a regular tailor, that's for sure! My outward appearance, as we know, has no spiritual benefit.

Do I find it at church, in a prayer meeting or home group?

Not really!

I suggest that without this armour I am not likely to be found at any of those gatherings. These times with God come from the passion of my heart. This is guarded by the armour of God. Nakedness means I'm vulnerable, prey to any assault of the enemy who is totally committed to steal, kill and destroy everything of my life in God. I am powerless and subject to his deceits without this heavenly armour. The text infers that without God's armour, I will not stand. I will collapse into agreement with his satanic majesty, instead of standing and yielding to His Majesty, King Jesus, and King over all kings. When we really grasp the essence of this, we will be studious in our embracing of the urging of the apostle to so clothe ourselves.

None of us want to be vulnerable. The answer is to be clothed in God's armour. I will not trust in myself, my knowledge of the Bible, my history or place within the church. My trust will be set on Jesus. He is the answer! He provides the various parts of this covering in Himself.

That colleague at work who always rubs you up the wrong way; the pretty young thing who seems to offer something exciting, tantalising; the domineering spouse or controlling church leader - these are not our struggle. The struggle is with the spiritual forces behind these people, the forces which cause them to behave as they do. The devil is utterly malevolent. He has an extreme hatred of God and God's people. He is totally committed to our destruction.

That person who rubs you up the wrong way... are they living in conviction because of the light and salt your life is to them? Are they secretly jealous of who you are and how you live? The pretty young thing offering things beyond your wildest dreams... is she the one who desperately needs to know real love and acceptance - possibly freedom from abuse?

- What do these people present to us about ourselves?
- How secure in God and our relationships are we?

These people can be used to pull us down, to lead us into sins of a sexual nature, or an ungodly anger which destroys another. It is the forces in the heavenlies with whom we have to deal! Therefore we need spiritual weapons and means - hence the full armour of God!

You don't actually love that kind, thoughtful man at work, or that girl offering her body. That is illusion, lies from hell to pull us away from righteousness. The controlling church leader does not hate you. He is manifesting his own needs for healing, his own struggles and vulnerability. This is where love covers a multitude of sins. Satan will seek to use anyone and anything to bring us down and cause us to flounder and lose the truth of God in our life. Putting on and keeping on the armour of God enables us to see the truth. We wear the belt of truth around our waist. It is not for naught!

This belt is the first item mentioned. We must wear truth for it is in knowing the truth that we find freedom. For instance, when the truth is alive to us we don't fight against people but spiritual forces, because then we can see the people as more like 'victims' to demonic influence than perpetrators of it. It is a profound truth that 'hurt people hurt people'. Jesus is the truth; as we fasten around us the being of Jesus in the fullness of the Holy Spirit, so we are secure in knowing who we are in Him, our eternal security, the forgiveness He has given us, the hope that is in us, the glory of the gospel, and so much more. We are freed from doubt and questioning when we are embraced in His truth: righteousness, the breastplate covering our heart. We are made righteous by and in Jesus.

Being right with God and right with man is what righteousness is. It means we are made so as to conform to His will, to have God-likeness upon us. How terrible a concept this is - sinful humanity being elevated and transformed to show God-likeness! What a powerful work the death and resurrection of Jesus have produced. With our hearts guarded by righteousness, we are less prone to the prey of the 'roaring lion' that goes about looking to see who he can devour.

This knowledge - that God is positionally and experiencially conforming us to the likeness of Jesus - empowers and equips us to counter the lies of Satan, who would like to convince us that we are weak, failing sinners. Our hearts are guarded by truth.

Prov.4:20-23 (NKJV)

My son, give attention to my words, incline your ear to my sayings. Do not let them depart from your eyes. Keep them in the midst of your heart; for they are life to those who find them and health to all their flesh. Keep your heart with all diligence for out of it spring the issues of life.

We fit our feet with the gospel of peace. Isaiah says:

Isa.52:7

How beautiful on the mountains are the feet of those who bring good news, who proclaim peace, who bring good tidings who proclaim salvation, who say to Zion, 'Your God reigns'.

Peter follows this up by urging us to "always be prepared to give an answer to everyone who asks you to give the reason for the hope you have" (1 Pet.3:15). We stand on the unshakeable Rock, Christ Jesus. He is our salvation. Our footwear is what we stand on and walk in.

- How well do you know the gospel?
- Are you secure in all that it is?
- Do you doubt the reality of salvation and life with God in Jesus?

This is a gospel of peace. We have inherited peace in salvation. It is peace with God through our Lord Jesus Christ having been justified through faith in Him (Rom.5:1).

'Justified' means 'just as if I had never sinned'. Therefore I have peace with God because in His eyes I am as if I had never sinned. So, *I* have peace with God, *you* have peace with God, *we* have peace with God - therefore with each other. He is our Peace. His gospel is a message of peace: God in Christ reconciling the world to Himself.

Matt.5:9

Blessed are the peacemakers for they will be called sons of God.

How urgent it is in these days to be those who speak peace and minister peace through our lives. The church is fractured and in pain. It is riddled with the divisiveness of denominations, plagued with the pride of empire builders, confused by the propagators of ungodly ideologies within her midst, and cowering in cowardice before the merciless assaults of demonic enlightenment and arrogance of men. How desperately she needs the healing peace of God to restore, revive and revolutionise her brokenness. Our generation is fragmented in every direction - man at war with himself, his family, his nation, his neighbours. Racism is rampant, religions rife; puffed up politicians prattle platitudes; businesses bully by economic sanctions; and the poorest, weakest, most vulnerable fall by the wayside as globalisation juggernauts onward, careless and indifferent to the cry of the disenfranchised. Into this morass of pain and greed we must bring the good news of peace through our Lord Jesus Christ, that the hearts of the fathers may be turned to the children and the children to the fathers and His kingdom come on earth as it is in heaven, as we so often pray.

This peace is not only the absence of war; it is something more. It speaks of peace, wholeness, unity, completeness. Only God gives this. We only know this peace when we know He who is our peace. Such knowing releases us into living this peace - enabling and empowering us to give it to others.

Add to this the helmet of salvation, and we are fully covered and protected. The helmet, of course, covers our head and protects our minds. Our head is covered as we place ourselves under the headship of Jesus. He is our authority. This helmet protects our mind from every lying, deceitful, devious, compromising thought of the 'father of lies'. The full truth of salvation releases us from such deception and into the power of resurrection life in the Spirit.

What 'salvation' do you embrace?

- Is it the complete, for all time, irreversible, 'effective whatever I do or don't do' salvation?
- Or is it a lesser salvation that still leaves you in fear of ultimate rejection because of failures?
- Or a salvation that demands specific, continuous works to retain its validity?

Eph.2:8
By grace you are saved through faith, and this is not from yourselves, it is the gift of God, not by works so that no one can boast.

Armed with true knowledge we safeguard our hearts from fear and our minds from unbelief. We stand in the security of God's truth that sets us free into the freedom of an abundant life in the Spirit, to be enjoyed in our bodies, mind and spirit. Notice how we are urged to "take the helmet of salvation". It is offered/available/found on the banqueting table that accompanies us every step we take, every challenge we face, every joy we embrace. Unless we take it up, fit it snugly and live under its truth, we will flounder. Doubt and unbelief will haunt our way and weaken our walk and witness.

So it is with the shield and sword. They are not clothing but are essential to the completeness of this uniform. The shield of faith blocks, deflects and extinguishes the lying accusations of the enemy. Our faith is in the faithfulness of God. It is who He is, the truth He is, the promises He gives which cannot fail. Faith is not in our ability to try to believe Him. It is the security of knowing that He does *all* that He says. Our ability is in trusting Him, not working up a belief that He can do it. The more we know His truth in the nature of who He has revealed Himself to be and in our knowing of the scripture, the more we can stand in the truth as we put into practice what He has said and overcome the evil one.

The sword, which is the word of God, is the victorious weapon of declaring the truth – just as Jesus in His desert temptation thrust God's word at every lying challenge and won the day. Jesus is the Truth. The more of Jesus we embrace, the greater our sword, and the more effective its use, the more powerful its accomplishments!

As we wear these garments - the armour of God, to stand against every lying attack of the evil one; humility, to acknowledge Christ is all and in all, and we are all that He has made us to be as His Spirit indwells us; compassion, to feel and love as He does, to see through the facade to the precious beloved of God in everyone we meet; kindness, in which to demonstrate His compassion with gentleness and patience; over-covering all with the garment of love which "binds them all together in perfect unity"(Col 3:14) - so we grow up into Christ who is the head over all things for the church which is His body. As the Head, Jesus brings us to the unity of His heart, namely "that they may all be one, Father, just as You are in Me and I am in You, may they also be in us." (Jn.17:21)

Unity is the very heart of the heart of God. Unity is the greatest need of the church - to love one another as He has loved us.

Ps.133

How good and pleasant it is when brothers live together in unity. It is like precious oil poured on the head, running down on the beard, running down on Aaron's beard, down upon the collar of his robes. It is as if the dew of Hermon were falling on Mt. Zion. For there the Lord bestows His blessing, even life for evermore.

Like oil running down on the collar of his robes... This is the priestly anointing oil that sets apart and empowers the priest for his role before God. Beloved, we are a kingdom of priests to God. In our unity the oil of the Holy Spirit is poured down upon us – not just a spot on the forehead but running down onto our priestly garments - abundance of grace! Our garments are covered in the oil of anointing, that we too carry the power and authority of the King. Each believer is a priest unto God, as Peter reminds us.

1 Pet.2:9

You are a chosen people, a royal priesthood, a holy nation, a people belonging to God, that you may declare the praises of Him who called you out of darkness into His wonderful light.

We can all come boldly into His presence on the merits of the blood of Jesus - no need for any other mediator, for there is only one mediator between God and man: the man, Christ Jesus (1 Tim. 2:5).

Ezekiel speaks of the priests taking off the clothes they have worn whilst ministering, so that they do not consecrate the people by means of their garments (Ezek.44:19). How glorious it is that the very clothes they have worn carry the anointing of God.

Remember the woman who came and touched Jesus' robe?

She was convinced that if she could just touch His clothes she would be healed, and she was! Pieces of cloth were sent out to the sick and they were healed and freed from evil spirits because these cloths had come from Paul's body (Acts.19:11-12).

It suggests in Acts 5:15 that people were healed because Peter's shadow carried the anointing of God's healing power. This is a deep mystery. Jesus alone is the healer, yet scripture shows that somehow, something of the glory of God resided in the clothes and presence of Jesus, Paul and Peter. How great will be that day when God's church comes into the unity where Holy Spirit is poured out upon us, covering our spiritual garments with such anointing that our communities are transformed.

He did it with Peter and Paul; why not with us?

We don't come in and go out as the ancient priests did in their allotted times. We live always in the presence of God, worshiping and offering our sacrifices of praise. So we never remove our priestly robes. We are always clothed in righteousness and salvation. There is never a time when the armour of God is not needed, or the garments of humility, compassion, patience etc are not be worn for the display of His majesty and glory. Every situation in life demands a response in the Spirit. For this we need to clothe ourselves, for the display of His glory adds something more: fragrance!

In chapter 4 verse 11 of the beautiful Song of Solomon, our lover, Jesus, is expressing His absolute delight in His beloved, you and me. He makes this declaration:

SS 4:11

The fragrance of your garments is like that of Lebanon.

Lebanon was known for its great fragranced wood. Frankincense was the foremost gum extracted from Lebanon's numerous woodlands and forests. Hosea draws the same analogy as he speaks of the graces accompanying Israel's repentance.

Hos.14:6-7

Like a cedar of Lebanon he will send down his roots. His splendour will be like an olive tree, his fragrance like a cedar of Lebanon... and his fame will be like the wine of Lebanon.

The cedars of Lebanon were used in the building of the temple. This wood had to have been the best possible to be deemed suitable for such a task. Throughout scripture the cedars of Lebanon are elevated above all other trees as the greatest and most beautiful.

"The balsamic juice of the cedar exudes from every pore. Large beads and nodules of the fragrant resin form on the uninjured branches. An incision into the bark is followed by copious distillation of the same. Where two

branches meet and rub together, they each pour out the life giving sap,
which cements them , so that they grow fast to one another." 2

Imagine, if you will, a mountainside covered with magnificent trees, each one exuding the sweet gum which nourishes and restores it, while flooding the atmosphere with such fragrance. What a picture to bring to the 'fragrance of Lebanon' in the garments of Christ's beloved bride.

2 Cor.2: 14-16

Thanks be to God, who always leads us in triumphal procession in Christ and through us spreads everywhere the fragrance of the knowledge of Him. For we, are to God the aroma of Christ among those who are being saved and those who are perishing. To the one we are the smell of death; to the other the fragrance of life.

Throughout the instructions about the sacrificial offerings, God emphasised that the correct offerings made in the correct way by the correct people was to His nostrils a pleasing smell, a desired fragrance. As our lives are laid down in daily offering as living sacrifices, so the sweet-smelling fragrance pleases our God. As we are trying to show in this chapter, the garments we adorn ourselves with demonstrate those living sacrifices as we choose to take on the character of Christ in all His rich varied manifestations. Such a heart is a fragrant offering to our Beloved Father. We bless those around us with the fragrance of our lives. Those who walk the way of Christ with us smell the sweetness of life. Those rejecting the grace of God are repelled, smelling their own death, for we represent the very life they reject. Thus they are choosing the death their attitudes bring. Because we have chosen a life in contrast to theirs, they see us as those who are not living a real life. We are the walking dead, because we daily take up the cross to follow the Saviour.

2 Cor.2:14-16 (The Message)

Everywhere we go, people breathe in the exquisite fragrance. Because of Christ, we give off a sweet scent rising to God, which is recognised by those

---

2 Hastings Dictionary of the Bible, Vol.1, Topic: Cedar.

on the way to salvation, an aroma redolent with life. But those on the way to destruction treat us more like the stench of a rotting corpse.

One more thought about the fragrance: the gum from the trees glues two damaged branches so that they are restored and now grow as one, joined in the place of their 'rubbing each other up the wrong way'. In the natural we hurt one another. We are often rubbing each other up the wrong way. In Christ, the fragrance of 'laid down serving hearts' enables us to heal and restore one another and grow stronger together in Him. We create a place of wholeness where once there was brokenness and pain.

Ezek.44:17-18

When they (the priests) enter the gates of the inner court, they are to wear linen clothes; they must not wear any woollen garment while ministering at the gates of the inner court or inside the temple. They are to wear linen turbans on their heads and linen undergarments around their waists. They must not wear anything that makes them perspire.

The priests had to wear linen against their bodies. This was to prevent perspiring. King David's robe was linen, as were the robes of the Levites and the singers, when the Ark was brought to Jerusalem (1 Chron.15:27). The veil of the temple was of fine linen (2 Chron.3:14). The temple musicians wore linen (2 Chron.5:12).

In the Revelation of John we read of the Bride making herself ready with fine linen, bright and clean which was given her to wear. The fine linen stands for the righteous acts of the saints (Rev.19:7-8). The armies of heaven who follow 'He who is called Faithful and True', riding on white horses, are dressed in fine linen, white and clean (Rev.19:14).

Linen represents the lack of human effort, lack of perspiring. In truth there is no human effort in 'kingdom busyness'. Kingdom busyness is conducted by the Holy Spirit. We are co-operators and achievers only through the indwelling Spirit of God. So we clothe ourselves with linen. No human endeavour can fulfil Kingdom purposes. We need to separate human desires and doings from Spirit-initiated activities. Our zeal for the Lord and the needs of the world must be filtered through the Spirit's judgments. Flesh breeds and fulfils flesh. Spirit gives life to spirit.

The writer to the Hebrews outlines this when he opens up something from Israel's history to show how many failed to enter into God's rest in the Promised Land. He concludes:

Heb.4:9-11

There remains then a Sabbath rest for the people of God; for anyone who enters God's rest also rests from his own work, just as God did from His. Let us therefore make every effort to enter that rest, so that no one will fall by following their example of disobedience.

This is the rest from human striving and stoicism, the rest from earning approval or striving for acceptance. It is the rest of knowing that in Jesus absolutely everything is once for all completed and achieved. The cry "It is finished!" rings out triumphantly declaring that all the purposes of the Father are accomplished. The job is done! No human effort, reason, philosophy, religion or ritual is needed. Everything is from God, through God, by God, and for God. We are the thankful recipients. By faith we receive and embrace the grace of God in salvation and new life in the Spirit; and we contributed nothing to the plan or its fulfilment. In this new life in the Spirit, we rest from the pressures of the flesh to rely on the promised indwelling Holy Spirit to walk the resurrection life. Paul speaks of being crucified with Christ - that he no longer lives, but Christ lives His life in Him. That which is crucified is dead. It is at rest. It has stopped.

This 'rest' is the subject of our next chapter.

SEATED: Promised Rest

Ps.37:7

Rest (be still) in the Lord and wait patiently for Him. Do not fret when men succeed in their ways, when they carry out their wicked schemes.

Isa. 30:15

In repentance and rest is your salvation. In quietness and trust is your strength.

We are seated at the banqueting table. It is a feast, not a buffet! These words are filled with longing and promise. I can almost hear some of the comments: "Yes, but it's not like that for me", "It's okay for you to quote scripture at me; you are not in my shoes". This is true, but so are the words of God. He never taunts us with promises beyond their realising. I want, in this chapter, to explore this idea of resting, of being seated in Christ. It is a frequent image across the pages of scripture.

Let's first look at where it is not good to be seated. Then we will be free to focus on the good place to be.

Ps.1:1

Blessed is the man (or woman) who does not walk in the counsel of the wicked or stand in the way of sinners or sit in the seat of mockers.

- Where do we receive our understanding?
- Where do we go to nourish our spirits?

1 Cor.15:33

Bad company corrupts good character.

Taking on board the philosophies of unbelievers, their 'wisdom' and ideals, will not build up the believer. Jesus is our Wisdom. His words are words of life. Mockery is a cursed thing which only leads to pain and destruction unless, as Elijah, you are revealing the impotence of idols (1 Kings.18:27). His words were directed to the idols rather than the people.

145

Jesus was mocked prior to His crucifixion. He presented a figure of ridicule to the soldiers. They could not see the King. So they mocked Him, made sport of Him, despised Him in their own eyes. See the dignity with which He withstood their cursing. Note also the humiliation of the mockers as they observed His quiet, loving grace toward them. He died for those who mocked Him. It is so easy for us to mock, to laugh at the ways of people. I have observed at first hand the disabled being mocked. I can still recall a comment from my early days as a teacher, a comment so disrespectful it is not printable.

Politicians somehow seem to contrive to make themselves objects of mockery. Scripture urges us to pray for those in authority, kings, presidents, prime ministers, local political representatives, council officers... (1 Tim.2:1-3). How about adding parents, teachers, church leaders to that list?

"All in authority" includes all in authority. Let us not be found among those who turn to scorn and mockery of leaders. Should we not seek to separate the person from the policy? The person is precious to God; they should be honoured. The policy is to be evaluated according to biblical criteria and, where necessary, shown up for what it is, while supporting that which can be accommodated within our Christian remit. Paul tells us the good result of praying for such leaders "that we may live peaceful and quiet lives in all godliness and holiness."

Let us be careful to take all our counsel from God and godly people. After all, it is Jesus who is the Truth. Every word out of alignment with Jesus is falsehood. The number of 'ologist's, the number of letters after a name, is no guarantee of truth. Truth is in God. Let us cleanse our minds by embracing God's true words in our lives and turning from, and repenting of, the philosophies of men.

Ps.119:97-99

Oh, how I love Your law! I meditate on it all day long. Your commands make me wiser than my enemies, for they are ever with me. I have more insight than all my teachers for I meditate on Your statutes.

The way of the wicked and the mockers is to be a place where God's loved ones are not found. Another wrong place for us to sit is outlined in

James where he shows the evil of favouritism. Elevating one person above another, despising the one and glorying in the other, is so wrong within the community of believers. He paints a picture of a rich, well-dressed man arriving at church and being shown the best seat while a poor man in rags arrives and is dismissed to a corner or a place on the floor. Such favouritism makes us guilty of judgments we have no right to make. It shows the shallowness of our hearts and a gross lack of love. It reveals our prejudices and despises someone whom God loves as He loves Jesus.

I believe in honouring those in leadership within the church. I honour them for who they are and the responsibility God has placed on them over my life and the flock of God. Nevertheless, I have always been uncomfortable with reserved parking places for them and a softer, more comfortable chair.

- Are we exalting man above his rightful place, showing preferential treatment?
- Are you less worthy of that parking place, having to walk from the far end of the car park and in the rain?
- Is he/she more worthy than you of the ease and comfort afforded?

I for one don't want a reserved parking place - I'm not that important. Please don't misunderstand me. I would happily walk across the car park in the rain to bless a child of God. I just want the option of choosing to bless rather than having it imposed. Jesus spoke into this sort of issue. Speaking to the proud religious leaders, He comments:

Matt.23:6

They love the place of honour at banquets and the most important seats in the synagogues.

He goes further when He tells the parable of the feast at which a man seats himself in a prominent position only to be humiliated by being sent to a lesser seat. What shame! Rather always choose the humble seat and, should it happen, be moved to a more prominent place. For those who exalt themselves will be humbled and those who humble themselves will be exalted (Lk.14:1-14). Never choose the wrong seat of prominence.

Grow a heart of humility with which you are happy to choose the insignificant, allowing God to exalt you or leave you where you are, and you are happy and content anyway.

So let us choose not to sit in places which lead us into error or into the fruitless 'wisdom' of our age. Let us not sit where we despise the grace of God through our attitudes and language. Such things should be alien to the experience of the children of God. Something else that does not belong is trusting or resting in anything that is not flowing from the grace of God. When we are seated, we are at rest. When we set our confidence in something or someone, we rest, take our ease in the assurance of that confidence. In this context let us be careful to keep all of our confidence fully in Christ Jesus. Paul cautioned the church in Rome about their reliance on the Law and their bragging about their relationship with God (Rom.2:17ff).

Putting trust and confidence in the Old Covenant written Law demanded full observance in every part. Failure to observe this meant failure in every part. We can have no confidence, no place of rest in anything we can do. Paul emphasises this when he declares:

Rom.7:17-18

I know nothing good lives in me that is in my sinful nature (flesh) for I have the desire to do what is good, but I cannot carry it out.

When we add to this the truth that 'knowledge puffs up but love builds up' (1 Cor.8:1), then we have a picture of humanity totally inadequate in its own abilities. All our self righteousness is like filthy rags. Apart from the glorious grace of Abba God we are utterly helpless and hopeless, just like flotsam bobbing about in the ocean, powerless to effect what happens, where it is driven by the tides, ignorant of the shore upon which it will be cast.

Have no confidence in the flesh. Paul pushes this to the limit, stating:

Phil.3:7-9

Whatever was to my profit I now consider loss for the sake of Christ. What is more, I consider everything a loss compared to the surpassing greatness of knowing Christ Jesus my Lord, for whose sake I have lost all things. I consider them rubbish that I may gain Christ and be found in Him, not having a righteousness of my own that comes from the law, but that which is through faith in Christ, the righteousness that comes from God and is by faith.

...this from the man who was head and shoulders above his colleagues in observance of the law.

He is actually saying that all our learning and degrees, our place in society, business, all our achievements and successes - though legitimate and worthy - are reckoned as dung in comparison to knowing Jesus. Wow! Also he is stating that such achievements have no value in knowing God and are worthy of the dung heap if they keep us from Him. Our private parking place, the plaque on the door, the trophies in the cabinet, the glass-domed mega-building, the millions in the bank, the public exposure through TV, music or literature - all is as garbage when compared to knowing Jesus and living in Him. So great is our God!

The scripture carries a warning to all those who practice another way of 'following God'.

Ps. 95:10–11

For forty years I was angry with that generation, I said they are a people whose hearts go astray, and they do not know my ways, so I declared an oath in my anger, they will never enter my rest.

For those who persist in their ambitions, who think that God needs their help and wisdom, for those driven by a need to prove something, those who feed off the adulation of the audience, there can never be a place of rest or satisfaction or peaceful assurance. There can only ever be a pursuit of the drug that is driving them: more books, bigger church, shiny car - the list is endless.

Matt.5:3

Blessed are the poor in spirit for theirs is the kingdom of heaven.

For us, it is the lowest seat, the choosing of the 'insignificant'. Jesus, at dinner, opens up one of the most beautiful stories of the Gospels. It's the story of the woman who came and anointed Jesus with the very expensive perfume, who wept at his feet, washing them with her tears, kissing them, drying them with her hair, and pouring the perfume on them. This woman was not a respectable lady who had been invited with her husband. Nor was she a servant of the house, overwhelmed by the wonder at the person of Jesus. This woman was known for her sinful living. She withstood the disgust and the despising of the guests. How she managed to gatecrash the party I'm not sure, but she made it to the feet of Jesus - rather like the persistence of the woman who fought her way through the crowds to get to Jesus to touch the edge of his garment and found healing in her determination.

Outrage follows her public expression of abandonment and love. Embarrassment and shock fills the room. This 'sinner' had dared to come into the home of a Pharisee! Jesus has allowed her to lavish her love on Him! Disgusting!! Doesn't He know? No self-respecting rabbi-cum-prophet would allow such behaviour. He's made Himself unclean by consorting with such a creature. He must be a fraud.

Jesus graciously opens up what has happened by telling a story. It is a story about forgiveness, being released from debt, being freed from the chains of fear and judgement. The one with the most to lose is the one who will most extravagantly show love to the forgiver. He goes on to illustrate the carelessness of His host who has failed in the common courtesies of foot washing and greeting. Is this Pharisee so attentive to his own place, to the quality of his food, and the entertaining of his guests that he overlooks the mundane? This 'sinner' has 'rescued' the host from his lack of love and courtesy by doing it for him and bearing the reproach of her actions.

In another account of this story, Jesus declares that her story will be told around the world. The proud Pharisee is humiliated; the humble sinner is exalted. In Mark's account, Jesus is quoted as saying, "She has done a beautiful thing to me" (Mk. 14:6) - not she has done a beautiful thing *for* me, but *to* me.

Are our acts of love to Jesus or for Jesus?

This is not dissimilar to the culture in which I was raised in northern England. It is too easy to avoid intimacy through actions or by actions:

"Of course I love you; I work to provide all that you have", "Of course I love you; I cook the meals and clean the house".

Do you see my point?

The actions are meant to reflect the love, yes, but can easily hide a lack of intimacy and deep love. To tell your loved ones that you love them, to take a few moments to demonstrate it with a hug, a smile, a kiss, to look them in the eye and say, "I love you" is so important. Let us grow in 'beautiful to me' expressions of love, to God and to each other.

"Dutiful roses are a contradiction in terms."

- John Eldridge, 'Desires'

"Like an alabaster jar poured out at your feet,
A pure and broken vessel with a fragrance that is sweet,
A perfume full of worship that rises to your throne,
Like an alabaster jar."

- Michael John Hughes, Kelly Warren, 'You are beautiful.'

This act of utter selfless devotion to Jesus has been told throughout the world as this story has been recaptured. Would you like the story of your life to be told around the world? The answer is in these words.

While thinking of Jesus at dinner, let's see another incident that may stir our hearts to further Christ-likeness. In Matthew chapter 9, we read of Jesus dining at Matthew's home. Jesus has just invited Matthew to join Him as a disciple. At dinner many of Matthew's friends of dubious character are present. Jesus is comfortable here, just as He was at the home of the Pharisee. The Pharisees seize the opportunity to challenge Jesus. Their law forbade association with such 'sinners'. Ceremonial uncleanness was inevitable, plus the loss of reputation (Matt.9:9-13).

- How comfortable are we being seen eating with the 'great unwashed' of our towns?
- How secure are we in the company of those whose lives are less overtly respectable than our own and our colleagues?

Jesus wrapped the towel around His waist and washed the feet of those who would betray and desert Him.

"Love one another as I have loved you."

Perchance you will entertain angels without realising it. In this gathering Jesus is serving the ones around Him. He gives them respect, honour, Himself. He defends them; he does not judge or condemn. We all need to be familiar with honouring and strangers to criticising.

Mark 12:30-31

Love the Lord your God, with all your heart, with all your soul, with all your mind and all your strength. Love your neighbour as yourself; there is no command greater than these.

Jesus, being tired, sat by the well in the town of Sychar. Again He gives Himself in serving to the woman who comes to fetch water. The sixth hour was the hottest time of day. Could she be coming then because her history and reputation separated her from the other women of the town? Jesus speaks love into her heart. Even His revelation of her marital status does not cause her distress. She recognises His prophetic anointing. He leads her to salvation and freedom, and He equips her as an evangelist to draw the town to him. What was it that Peter said?

1 Pt.3:15

Always be prepared to give an answer to everyone who asks you to give the reason for the hope that you have.

Timothy reads like this:

2 Tim.4:2 (Amplified)

Herald and preach the Word. Keep your sense of urgency (stand by, be at hand, and ready), whether the opportunity appears to be favourable or unfavourable. (Whether it is convenient or inconvenient, whether it is welcome or unwelcome, you as preacher of the Word are to show people in what way their lives are wrong.) And convince them, rebuking and correcting, warning and urging and encouraging them, being unflagging and inexhaustible in patience and in teaching.

Jesus said:

John 4:34
My food is to do the will of Him who sent me, and to finish His work.

How easy to let tiredness overwhelm us or deflect us from one of the greatest privileges known to man - making Jesus known! How easy, at the end of a busy day, to prefer the comfort of the couch to time in a prayer meeting. Jesus was consumed with desire to fulfil the will of the Father. God is never impressed with our excuses.

Nehemiah 8:10
Joy of the Lord is our strength.

Ps.27:1
The Lord is the strength of my life.

Deut.33:25 (NKJV)
As your days, so shall your strength be.

The 'rest' of being seated in Christ is not about idleness or laziness - it is about living out of His love, life, grace and faith, as we shall see.

Hospitality is a great gift, which I believe we all have, though some are gifted to excel in this ministry. Inviting people to eat with us affords them honour, recognition, and assures them that they are important to us, valued by us and that we love their company.

What a great environment for 'gossiping the Gospel' in encouragement and ministry. This is a great service to God and the people He loves, and let's add this admonition of Jesus:

Lk.14:12-14
When you give a lunch or dinner, do not invite your friends, your brothers or relatives, or your rich neighbours, if you do they might invite you back, so you might be repaid. But when you give a banquet, invite the poor, the crippled and the blind, and you will be blessed. Although they cannot repay you, you will be repaid at the resurrection of the righteous.

Jesus is always looking for servant hearts, even at the dining table.

Let's now look at one of the most famous stories of 'sitting' in the Gospels. Jesus is staying with his very dear friends Martha and Mary, the sisters of Lazarus. Martha is distracted by the busyness of preparing food to serve to Jesus and the twelve - no mean task! Hands up to volunteer to prepare food for at least fifteen people! Notice: Martha is distracted. Jesus is in the house, and she is distracted. There is so much distraction going on across the Church. We have programmes for everything and everyone. We have diaries crowded out with events, appointments and happenings. Don't misunderstand me; I am not suggesting this is wrong per se, but Jesus is in the house and we are busy.

- Do we know He's in the house?
- Would there be a difference if He were not in the house?

Sometimes we concentrate so much on our smooth-running organisation, we seem more like a successful, or not so successful, corporation providing religious/spiritual facilities for the benefit/entertainment of one another and hopefully the alienated non-members who rarely, if ever, come and sample what is on offer.

At our 'worship meetings', or regular Sunday services, we concentrate on our PowerPoint presentations, we fuss over the flowers, which robes we wear this week, have we got enough of...? There's so much going on in so many places. Sadly, in many churches everything will proceed from start to finish whether Jesus is in the house or not. Our prayers and responses are all written down for us. We know when to stand, sit, speak in the same predictable format, week by week and year by year. In fact there is no need for Jesus to be there; we are very accomplished at what we do. We do not need the Holy Spirit to be able to do it. Even our modern PowerPoint praise meetings can be so slickly orchestrated – timed-to-perfection, glossy, colourful presentations.

Again, don't get me wrong; such things can be helpful but must *never* become a distraction.

- Should preachers pause and wait for the 'points' to catch up and flash on the screen so we all get the point? How much of our busyness spirit is inspired and initiated by God.

- How many of the exhausted volunteers are touching Jesus in their pressurised kingdom service?

"Martha, Martha," said Jesus, "you are worried and upset about many things." Is this a fitting verdict on what happens 'in church'?

Worry is a lack of faith, and without faith it is impossible to please God. Contrast this with Mary who "sat at the Lord's feet, listening to what He said".

"Jesus is in the house. I am consumed with desire for Him, sitting at His feet among the men! This is not a proper place for a woman, but Jesus is in the house, and I don't care about propriety or culture. I just know I have to be with Him. I want to be where He is. I want to smell the sweet fragrance of His nearness. I want to feel His hand resting on me. I want to gaze on Him, drink in His beauty. I want to listen and take hold of every word He utters. My beloved Jesus is in the house."

"Only one thing is needed. Mary has chosen what is better and it will not be taken away from her," said Jesus.

That is His verdict! How can I come back at Him with my 'yes but' or my 'however Lord if' when Jesus says, "Only one thing is needed and that one thing is better"?

Church programmes are not necessarily wrong. I'm trying to arrive at the place of Jesus' heart in all this. For some churches, cancelling all programmes would be the best thing, to clear everything out of the way, to set hearts to seek after and find this 'one thing needed'. Only you and God know how this precious 'better' choice is working out for you. Make no mistake - there are very many Christians who have a real love for God, for the church and the lost. They are busy in well-doing, giving themselves to God through church programmes. They are exhausted, running on empty, dry, joyless, work- and performance-driven. Deep joy and intimacy with Abba are a distant painful memory - leaders and pastors, preaching when the well is dry, declaring truths which are not working in their own lives.

There is a solution. Quit the distracted life! Put down everything that is dimming your view of 'Jesus is in the house'. Set your hearts to seek His face. Pray, "Oh Lord, make me into a Mary; I want to be a Mary. I want to sit in Your presence, feel your touch, hear Your words. Nothing matters but You, dear Jesus, only You. Oh Lord, it's been such a long time; I need to hear and know that You take great delight in me. I need to feel you quiet me with Your love. I need to hear you rejoicing over me with singing. I need your presence, Your love, Your grace (Zephaniah 3:17).

"Lord I repent of my busyness, the things that distract me from You - all those good and worthy things that drain my energy, sap my strength, and cause me to function as a robot - saying the words, doing the action, while lacking that vital heart-to-heart relationship. Teach me to rest - to rest in You, to be still and at peace before You."

So what is this rest and how do we find it?

This 'rest' is the place of ceasing from our own works or our own effort (Heb.4:10). Our works amount to everything we do, say and work through, which have not been initiated, empowered, enabled and accomplished by the Holy Spirit.

Hebrews 3:16-19 tells us that it was the rebellious and unbelieving Israelites who never made it to the Promised Land. Reading the history of Israel's journey to the land, it is a story of rebellion, unbelief, and downright idolatrous revolt. It seems the only times the people were faithful and obedient was when everything was going well for them; when their bellies were full and their enemies put to the sword, they loved God. When any hint of trouble or danger appeared, they turned against Him. How easy it is to love God when the sun is shining. The children are happy and well-behaved, your spouse 'loving on you', your job secure and your freezer full. "Yes sir, that's my kind of God. I love Him!"

No sir, that's your kind of Santa Claus, and your kind of Santa Claus is not the God of the Bible! God of the Bible leads His beloved into the desert. He calls His beloved to fasting. He says that in this world you will have trouble. He says that you will be hated for his sake. No bed of roses here!

When Israel rebelled they were saying, "We do not trust You, God. We do not feel right now, in this situation, that You have the answer and have everything in control. We are going to try our own ideas. Will you please bless us for the success we hope for?"

So often, rather than waiting for the Holy Spirit to speak, we plan our new season's programme. We fill it with sermon headings to complement our scheme; we direct our group activities to this end; and, having printed it all off, we settle back for a successful few months. Our teaching programme is good, theologically sound, well-structured;

everyone is going to benefit from this. God will be pleased. We will all benefit from head knowledge of the Bible and being active again. If we are busy, we are doing God's will, aren't we?

- Does God count success as we do?
- Does the Lord delight in burnt offerings and sacrifices as much as in obedience to the voice of the Lord?

1 Sam.15:22–23

To obey is better than sacrifice and to heed is better than the fat of rams. For rebellion is the sin of divination (witchcraft) and arrogance like the evil of idolatry.

The literal Hebrew and the literal Septuagint (the Greek translation of the Hebrew) both state that rebellion is witchcraft. Sin entered into the arena of human experience through the rebellion (disobedience) of Adam and Eve. Rebellion is sin, sin is lawlessness (1 John 3:4), and rebellion is witchcraft; therefore sin is witchcraft, witchcraft is lawlessness and all permutations of these words.

Is it really possible that so much of what we do as churches could have its roots in witchcraft? What do I mean by this? Well...

- Is our life being lived in reliance upon the Holy Spirit?
- Is what I am involved in right now Holy Spirit initiated and enabled?
- Am I just following in the usual routine?

You see, if God has not spoken, then I have made an independent decision; my independence is rebellion against God. Rebellion is spawned by unbelief; unbelief is about making God less than He is. When, in our eyes, we have made God less than He is, we have turned Him into an idol. We are worshipping a God who we do not trust, a God whom we expect to fail and let us down, a God who so often seems impotent. Because of this we construct Plan B, to help God out of His 'inadequacy'. If we can keep busy, this will disguise God's 'impotence'. So often we substitute busyness for reality; equally we steer clear of declaring 'the whole council of God', just in case. How many faithless prayers are said over the sick? How rare it is to hear, "Be healed in Jesus name!" How common to hear

157

right-sounding piety about "if it be Your will" and "bless them through this trial" etc. We have to find a 'safety net' just in case God does not come through as we have prayed. Every expression of unbelief is giving birth to rebellion.

How do we learn to move from unbelief into faith?

Fiery zeal for God and His glory, coupled with compassion for people, so often drives us into territory where we stick our neck out with the best of intentions and end up in embarrassment as, once again, our prayers and preaching produce nothing tangible. I don't mind the embarrassment; I can live with that. People usually make fun of followers of Jesus anyway. But it is the 'lack of action from heaven' which is the problem: why has God let me down again?

I am all too familiar with this scenario in my own experience. I also struggle with my passion and enthusiasm for God being bridled by the discipline of the Holy Spirit. Every time I encounter a sick person, I see an opportunity for God to show His love and glory by setting a body free. Then the people will believe. Then the people will praise Him. So 'all guns blazing' I anticipate moving into the situation in Jesus' Name. Make no mistake: the passion, desire and enthusiasm are of the Holy Spirit; the natural man is too self-centred to really be bothered. But, just as a runaway train is an impending disaster, so is a well-meaning, self-motivated Christian.

If we return to the healing scenario I mentioned earlier, have I prayed about how God wants to work in this situation? Have I sought His face and wisdom before opening my mouth? God may well be dealing with much deeper heart issues than the surface sickness suggests.

What if God gives me the answer I have prayed for and the person goes home better?

- Are they really better?
- Are they really healed?
- The physical sickness is gone, but what of the heart?
- Will God have to open up a fresh situation to touch that issue again?

Make no mistake, God desires we are well in our bodies.

3 Jn:2

Dear friends, I pray that you may enjoy good health and all may go well with you.

Lk.4:18-19

The Spirit of the Lord is on Me because He has anointed Me to preach good news to the poor. He has sent Me to proclaim freedom for the prisoners, and recovery of sight for the blind, to release the oppressed, to proclaim the year of the Lord's favour.

He longs so much for our hearts to be healthy. It is love that transforms. His love has transformed us and is continuing that work until we become as lovely and loving as Jesus, till Christ is fully formed in us. In this way we show Him to the ones who as yet are strangers to that love.

Now that I am speaking from human logic, am I creating a dilemma for God by praying healing without His word of wisdom? Do I really want the 'desperate hope' and 'holding-of-breath anxiety' followed by the "oh well, let's keep plugging away; one day God will answer", and look away with another spiritual disappointment?

Is it not much better to enter into God's rest, to learn the 'unforced rhythms of grace', as Peterson puts it in The Message (Matthew 11:28-30)? It is more than time to stop trying to make things happen, to give up trying to pressurise God into our will. He will never give in to our pleadings. He wants to bring our hearts into agreement with His. This is the place of rest. In prayer and a deep intimate love relationship we choose to wait - to wait to hear. Only when we have heard do we move into what His word is saying at that moment. We do not live by bread alone but by every word that is proceeding from the Father. The word here is 'rhema', which is 'the new word for that moment'. What God said *yesterday* is history! What He said *an hour ago* is history!

What does He want right now?

"Speak, Lord; your servant is listening."

One of the hardest things for a caring Christian to learn is to say 'no'. I recall when, as a young pastor, Saturday was our family day. This meant an early rise and getting away from the area - leaving behind all the people and things which would unwittingly rob us of that vital family together time. I had to learn to ignore the nagging questions about "What if?" and "How will they manage if the pastor is away?" It was in the days when we didn't walk around with mobile phones strapped to our ears! God is the answer to our needs, not the pastor, youth leader, prayer co-ordinator, or whoever. Each of these ministries should always be pointing us to Jesus.

Matt.11:28-30

"Come to Me," said Jesus, "all you who are weary and burdened, and I will give you rest. Take My yoke upon you and learn from Me, for I am gentle and humble in heart, and you will find rest for your souls. For My yoke is easy and My burden is light."

The wonderful liberating truth of God is this: we do not have to do anything other than come to Him, turn to Him and receive Him. When we are united with God by faith in Jesus and the Holy Spirit indwells us, we are in a place of knowing we are perfectly loved. We can sit at the station and wait for the bus to come and take us to heaven, or we can die a death through exhaustion and disease in some far-flung corner of the world, giving God's love to the needy. In both cases we are equally, utterly, perfectly loved. Nothing can affect or influence God's love toward us.

This is the place of rest - resting in this amazing, unalterable truth of God. We are saved! We are children of God! We are eternally His! There is absolutely nothing in the whole universe that can in any way diminish this. We do not have to work, struggle, strive or conform. We do not have to attend, pay, dress, pray, read the Bible, witness... there is *nothing* in all creation that can separate us from the love of God which is in Christ Jesus our Lord (Rom. 8:38-39).

There is no 'have to' with God. 'Have to' is an assault on His grace. 'Have to' is unbelief. It claims that we have to do something to get God's attention, or find His favour, or... whatever. Rebellion is the fruit of unbelief, and rebellion is witchcraft. In our lives, we can opt for showing how spiritual we are by being at church every night of the week and all day Sunday. People will then see how much we 'love and follow Jesus'. What they won't see, of course, is my burnt-out heart, my frazzled failing family life or my lack of rest in my spirit.

Is that really what God wants?

Ps.46:10

Be still, and know that I am God.

These words are found in a psalm which speaks of God as our shelter and help - a help to the extent that no matter what is going on in the world, we have no need to fear. When we have learned to know God in this way, we can enter into His rest. The Hebrew word used here for rest is 'raphah' which means 'to cause to fall', 'to let go'. This implies releasing something burdensome. God's will is not burdensome. God's will is good, acceptable and perfect (Rom.12:2, KJV).

If things are burdensome, ask yourself, "Is this really God's will for me?" Don't misunderstand me. Following Jesus is the way of crucifixion. It is a path of trials and challenges. Yet, as Paul says:

2 Cor.5:14

The love of Christ compels us.

2 Cor. 12:10

For Christ's sake I delight in weaknesses, in insults, in hardships, in persecutions, in difficulties. For when I am weak, then I am strong.

If you take time to read of what he endured for the gospel, as in 2 Corinthians 11:23-33, you can see that he had something settled in his heart and spirit. The only thing that mattered was Jesus and preaching the gospel to everyone he could reach that they might be saved. I don't read here of fighting and fussing, of complaining, changing course. I don't read of pastor-bashing, changing church because of problems, no 'pom-pom' mentality ('poor old me'!) I read of quiet submission to a Father who works everything after the counsel of His will, working good in all of His life.

The secret of rest is "Christ in you, the hope of glory" (Col.1:27); "God who works in you to will and to act according to His good purpose" (Phil.2:13); "It seemed good to the Holy Spirit and to us ..." (Acts 15:28) - working in conjunction with His anointing. When we have the deep assurance within, we have confidence that we are walking rightly with

God, and blessing of eternal fruitfulness will be on us. Being seated at the banqueting table is about this freedom from self and about resting in His sufficiency.

Heb.4:10

Anyone who enters God's rest also rests from His own work.

Yet we are told we have been created in Christ Jesus to do good works which God prepared in advance for us to do (Eph.2:10). But this is it - these are good works which Father God has prepared for us to - not our works or ideas but His!

We are encouraged to "make every effort" to enter this rest of God - an interesting paradox: making every effort to rest. But, this does not come easy to us. It demands the humbling of our pride. It means recognising that our schemes, ideas and efforts at doing it for God are no more than that: our efforts. It takes courage to stop doing, to stop until God says, "Go!" It takes courage to learn stillness in trust. We fail and have to try again, believing God to be true and good and realising that He is able to do immeasurably more than all we ask or imagine according to His power that is at work within us (Eph.3:20). This is the 'rest' that God calls us to.

As well as a place of rest, being seated is also a place of acknowledgement, honour and victory.

Ep.2:6

God has raised us up with Christ and seated us with Him in the heavenly realms in Christ Jesus, in order that in the coming ages He might show the incomparable riches of His grace, expressed in His kindness to us in Christ Jesus.

Seating us with Him in the heavenly realms is an acknowledgement of acceptance, ownership, fatherly love, pleasure and accomplishment. Ephesians 1:6 speaks of being "accepted in the beloved" (KJV). Isn't that such a beautifully expressed truth - accepted in the beloved? How beyond words is this wonderful truth! God - the Creator and Sustainer of all things, the One and only True and Living God, the All-Holy, Righteous,

Highly Exalted, dwelling in unapproachable Light, without Beginning or End, the All-Knowing, All-Seeing, Ever-Present God - has accepted us as His beloved children, adopted, purposefully chosen by name to be His.

Does not your heart burn within you at this awesome declaration of eternal love?

Love beyond comprehension - amazing! A self-centred, proud, weak, failing speck of dust has been lifted up to sit in the bosom of Father God in heavenly realms. This has been the Father's desire since before creation. In the Garden He walked and talked with Adam - Adam, His masterpiece of creation, sharing sweet communion with Almighty God.

Such has it ever been, such will it ever be the will of God. Because of all that Jesus accomplished in His obedience to the Father, we are seated with Christ in God in heaven. There is no fear, shame, guilt or embarrassment in this place - only acceptance.

"Come up here, come up now, My beloved," is the cry of the Father. Because of Jesus, Abba God says, "This is where you belong - in My presence, in My glory, in My heart."

We are God's creation. He made us; we are His.

1Cor.6:19-20

Do you not know that your body is a temple of the Holy Spirit who is in you, whom you have received from God? You are not your own; you were bought at a price. Therefore honour God with your body.

In the Psalms we read:

Ps.24:1

The earth is the Lord's and everything in it, the world and all who live in it.

We belong to God twice over. We are His by creation and His by redemption. Sin had separated us from this reality of life in God. Through Jesus this has been restored. In seating us with Him in heavenly realms, God has declared His ownership afresh: "You are Mine. I made you. I paid for you. This is where you belong!"

Paul tells us:

2 Cor.1:22

He anointed us, set His seal of ownership on us and put His Spirit in our hearts as a deposit, guaranteeing what is to come

We all know what it is to put a deposit on an item to secure ownership. You walk past a house and say to yourself, "That's mine. In a few weeks I'll be living there" - guaranteed by the deposit. It is the same with a car, painting, or a holiday - all are secured by deposit! God has put a deposit in us. Even though we are living here, housed in flesh, a day is coming when full ownership will take place.

Col.1:27b

Christ in you, the hope of glory.

God has guaranteed through this deposit that He will take up full residence in us, and we in Him. "Behold, I am coming soon."

In Ephesians, Paul puts it this way:

Eph.1:13-14

You also were included in Christ when you heard the word of truth, the gospel of your salvation. Having believed, you were marked in Him with a seal, the promised Holy Spirit who is a deposit guaranteeing our inheritance until the redemption of those who are God's possession, to the praise of His glory.

He continues with a word of caution:

Eph.4:30

Do not grieve the Holy Spirit of God with whom you were sealed for the day of redemption.

The Holy Spirit is the ownership seal of God. We have been branded by God as belonging to Him. The red hot mark of Holy Spirit has been deposited in us, purifying us as in a furnace, sanctifying us as 'holy unto the Lord', marked out, carrying a different mark to the rest. The Spirit of grace and glory rests on us. We are God's! God's solid foundation stands firm, sealed with this inscription:

2 Tim.2:19

"The Lord knows those who are His" and "everyone who confesses the name of the Lord must turn away from wickedness."

I remember hearing of a machine used by Canadian lumberjacks. This machine was used for marking or branding logs with the seal of ownership, so that when the logs arrived at the end of their river journey, owners could claim the wood. This machine apparently struck the end of the log with such force that the brand travelled the length of the log. Cut the log at any point and the owner's brand was visible! I want to be so full of God that should anyone assault or abuse me in any way, the only thing that would come out would be Holy Spirit. Should you praise and honour me, the only thing I want to be seen is the Holy Spirit.

Don't you want this to be true of you also?

Being seated with God in the heavenlies demonstrates His ownership. We have this confidence that, whatever occurs in life, God's ownership is on us. The Holy Spirit guarantees that we are God's.

Rom.8:9

If anyone does not have the Spirit of Christ, he does not belong to Him.

Hosea 11:1-4

When Israel was a child, I loved him, and out of Egypt I called My son. I led them with cords of human kindness, with ties of love. It was I who taught Ephraim to walk, taking them by the arms.

Could there be any doubt about the love of God the Father?

Heb.2:11

Both the One who makes men holy [God] and those who are made holy [us] are of the same family so Jesus is not ashamed to call them brothers.

Jesus is seated at the right hand of the Majesty in heaven. *We* are heirs and co-heirs with Christ (Rom.8:17). How amazing is that!! What Jesus inherits, we inherit in Him. As He is seated, so are we. God has raised us up with Christ Jesus and seated us in Him in the heavenly realms, in Christ Jesus. Wow! Such love!

As the father in the story of the prodigal welcomes home his son, not as a servant but to his rightful place as a son, so Abba God leads us into sonship and a welcome in the family home.

Jn.14:2-3

In My Father's house are many rooms ... I am going to prepare a place for you ... I will come back and take you to be with Me that you also may be where I am.

Jesus is seated at the right hand of the Majesty on high. We are in Him. This is our legal position in God. So we are seated in Christ because of the love of the Father. When we realise where we are, we realise that it is love that has brought us there. I know I am beloved of God because I am seated in heavenly realms in Christ. I know I am seated in heavenly realms in Christ because I am beloved of my Father. I do not belong in a barn. The hovel is not my home. We have an old-fashioned expression in the UK which speaks of the 'family seat'. It refers to the property which is handed down from generation to generation. We are the inheritors of a family seat. It is the kingdom of God.

Lk.15:31

[The father said,] "My son, you are always with me, and everything I have is yours."

Romans chapter 4 tells us that Abraham received the promise that he would be 'heir of the world'. This promise comes by faith so that it may be by grace and is guaranteed to all Abraham's spiritual offspring (Rom.4:13-17). Galatians reminds us that if we belong to Christ, then we are Abraham's seed and heirs according to promise (Gal.3:29). What an inheritance our Father has prepared for us in His love - and all for the Father's pleasure! Blessing us with riches beyond comprehension brings pleasure to the Father.

Eph.1:5

He predestined us to be adopted as sons through Jesus Christ in accordance with His pleasure and will.

You know what it is like when a child has a birthday coming - the excitement, anticipation, knowing some gift is on its way - but as the giver, how much joy there is in seeing such happiness and excitement. The parent has just about as much fun and joy as the child!

Why does Abba God sit us in heavenly places in Christ?

Because it gives Him pleasure. Just as the child is in wonder, surprise, amazement, with love and gratitude in the eyes, with impulsive, spontaneous outbursts of affection, so the Father derives pleasure in us.

No, we do not deserve such gifts. No, we can never earn them. No work or sacrifice can cause the Father to give. He gives because He loves. He loves because He is God. We are lifted out of the pit. We are brought to stand on a rock that can never be shaken. We are seated in Christ in the heavenlies, just because it pleases the Father. We are the evidence of the success of the Father's plans.

Eph. 3:10-12

His intent was that now, through the church, the manifold wisdom of God should be made known to the rulers and authorities in the heavenly realms according to His eternal purpose which He accomplished in Christ Jesus our Lord. In Him and through faith in Him we may approach God with freedom and confidence.

There it is simply spelt out! In and through Jesus, the Father has created His new creations of humankind, who are fitted to be in His presence with freedom and confidence.

How can this happen?

Paul talks of the commission given him by God:

Col.1:25-27

To present to you the word of God in its fullness, the mystery that has been kept hidden for ages and generations, but is now disclosed to the saints. To them God has chosen to make known among the Gentiles the glorious riches of this mystery, which is Christ in you, the hope of glory.

In His wisdom, God the Father, through Jesus the Son, has redeemed and purified for Himself a people - a people who were corrupt by nature, centred on themselves - through the wonderful sacrifice of Jesus, by His blood poured out on a Roman cross, in which He gave His life. Through the power of a resurrection life He brought forth this transformed community who, filled with the Spirit of God, now cry, "Abba Father." This is the accomplishment of the Father. He places us in Jesus, seated at His side. From there He shows to all the forces of darkness just how perfect His ways are. All of this was determined in eternity before one word was spoken into time and creation began. This is all through His amazing grace which He freely, lovingly lavishes on us in abundance, so that together with Jesus, in Jesus, everything of creation will be brought under His headship.

What a 'wow' of a plan! It was determined in eternity before any mistakes, disobedience, or rebellion had ever happened - joining all believers through all time with the guarantee of the Holy Spirit, proving His promises to be real and that the inheritance offered us will be realised - all for His pleasure and glory and for our salvation. This is what it means to be seated in Christ. This is our new legal position in Christ Jesus, unaffected by what happens with us on this earth. We are in Christ. From this place He calls us to walk out our relationship and inheritance.

Ezekiel went and sat among the exiles. He spent seven days experiencing their experiences. It overwhelmed him. We, from the security of the heavenly realms, can sit where others sit and share their experiences. Jesus came and 'tabernacled' among us. He pitched His tent alongside ours. He lived out the love of the Father in sitting in our place, sharing our joys, sorrows, pain, hopes, failures and successes. He brought the relevance of Father to our world. So must we.

What else can such love cause us to do but to give it away?

We are to sit where the people sit and make the Father relevant to them!

Jeremiah, on the other hand, found himself sitting alone, separated from company.

Jer.15:17

I sat alone because Your hand was on me, and You had filled me with indignation.

The burden of God's heart was strongly on him. He could not party. He had to pray and weep. He found his seat an unpopular one - cast into a pit, turned against, hunted and despised.

Why?

Because he cried out God's truth in his generation. What a need in our day! Oh yes, it is a costly seat. Even many in our churches do not want to hear the truth. It is only from the position of knowing that we are seated secure in Christ that we can endure and embrace the seat of isolation. Both these great prophets knew the wreckage of their nation. They knew the collapse of true religion and worship of God. They knew something of the pain in the heart of God, and they gave themselves to Him to call His people back to their God. Isaiah illustrates this heart in the prophet:

Isa.62:6-7

I have posted watchmen on your walls, O Jerusalem. They will never be silent day or night. You who call on the Lord, give yourselves no rest, and give Him no rest till He establishes Jerusalem and makes her the praise of the earth.

As stated above, rest is not idleness. It is confident living from the place of the Spirit. So we do not rest until the cry goes up, "God has triumphed! His work is complete. The earth receives her Lord."

Isaiah calls us to 'nag' God, give Him no rest, get Him so fed up with our prayers, that for the sake of peace and quiet... He will respond. This is the picture Jesus gives of the judge who comes to that point over the woman who demands justice (Luke 18:1-8). Remember, we are calling on Abba God, our Father, the Father who loves to release His children's godly requests.

Jn.16:23-24

I tell you the truth, My Father will give you whatever you ask in My name. Ask and you will receive, and your joy will be complete.

2 Chron.6:41

Now arise O Lord God, and come to Your resting place, You and the ark of Your might. May Your priests, O Lord God, be clothed with salvation, may Your saints rejoice in Your goodness.

One more thing, no less important, no less relevant:

Matt.20:20-23

Then the mother of Zebedee's sons came to Jesus with her sons and kneeling down asked a favour of Him. 'What is it you want?' He asked. She said, 'Grant that one of these two sons of mine may sit at your right and the other at your left in Your Kingdom.' 'You don't know what you are asking, Jesus said to them. 'Can you drink the cup I am going to drink?' 'We can,' they answered. Jesus said to them, 'You will indeed drink from My cup, but to sit at My right or left is not for Me to grant. These places belong to those for whom they have been prepared by My Father.'

This account assures us that Abba God has already prepared our specific place in His Kingdom. "I go to prepare a place for you," said Jesus.

There is a place prepared for you with your name on it. It is not a 'free for all' at the table of the Lord. It is not 'first come, choose your seat'. We all have a unique place in the heart of the Father. We all have an individually appointed seat at the feast, at the throne.

1 Pet.2:5

As living stones we are being built together into a holy habitation in the Lord.

Building involves each stone being fitted into its right place. Under God's direction the whole body is fitted together perfectly. As each part does its own special work it helps the other parts grow so that the whole body is healthy and growing and full of love.

Rom.12:5

In Christ, we who are many form one body, and each member belongs to all the others.

1 Cor.12:18

God has arranged the parts in the body, every one of them, just as He wanted them to be.

These scriptures emphasise the care and detail with which God has put together His building, His body, His bride. As we walk in obedience to Him, we find that we are joined to the right ones; we are related to the ones we can bless and be blessed by. Often this is for a season in our life, and we are then moved to a fresh part of the building or body. All the time Father is perfecting Christ in us and enabling the bride to make herself ready. We all have a particular seat at the banquet, just as at a wedding where our name tag tells us where we sit for the feast. This is the place that best pleases the bride and groom. And always, as Jesus demonstrated, we opt for the lowest, humblest place.

STUDY: In the Shade

SS 2:3

I delight to sit in His shade, and His fruit is sweet to my taste.

Ps.91:1

He who dwells in the shelter of the Most High will rest in the shadow of the Almighty.

Hos.14:6-7

His splendour will be like am olive tree, His fragrance like a cedar of Lebanon. Men will dwell again in His shade.

Ps.17:8

Keep me as the apple of Your eye. Hide me in the shadow of Your wings.

Is.49:2

In the shadow of His hand, He hid me.

Is.32:2

Each man will be like a shelter from the wind and a refuge from the storm, like streams of water in the desert and the shadow of a great rock in a thirsty land.

Jn.10:28-30

I give them eternal life, and they shall never perish. No one can snatch them out of My hand. My Father, who has given them to Me is greater than all, no one can snatch them out of My father's hand. I and the Father are One.

Ps.36:7

How priceless is Your unfailing love, both high and low among men find refuge in the shadow of Your wings.

Ps.57:1

I will take refuge in the shadow of Your wings until the disaster has passed.

Ps.121:5

The Lord watches over you. The Lord is your shade on your right hand.

Ps.63:7

Because You are my help, I sing in the shadow of Your wings.

Sitting in the shade in the Lord is a place of...

- Rest: Ps. 91:1
- Dwelling, somewhere to live: Hosea 14:7
- Hiding: Isa.49:2
- Safety, security, protection: Jn.10:28-30, Ps.17:8
- Refuge for all, great and small: Ps.36:7
- Refuge from disaster: Ps.57:1, 121:5
- Shelter in the shade of a great rock in a thirsty place: Isa. 32:2
- Worship and praise: Ps.63:7

It is not surprising that we can say, "I delight to sit in His shade."

Sitting at the banqueting table means that someone has to attend to our needs and serve us. This is the topic of the next chapter.

SERVANTS: Angels and Men

Who are the ones whom God has commissioned to serve and minister to us?

The angels!

Heb.1:14

Are not all angels ministering spirits sent to serve those who will inherit salvation?

There are myriads of books giving extensive teaching and studies on angels. I only wish to outline some examples of the service these spirit beings bring.

The first mention of an angel in the Bible is when Hagar is in the desert and the angel comes to speak encouragement and prophecy into her life (Gen.16:7). Two angels arrive in Sodom to rescue Lot and his family from the coming judgment on that city. On this occasion they are recognised as humans. Angels play significant roles in the life of Abraham. They call to him from heaven and they visit him. They bring words of prophecy into his life. It was an angel who appeared to Moses at the burning bush, grabbing his attention and releasing God's call on his life. It was an angel who was to lead the way through the desert.

Ex.23:20ff

See I am sending an angel ahead of you to guard you along the way and to bring you to the place I have prepared. Pay attention to him and listen to what he says. Do not rebel against him. He will not forgive your rebellion since My name is in him.

Yet on another occasion, Moses, while lamenting his lot, pleads with God, "You have told me to lead these people, God, but how am I going to do it? Who is going to lead me? I need all the help I can get!"

God replies:

Ex.33:14

My presence will go with you, and I will give you rest.

We must be careful to not become sidetracked by seeking angels or attributing to them the presence of the Holy Spirit. They are there, they are here, ever ministering to us for our good as God determines. Sometimes it is obvious, other times not so. Sometimes they may be seen, sometimes not. There are probably many times when we have been unaware of their activity. God told Moses he was sending His terror ahead of the people to throw into confusion every nation which they would encounter. This happened before the Hebrews experienced the outcome. So it is with us. Often, ahead of us in our walk with God, the ministering spirits have prepared the way at the command of our Father God. We can always give thanks, in faith, for such activity on our behalf.

We can always believe for angelic ministry in every situation, but our focus must always be on the Father. Angels are recorded as acting on behalf of God's people throughout the scriptures.

Balaam was stopped in his tracks when an angel revealed himself to the donkey he was riding. This caused the prophetic curse to be turned to blessings (Num.22). Gideon encountered an angel whose ministry turned the whole course of his life around, bringing deliverance to Israel (Jude 6). The birth of Samson was heralded by an angel (Jude 13). An angel ministered to Elijah preparing food for him and sending him on his way (1 Kings 19). After Isaiah prophesied deliverance for God's people, an angel was sent to execute judgement against the Assyrians (2 Kings 19). King David saw an angel when God's judgment came on his people following David's sinful census (1 Chron.21). Daniel testified to an angel closing the mouths of the lions (Dan.6).

The birth accounts of Jesus include prominent angelic ministry. Jesus speaks of angels throughout His ministry as in Luke 12:8:

Lk.15:10

I tell you whoever acknowledges Me before men, the Son of Man will also acknowledge him before the angels of God. In the same way, I tell you there is rejoicing in the presence of the angels of God over one sinner who repents.

On the night of His arrest and trial we read that He was strengthened by angels. At His resurrection it was angels who moved the stone and who testified to His resurrection. As we move into the life of the early church we find angels releasing the disciples from prison. An angel told Philip to leave the revival and go to the desert to preach to the Eunuch. Before he was truly born again, Cornelius saw an angel in a vision, which led to Peter's visit and the salvation of himself and his whole household as the gospel penetrated the Gentiles. Herod, in his arrogance, was struck by an angel and died. When Paul was facing shipwreck on his way to Rome, an angel spoke to him, and he and all on board were saved. Throughout his writings Paul refers to angels (Gal.4:14, Col.2:18, 1Tim.3:16). The writer of Hebrews often speaks of angels. In Revelation there are over sixty references to them.

This shows us that throughout scriptures angels are very real and active in the purposes of God. There are numerous testimonies to the recognised ministry of angels in our day which are in agreement with the biblical examples. This heightens interest, and it is important with all the stories we hear that we filter them through what the scriptures show us and at the same time to not lightly dismiss them. I heard recently of a young woman who was saved from very serious assault by what can only be concluded as the presence of angels. The people involved in this are still around today to bear witness to it, as were the people of the Bible. So, let us give thanks to God for the ministry of angels in our lives. Let us expect it, seek it from Father, and not be surprised when they turn up!

- The generations before Jesus testified of angels.
- Jesus testified of angels.
- The generations of the New Testament testified of angels.
- People today testify of angels.
- It would be foolish to dismiss this reality.

Angels are sent to serve; how do they do this?

By ministering the provision of God into our lives! The Bible shows they brought revelation, gave strength, executed judgement, affected nature, removed hindrances, provided food and drink, brought God's word, fought battles... To us they bring whichever course of our meal we are most in need of. We are seated at the banqueting table, under a banner of love, receiving from Father whatever we need. The angels are at hand to do this task. We should not doubt or ignore the angels, nor relegate them to stained glass windows or iconic attachments. We are potentially denying the grace of God to us should we turn from this truth. Let us open wide our hearts and minds, not fearing some weird, mystical experience but embracing the good, safe, gracious favour of the Father. Sometimes we may be entertaining angels and not realising it.

Angels are not the only servants. We are all called as servants to serve one another. The apostle Paul delighted to own the title of servant. To him it spoke of honour and high calling:

Rom.1:1
Paul, a servant of Jesus Christ, called to be an apostle.

Rom.1:9
God whom I serve with my whole heart in preaching the gospel of His Son.

Throughout his letters he speaks of serving: of serving God, the church and the cause of the gospel.

Gal.5:13
You my brothers were called to be free. But do not use your freedom to indulge the sinful nature; rather serve one another in love.

He demonstrates this when in the letter to Corinth he speaks of his freedom to eat meat, but that he will not do so if it causes offense to another.

1 Cor.10:23-11:1
So, whether you eat or drink or whatever you do, do it all for the glory of God. Do not cause anyone to stumble whether Jew, Greeks or the church of God... for I am not seeking my own good but the good of many, so that they may be saved.

Right throughout Paul's ministry, this is prominent. He refuses to be financially dependent on the churches. His preaching is all about Jesus, never himself, as his words to the church in Corinth illustrate:

2 Cor.4:5

*For, we do not preach ourselves, but Christ Jesus as Lord, and ourselves
as your servants for Jesus' sake.*

The Greek word 'doulos' is used here. As well as 'servant' the word
strongly means 'slave'. Paul is allying himself with the idea of being a slave.
He sees himself as such in his relationships with fellow believers. Possibly
the greatest apostle, evangelist, theologian in the history of the church, he
sees himself as nothing more than a slave to the ones whom he daily
strives, in love, to care for and bring to Jesus. What an example to
challenge us in our daily walk with each other.

- How many Christians rush to serve coffee?
- To sweep the hall?
- To stand in the rain and supervise a car park?
- How many preachers and platform speakers see themselves as
  servants of the humblest one in the audience?

I confess I struggle to make sense of silk suits, expensive cars,
private aircraft, mansions, etc - somewhat out of place in this scenario. But
(myself included) each one of us has a walk in the Lord which is unique to
us, and He is the One who sees all and acts upon it.

In Romans chapter 6, Paul illustrates how being a slave or servant
means we are to follow obediently whatever is demanded of us. God calls
us to the obedience of righteousness. This means that choosing to serve
one another is not really an option. It is the obedience of righteousness!
We just have to do it to be faithful, obedient children. Yet God desires
that it comes from a willing heart, not an indifferent or resentful one. If
someone needs a lift to the church or market, we do it willingly, to bless
them by serving them. This is also a service to the Father, as even a cup of
water in His name is done unto Him. Jesus said:

Jn.12:26

*Whoever serves Me must follow Me, and where I am, My servant also
will be. My Father will honour the one who serves Me.*

"Whoever serves Me must follow Me"... Turn the pages to chapter 13 and follow Jesus as, on His knees, before the disciples whom He knows will desert, disown and betray, He washes their feet. He concludes with the words:

Jn.13:15-17

I have set you an example that you should do as I have done for you. I tell you the truth; no servant is greater than his master, nor a messenger greater than the one who sent him. Now that you know these things, you will be blessed if you do them.

No servant is greater than his master. Therefore, if Jesus humbles Himself and washes my feet, you have no foundation on which to not follow suit. To refuse or ignore is to make one greater in one's own eyes than Jesus.

Luke 22:25-26

The kings of the Gentiles lord it over them; and those who exercise authority over them call themselves benefactors, but, you are not to be like that. Instead the greatest among you should be like the youngest, and the one who rules, like one who serves.

Now, there is serving and there is serving! Remember the older brother in the story of the Prodigal?

Lk.15:29

All these years I've been slaving for you and never disobeyed your orders!

This son was a reluctant, hurting, aggrieved, jealous 'servant' - somewhat like the vineyard workers in the story Jesus told. These hired men agreed a wage for their work. They worked through the day to receive it. Noticing that those who had worked for only an hour received the same wage, they expected more. How angry they were when the owner paid them what they had agreed. To them this was unjust; they felt cheated. Possibly in the natural they had a point, but in *kingdom* terms they completely missed the point. What could be more wonderful, glorious, fulfilling and exciting than knowing at the earliest possible moment in life that we have our 'wages' of the 'eternal life in/through Christ Jesus our Lord'?

How privileged and honoured to live a life of devotion to Jesus! What greater joy and satisfaction can there be than living and serving our beautiful Shepherd-King? How amazing that we can please Him with our lives! There is absolutely nothing in the 'old life' to compare with Him, is there?

The 'losers', as it were, are those who have missed out on a lifetime on earth of getting to know Jesus and only come to Him at the end of their days. I know eternity will fill up the 'loss', but knowing and loving Father today has no challenger in this life. No, serving the Father in following Jesus is the real joy of life. In the same way, following Jesus as servants of one another is to find the joy of life.

Rom.12:10

Be devoted to one another in brotherly love. Honour one another above yourselves.

"You mean that organist who refuses to change and allow different music?"

"Yes!"

"That usher who bosses everybody and acts as if he owns the building?"

"Yes!"

"You tell me to be like a slave to that person with the very loud voice who is always rude and never washes properly?"

"Yes!"

1 Peter 4:8-11, The Message

Most of all, love each other as if your life depended on it. Love makes up for practically everything. Be quick to give a meal to the hungry, a bed to the homeless, cheerfully. Be generous with the different things God gave you, passing them around so all get in on it. If words, let it be God's words; if helps, let it be God's hearty help. That way, God's bright presence will be evident in everything through Jesus, and He'll get all the credit as the One mighty in everything, encores to the end ... oh yes!

Everywhere I turn in the scriptures, I keep bumping into this truth, that 'servanthood is greatness in the eyes of God'.

Phil.2:3-11, emphasis added

Do nothing out of selfish ambition or vain conceit, but, in humility, consider others better than your selves. Each of you should look not only to your own interests but also to the interests of others. <u>Your attitude should be the same as that of Christ Jesus</u> who, being in very nature God, did not consider equality with God something to be grasped, but made Himself nothing, taking the very nature of a servant, being made in human likeness. And being found in appearance as a man, He humbled Himself and became obedient to death- even death on a cross! Therefore God exalted Him to the highest place and gave Him the name that is above every name, that at the name of Jesus, every knee should bow, in heaven and on earth and under the earth and every tongue confess that Jesus Christ is Lord, to the glory of the Father.

This is the glory of our life: to become like Jesus. He has given us the example for us to follow in His steps. His steps led Him to a cross, led Him to death, and led Him to an exalted seat at the Father's side, the highest place.

Through taking up the cross daily, we pass through the death of our flesh nature to joyfully embrace His life in the Spirit. We serve Him in worship and devotion to His Bride. As a consequence He leads us also to that exalted place, seated with Him in heavenly realms.

Being seated at the banqueting table, under the banner of love, served by the angels and serving one another, striving to outdo each other in zeal, we find the grace we need to live in servanthood through the abundant provision laid out on the table. Reach out and take, taste and see... We come full circle. Here we are sitting as honoured children in the presence of the Father, serving and being served. As Jesus said:

Jn.15:20

Remember the words I spoke to you, no servant is greater than his master.

Jn.15:14-17

You are My friends if you do what I command. I no longer call you servants, because a servant does not know his master's business. I have called you friends for everything that I learned from My Father I have made known to you. You did not choose Me, but I chose you and appointed you to go and bear fruit; fruit that will last. Then the Father will give you whatever you ask in My name. This is My command, 'Love each other'.

Jesus told His disciples that those who sit at table are greater than those who serve them. Yet He is the One who serves. He assured them that because they had stood with Him in His trials, He would give them a Kingdom and they would reign with Him. They would find themselves eating and drinking at His table. How wonderful is that!

This is it; do you see it? We are servants, yet called to be friends and brothers, sons of God. Therefore we are seated at His table eating and drinking from the abundance of who He is. Yet because of who He is, our Servant King, we get down from our seats to serve one another, only to be seated again by those serving us. This is the way of the Kingdom. This is the heart of the Father.

TASTE AND SEE: Free Samples

Luke 22:30

So that you may eat and drink at My table in My Kingdom.

What does it mean to eat and drink at the table with Jesus?

We can project this into the future when we all share in the 'Marriage Feast of the Lamb'. We can project it into the future as imagery of our eternal home in heaven; and so it is. But, I believe we can apply these words to our life today. Jesus said the kingdom of God is within us. Thus, when He lives in us by the Holy Spirit, then that kingdom has come. Heaven has invaded earth because we have been made citizens of heaven here on earth. The Psalmist said:

Ps.34:8

Taste and see that the Lord is good.

Also:

Ps.119:103

How sweet are Your words to my taste, sweeter than honey to my mouth.

Obviously these words do not apply to literal eating but to receiving into our being the life and truth of God. The testimony of the writer is that this is good; this is sweet, pleasant, acceptable and desirable. So it is we prove for ourselves that, receiving Christ day by day as our life, He is so good for us.

Jesus said that those who keep His word will never see death, to which the Jewish leaders responded:

John 8:51-52

You are demon possessed! Abraham died and so did the prophets, yet You say that if anyone keeps Your word he will never taste death.

See how the same idea crops up again?

"Never taste death" - never *experience* death. This is contained in the meaning of the word 'taste' in the NT; the Greek word 'genomai' means 'taste, experience'.

Peter uses the same thought as he writes:

1 Peter 2:3

Like newborn babies crave pure spiritual milk, so that by it you may grow up in your salvation, now that you have tasted that the Lord is good.

Babies have such a drive for the breast and will not relent until they taste the milk sliding down their throat. Then they suck and suck with a desperation until they are satisfied. That is how we should be with Christ and with His word. "Show desperation," says Peter. "Now that you have experienced Jesus in your life, never be satisfied with anything else. Be desperate, crave, and yearn for Him; drink deeply of Him. Take Him into your being, keep drinking, keep hungering, keep thirsting, and then you will be filled."

Jn.7:37-39

On the last and greatest day of the feast, Jesus stood and said in a loud voice, 'If anyone is thirsty, let him come to Me and drink. Whoever believes in Me, as the scripture has said, streams of living water will flow from within him.' By this He meant the Spirit, whom those who believed in Him were later to receive.

It is only at that place of thirsting that Jesus becomes relevant to us. While the things of this life seem to satisfy, we give Him no real thought. As the shallowness and insecurity of life seeps into our consciousness, into our soul, we begin to question, to seek. It is here Jesus says, "If you are thirsty, come to Me and drink."

When we have tasted Him, when once His life has touched our hearts, we find that nothing can compare with His presence, His touch. Life is all about living in the reality of that presence, to drink of His love and know His grace. It is to find yourself the object of all of His goodness, His love, His joy. It is to appreciate the inestimable value He places on us. The result is that He becomes the all-consuming passion of our lives. That is why we continue to hunger and thirst: "I must have more of You!" He is an addiction to our souls!

Reflect for a moment on the void, the emptiness, fear, despair, longing and loneliness that comes over our hearts when he seems so far away. He causes us to desire Him beyond all the beauties of the earth, beyond all the honour and applause of men, beyond all the riches and luxuries life can bring to us.

Taste and see that the Lord is good! The Lord is good. It is who He is. As He is Love, so He is good. He is good all the time. He never changes. The goodness we acknowledge and celebrate in the smooth, comfortable, successful times is the same goodness that is about us in the darkest experiences. He never changes. He is good. These dark, desperate, painful, hopeless days are the days to discover that He is good.

"Come to Me and drink."

Look at Job; see the example of his life. As the disasters fall upon him, as he ends up bereft of all the good things that marked his life, with his family gone, his wealth gone, his body afflicted, his wife taunting him, he responds:

Job.2:10

Shall we accept good from God and not trouble?

Job.1:21

Naked I came from my mother's womb, and naked I will depart. The Lord gave and the Lord has taken away, may the name of the Lord be praised.

Why disaster strikes in people's lives, I do not know. I do know that the Lord is good. It is His ever-present truth to my life. Yesterday, God was good. Today, He is good. Tomorrow, whatever it brings, The Lord is good. Get this settled in your heart. Let's allow this truth to renew our minds, so that we may be transformed and live more in the good of His truth, and less in our confusion, bitterness, fear and self-pity, despite the situations of life. When we confront the situations before us, we begin, not with "Why me?" or "Now what?", not with "What have I done to deserve this?" but with "My Father loves me. He is always good. How do we, my Father and I, walk through this?"

Father I place into Your hands, the things I cannot do.
Father I place into Your hands the things that I've been through.
Father I place into Your hands the way that I should go,
For I know I always can trust You. [3]

That is the testimony that comes out of the other side of "taste and see that the Lord is good" - the knowing that, in our unknowing, He knows.

Is life so messed up that there seems to be no way forward?

Look again at Elijah, "a man just like us" as James says of him. He has shown Israel that God is true and their idol worship is in vain and demonic. Trouble is, the queen instigated the idol worship! He has just demonstrated and witnessed the mighty power of God to send fire and consume the true offering and to break the drought by the sight of a hand-sized cloud. Now, at the threats of a woman, he runs for his life. We find him in despair, crying out to God to take his life. He has hit rock bottom, big time. He is full of self-pity. He wishes he were dead. He falls asleep under a tree, to be awakened by an angelic chef who has prepared fresh bread and water for him. He eats and sleeps again.

Sounds a bit like depression doesn't it?

The angel wakes him again, offers more food. After eating we find a strengthened Elijah who lives now for forty days off that food until he comes to the cave where God reveals Himself afresh in the still small voice. Elijah confesses to feeling sorry for himself. He is unable to see the bigger picture because of his self-pity. He was unaware of God's provision in the faithful followers who had not bowed to Jezebel. He is restored and commissioned anew for the task of bringing the purposes of God into being and conferring the prophetic anointing on Elisha. Elijah has received God's healing ministry into his hollow heart. He has eaten the provision God gave him for his need. He is thereby strengthened and enabled to see God clearly, again.

---

[3] Jenny Hever, Thank You Music, 1975

Father God provides us with the indwelling Holy Spirit, with scripture, with the Christian community we relate to. By these we feed on Him. By these we taste and see that the Lord is good.

What is it all about when we get fed up with God?

"Oh, I'm not fed up with God," you say.

"No?"

"No, I'm just fed up with life, my marriage, job, church, health..."

- Isn't God your heavenly Father into whose care you have placed your life?
- Isn't God the One who said that in all things He is working for your good because you love Him?

Well, if you are fed up with something in your life, you must hold God accountable somewhere. What really happens when we get fed up with God is that we stop eating of His life. Then prayer begins to dry up, the Bible gets dry, then dusty.

Church?

Missed again last week...

How strange that the times we most need to taste His love and goodness, we walk away from the table. All the while, His love hovers over us. His banner speaks love to our hurting, broken lives: "I will never leave you. I will never forsake you."

When we walk away from His table, we seek our nourishment elsewhere. Daniel, a young man in a strange land, with his companions who also loved and worship the Lord, turned away from the best food that Babylon had to offer - the king's own food - the best wines, meats and delicacies available. But this was Babylon. It was not home. This was the best a godless people could offer. Daniel knew it would defile him, turn his heart and weaken his resolve to serve his God.

When we come to our sense, we see what the alternatives are really like. We see that there is nothing but that which will defile us. Getting drunk never removes the problem. Shouting at a loved one never helps to pay the bills. Gossiping about a brother in church never helps my loneliness. Such 'food' only defiles me. Daniel determined to remain faithful to God. He trustingly obeyed God, ignoring the best of Babylon for the vegetables of the Father's kingdom. He flourished and found favour with the king. There is no life for us apart from feasting on the Father.

God promises concerning those seasons of our life when we have eaten the food that defiles and have walked away from the table into famine and sorrow - that place where our hearts' yearnings cannot be satisfied, even though we devour more and more, growing weaker and weaker, seeing the light of His love grow dimmer in our vision. In this place of hopeless weakness and despair, He promises:

Joel 2:25. (RSV)

I will restore to you the years which the swarming locusts have eaten.

His faithful covenant promises mean He will never abandon us. He will never give up on us. He will restore. Once the Prodigal had come to his senses and returned to his father, he began to feast again on the riches of his father's house.

Is.55:1-2

Come, all you who are thirsty, come to the waters, and you who have no money, come buy and eat! Come buy wine and milk without money and without cost. Why spend money on what is not bread and your labour on what does not satisfy? Listen, listen to Me and eat what is good, and your soul will delight in the richest of fare.

Haggai graphically declares:

Hag.1:5-6

You have planted much but have harvested little. You eat, but never have enough. You drink, but never have your fill. You put on clothes, but are not warm. You earn wages only to put them in a purse with holes in it.

The problem with Israel at the time was neglect of the house of God. How easily we give ourselves to our temporal needs, and how difficult sometimes to give the attention we need to 'the dwelling place of God', our heart and spirit, the temple of the Living God. How futile to work and stress for money and things, which we have today and are valueless tomorrow, when we neglect the greater part: our relationship and life in God.

"Come, eat what is good and your soul will delight itself in the richest of fare."

Rom.14:17

The kingdom of God is not a matter of eating and drinking, but of righteousness, peace and joy in the Holy Spirit.

"Righteousness, peace and joy in the Holy Spirit" - not in the food that defiles, but in the provision of the table of the Lord.

The religious leaders of Jesus' day had this problem. John the Baptist, who neither ate bread nor drank wine, was said to have a demon. Jesus, who came eating and drinking, was accused of gluttony and drunkenness! Looking at things through natural eyes leads to wrong judgments. Using the utensils of this temporal life distorts spiritual truth.

Rom.14:2-8

One man's faith allows him to eat everything, but another man, whose faith is weak, eats only vegetables. The man who eats everything must not look down on him who does not, and the man who does not eat everything must not condemn the man who does, for God has accepted him.... he who eats meat, eats to the Lord, for he gives thanks to God, and he who abstains, does so to the Lord, and gives thanks to God. For none of us lives to himself alone, and none of us dies to himself alone. If we live we live to the Lord, and if we die, we die to the Lord. So, whether we live or die, we belong to the Lord.

God's kingdom is not about our diet; it's about our desire! My desire is to know You Lord, to feast at Your table, to daily taste and see that You are good.

1 Cor.8:8

Food does not bring us near to God; we are no worse if we do not eat and no better if we do

We need to be careful though that our freedom across every area of our life does not cause another to stumble. We have to work out with God how this applies to us personally. It is not what we eat or drink that harms us or makes us unclean but what comes out of our mouths. 'Unclean' in Jesus' context is in relation to religious purity. He is saying that food, table manners, associated rituals will not purify or dirty our hearts before God. It is what is in our hearts that makes us unclean. It is from our hearts that we make choices: choices such as not to cause another to stumble, or sadly, to ignore them and please ourselves. The externals of our life usually reflect the state of our hearts. A healthy heart enables me to enjoy a beer or glass of wine. An unhealthy heart leads me to excess and drunkenness. The alcohol of itself is neither moral nor immoral, spiritual nor unspiritual - it is what is in my heart that causes the drink to be either a blessing or become a curse.

So it is with all the externals of life. Other people see and make judgments on what they see. God looks at our heart. Taste and see: the Lord, He is good. When we are feasting on Him, He works in us to want and to do all that pleases Him.

Jesus said:

Matt.6:25-33

So, I tell you, do not worry about your life what you will eat or drink. Is not life more important than food?... So do not worry, saying, 'What shall we eat or what shall we drink? ...your heavenly Father knows that you need them. But, seek first His Kingdom and His righteousness, and all these things will be given to you as well.

There it is, again: God first, then everything else from His loving hands. Taste and see: the Lord, He is good. Always turn first to Him. Drink of His river of life, eat of His living bread, and you are sustained through the day.

When we learn this truth we are able to respond to Jesus' words, "You give them something to eat." This was the occasion when they stood before five thousand very hungry people without any food! The disciples replied, "We only have..." They had very little! It was impossible for that picnic to feed so many until it was given into the hands of the Creator of the universe. We don't have much to give. When we look at all the needs around us and across the world, we have so little. But, we *do* have! We have the truth that God is good all the time. Come and taste for yourself.

We have this testimony that we feed on Jesus and He satisfies. We have people around us whose lives we do not know; people who, honestly, are desperate for a bit of what, or rather who, we have; those who will gladly "eat the crumbs that fall from the master's table". The living of a life spent feasting on Jesus causes overflow, possibly twelve basketfuls, certainly some crumbs. We may not even be aware of other people feasting off the life of God in us. Our simple testimony, our gracious attitude, our compassion, integrity, all spill over into a place of blessing for others. Or, as Jesus said:

Jn.7:38
Streams of living water will flow from within him.

The Old Testament image of the land being a place of possession and dwelling for the Israelites carries with it many promises and blessings for us. Paul tells us that the history of Israel is an example for us in our walk with God. The 'promised land' for Israel is the promised life in the Spirit for the believer. It is certainly not heaven! We do not go to heaven and then have to fight the ungodly inhabitants. In heaven we will definitely not give in to sin and disobedience. Nor will we suffer defeat in battle. It is the life we come into when we have been baptised in the Holy Spirit, our own crossing of the Jordan; the land of entering into the fullness of our life in the Father that carries the blessed promise:

Deut.11:11-12
The land you are crossing the Jordan to take possession of is a land full of mountains and valleys that drinks in rain from heaven. It is a land your God cares for, the eyes of the Lord your God are continually on it from the beginning of the year to its end.

Our lives are full of mountains and valleys. The mountains are often seen as places of success, accomplishment, victory; the valleys, places of struggle, despair, darkness and defeat. Life is full of such experiences. The mountains and the valleys drink in the rain. The mountains and valleys of our life are to drink in the rain of heaven's grace upon us. As we 'taste and see' on the mountains and in the valleys, we produce in our lives "a crop useful to those for whom it is farmed".

God, of course, is the farmer. He is looking in all our mountains and valleys for a crop of His life in us as we walk through everything set before us. By welcoming the rain of His grace, we yield the fruit of righteousness. Getting mad at God, falling out with Christian friends, blaming everyone in sight, yields fruits of bitterness, strife and faithlessness. So let me encourage you to welcome His grace. Taste and see Him first in every situation. His grace is super-abundant above anything we can conceive of. Paul speaks of the constant supply of fresh, life-giving water in the parallel of the Israelites in the desert under Moses.

1 Cor.10:3-4

They all ate the same spiritual food and drank the same spiritual drink, for they drank from the spiritual rock that accompanied them, and that rock was Christ.

In the natural bursting of the water from the smitten rock - which flowed along with them in their journey, answering the thirst of the bodies - so Christ is our life-giving water, who accompanies us moment by moment. We can drink of Him and thirst no more for that which does not satisfy.

1 Cor.12:13

For we were all baptised by One Spirit into one body.... and we were all given the One Spirit to drink.

The Spirit is He who indwells us, fills us, overflows our life - the One who is ever with us. We may drink constantly for the joy of His presence and the need of the hour.

At the well in Sychar where Jesus met a woman of ill repute, He loved her into the place of finding the life-giving water of life.

Jn.4:14

Whoever drinks the water I give him will never thirst. Indeed, the water I give him will become in him a spring of water welling up to eternal life.

Or as He said on another occasion:

Jn.7:37-39

If anyone is thirsty, let him come to Me and drink. Whoever believes in Me, as the scripture has said, 'streams of living water will flow from within him'. By this He meant the Spirit, whom those who believe in Him were later to receive.

Can you see that we always have - as close as the breath we breathe - the beautiful Holy Spirit, empowering our walk, encouraging our faith, always bringing us to Jesus? Whatever life throws at us, there is One who is ever present, unchanging, constantly working the life of Jesus in us, available without an appointment to guide us, strengthen us, comfort, assure, focus us on Jesus; so that as we drink deeply of His love and life, we are sustained. Taste and see first. Then we don't need Plan B. The fruit of our drinking is the love we have to give to others from a heart of love to a heart of need.

Rom.12:20

If your enemy is hungry, feed him, if he is thirsty, give him something to drink.

Matt.25:35-40

Come, you who are blessed of My Father, take your inheritance, the Kingdom prepared for you since the foundation of the world. For I was hungry and you gave Me something to eat. I was thirsty and you gave Me something to drink. I was a stranger and you invited Me in. I needed clothes and you clothed Me. I was sick and you looked after Me. I was in prison and you visited Me. 'Lord, when did we see You hungry, thirsty, a stranger, needing clothes, sick or in prison?' 'Whatever you did for one of the least of these brothers of Mine, you did for Me.'

This comes out of the overflow of the love and life of Jesus in us. It comes from drinking deeply of Him. It definitely does not come from guilt trips perpetrated within the church. It doesn't come from a feeling of obligation. It can only truly come from a heart of love which is cultivated by constantly drinking of the life of Jesus.

THE MASTER'S MENU

Meat!

Jesus said:

Jn.4:32-34

I have food (meat) to eat that you know nothing about... My food (meat) is to do the will of Him who sent Me and to finish His work.

What do we understand from these words?

Jesus' nourishment and sustenance came from doing that which His Father desired. He is saying that the thing which strengthened and sustained Him, that which encouraged Him in times of weakness, vulnerability and temptation, was accomplishing the will of His Father.

He is also telling us that our natural needs are secondary to the fulfilling of Kingdom purposes. Being hungry is normal and natural, yet Jesus is saying that there is something even more important. Fasting gives us an indication of this. We choose to give up food for purposes of seeking God and hearing Him, growing closer and deeper.

Strange, is it not, that in the countries with a surplus of food there is also a multi-million pound business in looking thin! Obesity is a major health concern in the affluent nations, while in underdeveloped nations thousands die daily for want of nourishing food. The rich west gets fat on the back of poverty.

Television is filled with food programmes; chefs have become household names. Bookshops have hundreds of food and diet-related hardbacks. Supermarkets compete using thousands of products for the table, trying to outdo each other, for their profit and our gratification. 80% of the world population struggle to survive on 20% of its wealth. The rich 20% wallow in 80% of the earth's assets. Inequality flourishes, and we all play our part. Even as I write, our nation is expressing concern over the tons of half-eaten, unused food which finds its way into landfill every day.

There are value judgments to be made with every mouthful we consume. Kingdom life must permeate our kitchens. As Christians we have a responsibility for what we eat and why we eat. I am not advocating a 'hairshirt' approach to food, but I am advocating a 'kingdom' approach.

Gluttony is sinful. 'Comfort eating' is indicative of a real need for ministry to break negative beliefs and to release the life-giving truth of adoption and the Father heart of God into our spirits - to bring us into the truth of our security and acceptance in the heart of the Father. Our identity is completely found in Him. This book is about feasting, so you can see I am not averse to a sumptuous sit down, heaped-up plateful! But this feasting is that which will touch the 'everything' of every day, transforming it into tangible 'kingdom life' experience.

In these verses Jesus is saying that the whole purpose of His existence is to do the will of the Father and finish His work. There is no other purpose in Jesus being alive on the earth. He woke each morning for this end. He walked through His days, His words, actions, thoughts and desires centred on the Father and His pleasure. He has given us an example so that we should follow in His steps.

None of us want to feed our 'flesh' appetites. We want to be like Jesus. Only when we take our eyes off Him or allow the negatives to turn His truth into lies do we indulge and pamper our hurt pride. But when we do...

Am I alone in this, or do you sometimes and somehow dive into indulgence to appease the self-pity and damaged pride?

Eccles.6:7
All mans efforts are for his mouth, yet his appetite is never satisfied.

Oh, how true those words are! We feed our appetites only to end up empty and feel a void that only Jesus can fill and satisfy. The pleasures of sin no longer bring pleasure once we have tasted of the Living God. The pleasure turns sour even in its indulgence.

Isa.55:1-2
Come, all you who are thirsty, come to the waters. And you who have no money, come buy and eat! Come buy wine and milk without money and without cost. Why spend money on what is not bread, and your labour on what does not satisfy? Listen, listen to Me and eat what is good and your soul will delight in the richest of fare.

Jesus is the greatest satisfaction we can know. Food for our bodies is essential to life. Doing the will of the Father is essential to eternity. There is a table from which we can toy with the trinkets, or a table of treasures on which we can thrive - treats to thrill our hearts in the abundance and satisfaction of living out of the being of Jesus.

Milk

In the last chapter we thought about Elijah being fed on the food God provided for him. It strengthened, empowered and brought him back into a place of obedience and recognition of the greatness of his God. The writer of Hebrews states that feeding on God is nourishment to our souls. He is talking about Jesus as our High priest when he comes in with these scathing words:

Heb.5:11-14 (Amplified)

Concerning this, we have much to say which is hard to explain, since you have become dull in your (spiritual) hearing and sluggish (even slothful in achieving spiritual insight). For even though by this time you ought to be teaching others, you actually need someone to teach you again the very first principles of God's word. You have come to need milk, not solid food. For everyone who continues to feed on milk is obviously inexperienced and unskilled in the doctrine of righteousness (of conformity to the divine will in purpose, thought and action), for he is a mere infant (not able to talk yet)! But, solid food is for full-grown men, for those whose senses and mental faculties are trained by practice to discriminate and distinguish between what is morally good and noble and what is evil and contrary either to divine or human law.

The whole emphasis is on our spiritual nourishment. The KJV uses the term "strong meat" for "solid food". The Greek word for 'meat' here is 'trophe' which means 'nourishment'. The nourishment to our spirit and soul comes from the deep truths of God. The writer is unhappy that the believers have not grown to mature understanding of the Truth; so they still need elementary teaching, when the expectation is that they have grown in God and hunger for 'stronger' food.

What is this elementary teaching which is given to baby believers?

Heb.6:1-2

Let us leave the elementary teachings about Christ and go on to maturity, not laying again the foundation of repentance from acts that lead to death [or, as the footnote says, 'from useless rituals'], and of faith in God, instructions about baptisms, the laying on of hands, the resurrection of the dead and eternal judgment.

Wow! That is only the elementary, foundational teaching.
What more has God for us?

Every building is only as secure and strong as its foundation. So it is with our lives. When our foundation in God is strong, so is the building of our life. Without this foundation we will not grow. In fact, God will prevent us from growing until our foundation is established. Listen to these words from the same passage:

Heb.6:1,3, emphasis added

Let us leave the elementary teachings about Christ and go on to maturity... and God <u>permitting</u> we will do so.

We have to obtain God's permission, a permit from heaven that allows us, releases us, to pursue maturity.

Do you know that Abba God loves you too much to allow you to be destroyed by trying to build on a faulty foundation?

Now, we know that Jesus is the Rock of our salvation. He is the unshakeable Rock of foundation on which we stand, in whom we trust for all of life and eternity. These scriptures are speaking of our knowing who God is, our growing in truth into mature believers who understand and recognise what is God's good way and what is not, so that we are not as those who are "infants, tossed back and forth by the waves, and blown here and there by every wind of teaching and by the cunning and craftiness of men in their deceitful scheming" (Eph.4:14).

God will leave us feeding on milk if that is all we want! But, as Matthew Henry states, in his commentary on these verses:

Strong desires and affections to the word of God are a sure evidence of a person's being born again. If they be such desires as the babe has for the milk, they prove that the person is new born. They are the lowest evidence, but yet they are certain. [4]

This is the same sentiment that Paul uses when urging the Corinthian believers to "eagerly desire spiritual gifts". There is no room for passivity in this life in God, the idea that "if God wants to give me this or that then that's fine by me; if not, I'm okay as I am." God is always looking for those who are pursuing Him, who will press in, who will make every effort to enter, that will refuse to settle for less than everything, who only find contentment when Jesus is all in all.

Do we have this 'vociferous, hungry, impatience of a baby at its mealtime'?

As The Wycliffe Bible Commentary says of Peter's words:

1 Pet.2:2
Like newborn babies crave pure spiritual milk that by it you may grow up into salvation.

The scriptures have brought us to an understanding of salvation. Now, let's use them to feed ourselves so that we may grow into the fullness of spiritual life. This is Peter's message.

Jesus said:

Matt.4:4
Man does not live by bread alone, but on every word that comes from the mouth of God.

Let us pursue God for the cultivating of a greater desire for His words, rather than for the best gourmet offering at any high class restaurant. Yes, milk gets us started, we begin to find strength and growth through milk, as does every baby. But the scriptures make very plain that a milk diet will not sustain us.

In his instructions to the Corinthian believers, Paul states that the believers are not yet strong enough for meat. They are still babies in faith.

---

[4] Commentary volume 6: Marshall Brothers

Why?

There is division among them, jealousy and quarrelling. They have split themselves up into groups, the first form of denominationalism. Some boast in following Paul, or Apollos, others Cephas (Peter), even Christ. "Is Christ divided?" is his challenging question. While we cling to our tribal traditions and historic differences, we are fit only for spiritual milk - the food fit only for those who are not living as spiritual and mature saints but as people who live as mere men. This milk Paul is speaking of is not a cause of blessing or delight, but of shame (1 Cor.3:1-4, 1:10-17).

When God called Moses to bring the people out of Egypt, He promised them "a land flowing with milk and honey". When the spies returned from their exploration of the land, they testified:

Num. 13:27

It does flow with milk and honey, here is the fruit.

Of course it did! God had said the land would be like that.

- Why do we have to question His word?
- Why are we so susceptible to doubt?

Moses gave instructions: "See what the land is like.... what kind of land they live in... is it good or bad?... How is the soil, is it fertile or poor?"

This episode cost them forty years of wanderings and conflict, of death and despair. They should have inherited the land, as God promised. Now a whole generation died in the desert because of unbelief. Children buried their parents while they gazed in hope at a distant horizon.

How many more generations will die in unbelief with the promise a distant memory and emptiness the reward of a life of wilderness wandering?

The people of Israel in fear lost their inheritance. It was taken up by a new generation. They had been rescued from Egypt, yet never reached their God-intended life purpose; their carcases littered the desert sands, as do many today.

God, help us to trust You! Gift us the faith to believe that what You have said is as true for us today as the day You first spoke it. God, will You lead us from milk to meat? We want to lay hold of every good thing

You have prepared for us to enjoy and experience in this earthly part of Your Kingdom, while You perfect us for the heavenly one.

Manna

Before the Israelites entered the "land flowing with milk and honey, the most beautiful of all lands" (Ezek.20:6), they lived on the 'manna' provided by God day after day for forty years. Faithfully our Father fed the faithless. 'Manna', which means 'what is it?' is described as:

Ex.16:31
White like coriander seed, tasting like wafers made with honey.

This 'what is it?' arrived each morning - just enough for that day. You know a need is not a need until you need it. We only need grace for today. As the people were instructed to only take sufficient for that day, their daily portion, so we pray, "Give us today our daily bread."

"Don't worry about tomorrow," said Jesus. "Let tomorrow take care of itself."

In truth we only need grace for right now. That challenge you are facing right now will receive its portion of grace right now.

- What am I going to do right now with the grace for this evening?
- Where do I keep it?

I need right now the grace for right now. That is all. This is how we walk by faith, not by sight. The manna teaches us that day by day Abba God provides exactly what we need. There is never too little, never too much. He has an inexhaustible supply of everything needful. He knows what we need before we do. He has it prepared before we ask. He really does spread a table in the desert. The daily supply of manna is called the bread of angels. God gives to humans what He has provided for the angelic hosts (Ps.78:25).

Honey

Manna tasted like honey. The Promised Land flows with honey.

Prov.24:13

Eat honey my son for it is good.

Yes, it is. God has used it to illustrate the abundant provisions of His kingdom. As with manna, a surfeit leads to vomiting and spoiling (Prov.25:16). It becomes unhealthy. Overindulgence in manna meant it went bad. There is a way in which 'too much teaching' can go bad. We can feast ourselves on sermons, conferences, books, but if we are not allowing all that 'good food' to work its way into the depths of our spiritual being, it will become sour and meaningless to us. We will waste many precious truths by not taking them deeply into our spirits and minds, sufficient unto the day.

So, as you feast on God's word, be sure to eat only what you can digest at that time. As we grow up in Him, so our appetite increases. He assures us that:

Ps.19:9-10, 111:103

The ordinances of the Lord are sure and altogether righteous. They are more precious than gold, than much pure gold. They are sweeter than honey, than honey from the comb. How sweet are Your words to my taste, sweeter than honey to my mouth.

When we receive this truth into our lives in the knowledge that He loves us beyond comprehension, that its outcome will always be for our good, then it is sweet indeed. So often it seems not to be so. God's words seem harsh and cruel. Sometimes when we pamper our flesh nature because we feel hurt or let down, God's words come as hard and distant. But, in truth, His words are good and sweet to us as we apply them to our life and yield to His love.

Prov.16:24

Pleasant words are a honeycomb, sweet to the soul and healing to the bones.

Pleasant words are words of truth, affirmation and encouragement. When they are offered from love, they bring health. This is something we can experience as we receive them and something we can witness as we give them away. God's words to us are always true, always affirming, always encouraging.

During their wilderness wanderings, the Israelites craved food other than the daily provision of manna. God gave them 'quail' that descended so thickly on the camp that the ground was covered. They gorged themselves till they were sick. But also, in their grumblings, their minds became corrupt. They remembered the food in Egypt - an illusion, I am sure.

Num.11:5-6

We remembered the fish ate in Egypt at no cost, also the cucumbers, melons, leeks, onions and garlic...

This is a people who were slaves, who were forced to make bricks in great numbers while they had to search for their own straw. Whenever we move into unbelief, we move into thinking which is corrupted. It will pervert our outlook, lead us into wrong beliefs. When we demand of God what we want, we should be careful He doesn't give it, such that we find ourselves plagued with the consequences of our selfish cravings. The provision of the Father at His table of abundance is always good.

Apples

The apple that we know in the West is probably not the fruit that the scriptures speak of. The apple is not native to the area and appeared later than the biblical text. Every indication is to the 'quince', which is highly esteemed, historically and figuratively. A common tradition identifies the quince with the 'tree of knowledge of good and evil'.[5]

Nonetheless, the imagery we hold is of a fruit that is most pleasing in every way.

"Refresh me with apples, for I am faint with love," is the plea of the beloved in the Song of Songs (2:5).

---

[5] Hastings Dictionary of the Bible, Volume 2

There is sustenance in the fruit which brings comfort and strength. This whole passage from the Song is full of the imagery of this fruit. The lover, our Lord Jesus, is likened to the apple tree - a tree set apart from all others, a tree providing delight and shade, a tree whose fruit is sweet. Oh, taste and see that the Lord is good! It cannot be said too often - the Lord is good! Feasting on Jesus, in His love, grace, mercy, judgments, is sweet - sometimes uncomfortable, painful, confusing; but ultimately sweet.

Do you know what it is to be "faint with love", to be so overwhelmed with the Love who is Jesus that you lose all strength, motion, ability and find yourself fallen at His feet in adoration and delight? Oh, Jesus, so impact my heart that I am faint with love!

God speaks of us, His people, as the 'apple of His eye'.

Zech.2:8

Whoever touches you touches the apple of His eye.

These words were spoken to a people scarred with the humiliation of forced exile and defeat. They knew the disappointment of the abandoned restoration work on the temple in Jerusalem; they were a people unconvinced of the faithful covenant-keeping God of their ancestors. In his introduction to the book of Zechariah, in The Message, Peterson states:

> *Zechariah shared with his contemporary Haggai the prophetic task of getting the people of Judah to rebuild their ruined temple. Their preaching pulled the people out of self pre-occupation and got them working together as a people of God. There was a job to do, and the two prophets teamed up to make sure it got done.*

> *But, Zechariah did more than that. For the people were faced with more than a ruined temple and city. Their self identity as the people of God was in ruins. For a century they had been knocked around by the world powers, kicked and mocked, used and abused. This once proud people, their glorious history starred with the names of Abraham, Moses, Samuel, David and Isaiah, had been treated with contempt for so long that they were in danger of losing all connection with that past, losing their*

magnificent identity as God's people. Zechariah was a major factor in recovering the magnificence from the ruins of a degrading exile. Zechariah reinvigorated their imaginations with his visions and messages. The visions provided images of a sovereign God that worked their way into the lives of the people, countering the long ordeal of debasement and ridicule. The messages forged a fresh vocabulary that gave energy and credibility to the long term purposes of God being worked out in their lives.

But, that isn't the end of it. Zechariah's enigmatic visions, working at multiple levels and his poetically charged messages are at work still, like time capsules in the lives of God's people, continuing to release insight and hope and clarity for the people whom God is using to work out His purposes in a world that has no language for God and the purposes of God.

Is not this the background of today?

The church is despised, ridiculed, ignored. Christians are embarrassed, fearful, unbelieving, and desperate to see the God of the Bible as the God of the Bible. To you - yes, you - these words come: "you are the apple of My eye". Here is your identity, child of God.

Apparently, the pupil in the eye is the most tender, easily injured, irreplaceable thing. It is carefully protected by the surrounding matter. So you and I are in the eyes of Father God. He knows our frame; He remembers that we are but dust. His compassions never fail!

In the song of Moses, recorded in Deuteronomy, this thought is first brought to the attention of the Israelites.

Deuteronomy 32:10

In a desert land, He found him (Israel) in a barren and howling waste. He shielded him and cared for him and guarded him as the apple of His eye. Like an eagle that stirs up its nest and hovers over its young, that spreads out its wings to catch them and carries them on its pinions, the Lord alone led him; no foreign god was with Him.

Child, you are so precious to Abba God. His care of you is most loving, tender, and strong. You are never out of His sight or off His mind.

His thoughts concerning you are precious, so vast they are beyond number, as grains of sand (Ps. 139:17-18). We can always have confidence to cry, as the Psalmist:

Ps.17:6-9

I call on You, O god, for You will answer me; give ear to me and hear my prayer. Show the wonder of Your great love, You who save by Your right hand those who take refuge in You from their foes. Keep me as the apple of Your eye, hide me in the shadow of Your wings from the wicked who assail me.

May these words prove to be as "a word fitly spoken ... like apples of gold in settings of silver" (Prov.25:11).

Fruit

SS.2:3

His fruit is sweet to my taste.

It is not possible to define the effects of the fruit of Christ. He is so beyond everything of this natural experience. Only in the Spirit can one begin to taste something of the satisfying sweetness and healing balm that is the fruit of being in Jesus. In John chapter 15 Jesus uses the analogy of the vine to illustrate this.

Jn.15:15

I am the vine, you are the branches. If a man remains in Me and I in him, he will bear much fruit, apart from Me you can do nothing.

Remaining in Christ is the life we are called to live. The branches of a vine produce leaves and grapes only because they receive the necessary sustenance from the vine, its roots and the goodness of the soil in which it is planted. It is all about being joined.

Jn.17:21

I pray ... that all of them may be one, Father, just as You are in Me and I in You, may they also be in Us. So that the world may believe that You have sent Me.

Paul tells us that our lives are now hidden with Christ in God (Col.3:3). How true it is that only in Christ is there life; only in Him does anything make sense; only by choosing to remain in closeness to Him, to trust that He is our loving Father, that we are held in His hand, choosing to believe His words to our hearts; only in this place do we know life.

It is only from this position that the beauty of Jesus is seen in us. How easily when the going gets tough do we get going! We take our eyes off Him. We make decisions out of our fear or pain. Then we find ourselves struggling in our own strength and wisdom to respond to what has come our way. That is always the way of defeat. "Remain in Me" is the loving entreaty from the Father's heart.

As we yield ourselves to Him, He displays His life in us. This is the sweet fruit we taste when feasting on Him.

Gal.5:22

The fruit of the Spirit is love, joy, peace, patience, kindness, goodness, faithfulness, gentleness and self- control.

This is what we experience as we live in Him. Vine life produces in us the deepest fulfilment of our deepest desires. This fruit grows automatically in us as we remain in Him. It is inevitable. The branch produces the fruit which comes from being joined to the vine. We don't strive to be good or kind or full of love; it becomes the natural, or rather 'naturally supernatural', outflow of remaining in Christ.

Life outside of Jesus is extremely unpleasant. Its fruit is in direct contradiction to the life in Christ:

Gal.5:19-21

Sexual immorality, impurity, debauchery, idolatry, witchcraft, hatred, discord, jealousy, fits of rage, selfish ambition, dissensions, factions, envy, drunkenness, and orgies.

Not happy reading! Not a desirable lifestyle, nor something to aim toward.

Rom.1:29-31

They have become filled with every kind of wickedness, evil, greed, depravity, envy, murder, strife, deceit, malice, gossips, slanderers, God-haters, insolent, arrogant, boastful, invent ways to doing evil, disobey parents, senseless, faithless, heartless, ruthless.

What a way to live! I am sure each of us can see some reflections of our lives in this list. But as Paul says elsewhere:

1 Cor.6:11

Such were some of you, but you are washed, you are sanctified, you are justified in the name of the Lord Jesus Christ.

Is it not much more blessed to act in love rather than hate? To move in peace rather than discord? To live in joy rather than jealousy?

This is the inheritance of all who 'remain in Me'. The blessings of this freedom are as numerous and enjoyable as the never-failing compassions and morning-new mercies which are ours in His grace (Lam.3:22-23).

Eph.5:8-9

You were once darkness, but now you are light in the Lord. Walk as children of light, for the fruit of the Spirit is in all goodness, righteousness and truth.

Paul goes on to warn us to have nothing to do with the unfruitful deeds of darkness. The things of the flesh nature can only produce the fruit of the flesh nature, which is destructive, deceitful and imprisoning. Eternal fruit, fruit that will last, only comes from living in vine life with Jesus. Everyone wants to be loved, happy, and free of fear. Everyone wants to receive kindness, to be controlled in their actions. So, in remaining in Jesus, we find our God-given yearnings realised. We come into knowing the fruit of righteousness which is by Jesus Christ to the glory and praise of God (Phil. 1:11).

This fruit of righteousness is the knowing that we are free from guilt and shame, for we are made right with God through Jesus. It is in knowing the freedom from fear as God's judgments are piled on Jesus that we may walk free in Him - free from the fear associated with man as we live in goodness toward our neighbour, exercising obedience to the Spirit, living in peace and forgiveness, in humility and kindness. What riches are ours in the grace of God who loads His banqueting table with all these treasures!

We can learn to live in this good place as we seek after the wisdom of God which, James tells us, is "pure ... full of mercy and good fruit ... peacemakers who sow in peace raise a harvest of righteousness" (James 3:17-18). Learning to live out of the place of being at one in Jesus, exhibiting His grace, following His path, brings the good fruit of a righteous harvest. Oh, how good it is to be clean; how good to stand in the presence of Almighty God, coming boldly to that throne of grace knowing we are clean, knowing that the blood of the Lamb ever cleanses us from all sin - clean, free from shame, guilt, fear - called by name into the throne room of the Father. What joy! Led there by the Son, who brings us there claiming, "Father pour out Your grace; this one is seeking Your face. You know why I died, Father. You love this child. Look at My hands and feet. Grant mercy." [6]

Of course, this does not become our lifestyle experience overnight. We have to submit to the gracious disciplines of the Father, for the Lord disciplines those He loves (Heb.12:6). As earthly parents we exercise discipline toward our children. This comes from love - the desire to encourage them and develop in them the graces of life which we know will stand them in good stead throughout their life, bringing them into a personal love relationship with the Father. Abba God loves us so much more than we can possibly love our children. His disciplines are to encourage us to throw ourselves upon His grace, to press deeper into His heart. There is the place of healing. So often it is not fun! Discipline is not meant to be fun. It is about instruction, training; it's tough. But afterward it produces a harvest of righteousness and peace, and all because you are worth it in His eyes!

---

[6] Laura Woodley, from the album 'Home'

God has invested Himself in you. You matter to Him. He sees you as worth it. His whole purpose in salvation is that we may be with Him. His disciplines express love! The things that He allows into our experience all work good in us through His hands, because He sees us as worth it. He is investing in an eternal inheritance with every touch of His love on your life.

Prov.11:30

The fruit of righteousness is a tree of life.

There is a tree of life in the Garden of Eden, a tree whose fruit brings everlasting life. This is God's investment in order that His righteousness would be our righteousness that we may live in Him forever. Jesus declared at the beginning of His ministry:

Matt.7:18-20

Every good tree bears good fruit, but a bad tree bears bad fruit. A good tree cannot bear bad fruit and a bad tree cannot bear good fruit ... by their fruit you will recognise them.

Matt.12:35-37

The good man brings good things out of the good stored up in him, and the evil man brings evil things out of the evil stored up in him. But I tell you that men will have to give account on the Day of Judgment for every careless word they have spoken. For by your words you will be acquitted and by your words you will be condemned.

This is because out of the overflow of the heart the mouth speaks. When our hearts are nourished on the fruit of the Spirit, filled with all the fullness of Christ, they will overflow with words of life and worship. We cannot hide from God. He sees our hearts. He does not regard us from our outward appearance. That does not impress Him. He is seeking the heart of His Son in the children that His Son calls brother and sister.

There is only one way a tree can be good. It has to be the planting of the Lord. It is only as we are born again that we are made righteous and joined to the Father in the Son. Only then does the Spirit of God come to us and abide in us. Ezekiel paints a picture of the river of life flowing from under the threshold of the temple. As the river flows out from the temple it gets deeper and deeper until it becomes deep enough to swim in. On either side of the river, on its banks, grow an abundance of trees. It says of these trees:

Ezek.47:12

Fruit trees of all kinds will grow on both banks of the river. Their leaves will not wither, nor will the fruit fail. Every month they will bear, because the water from the sanctuary flows to them. Their fruit will serve for food and their leaves for healing.

Abiding in Christ is the place of fruitfulness. We receive His life which feeds and sustains us, as the waters are drunk up by the trees to bring fruitfulness. The fruit is exclusive to the tree on which it grows. A vine cannot produce figs, nor an olive, grapes; no more can we produce fruit that is not of Christ when we are joined to Him and drink in His life-giving grace.

Ps.92:12-15

The righteous will flourish like a palm tree. They will grow like a cedar of Lebanon, planted in the house of the Lord. They will flourish in the courts of our God. They will still bear fruit in old age, they will stay fresh and green, proclaiming 'the Lord is upright. He is my Rock and there is no wickedness in Him.'

How good is this - no growing useless with age! No retirement in the Kingdom of God. As we continue rooted, grounded, and established in Christ, so we can expect to stay fresh, green and fruitful. I have been a lover and follower of Jesus for more than fifty years. I might have expected a certain amount of sameness, of the mundane, of the predictable, same-as-usual stuff. But I find the longer I am in Christ, the more exciting He becomes, more marvelous in the revelation of His heart and depth of love. I find myself more passionate in my pursuit of Him. I am more secure in the certainty of being His beloved, adopted, chosen one; more convinced that He cannot fail, that nothing can separate us from His love. He keeps me fresh and green.

The joy of the Lord truly is our strength.

Ps.71:14-18

But as for me, I will always have hope; I will praise You more and more. My mouth will tell of Your righteousness, of Your salvation all day long, though I know not its measure. I will come and proclaim Your mighty acts, O Sovereign Lord, I will proclaim Your righteousness, Yours alone. Since my youth, O God, You have taught me, and to this day I declare Your marvellous deeds. Even when I am old and grey, do not forsake me, O God, till I declare Your power to the next generation, Your might to all who are to come.

I love these words. They are such a testimony to God's faithfulness, a testimony I have for myself of His greatness, a testimony I want to go to the grave declaring to those younger than I that they too may know this God. There is no retirement in the kingdom of God.

- Are you feeling tired?
- Washed up?
- Redundant?

Take the fruit of Christ again. Feed on Him; cling to Him. Let His vibrant resurrection power and life recharge your spirit and revitalise your body. Let Him inspire your faith and stimulate your prayers. Religion can never do or give what lies in the heart of God for you. We know that fruitfulness is the result of death.

Jn.12:24

Unless a kernel of wheat falls to the ground and dies it remains only a single seed. But if it dies, it produces many seeds.

Nature illustrates how fruitfulness comes only through sacrifice and death. The seed has to be planted, buried in the soil, that it might die and produce its fruit. Jesus gave Himself as a sacrifice, to die in obedience to the Father's will, to become the first fruits of a new creation. By His death we are made alive. We are the fruit of His sacrifice, the joy set before Him. Through death comes fruitfulness!

We have to follow the same path - to choose to die to our flesh nature daily, taking up the cross, yielding to the heart of the Father. Only in this way can we be fruitful in the kingdom of God. Pleasing ourselves, choosing our own way, creates a barrier which greatly hinders any growth of the fruit of Jesus in us. We need to constantly drink of His life-giving river, to feed on His life-giving words. We eat the fruit of who He is and produce the fruit of who He is in ourselves. We will see, and those around us will see, that we are joined to Jesus. He is our life; we bear the fruit.

COMMUNION: Simply Sumptuous

Wine

Jesus said:

Mk.14:25
I tell you the truth, I will not drink again of the fruit of the vine until that day when I drink it anew in the kingdom of God.

Wine - what a delight and a curse it has proved to be to mankind. The scriptures tell us it "cheers both God and men". Sadly we also have many accounts of the misuse of wine and the accompanying pain and destruction.

Wine is used throughout the sacrificial system of ancient Israel. It was obviously an acceptable offering to God. Leviticus tells us:

Ch.23:13
...together with its grain offering ... of fine flour mixed with oil, an offering made to the Lord by fire, a pleasing aroma and its drink offering of a quarter of a hin [about 1 litre] of wine.

This is typical of many verses describing the offering for sacrificial worship which is pleasing to God. The fruit of the vine pleases God. Paul tells Timothy to drink wine for the sake of his health. It seems a diet of water alone was causing Tim some health problems. Wine is used medicinally by the Samaritan who tends the victim of a street mugging as told in Jesus' famous story. In God's provision for His beloved, according to Hosea, is wine along with gold, grain, silver and oil (Hos.2:8). It is the cry of Isaiah the prophet:

Isa.55:1-4
Come, buy wine and milk, without money and without cost

God uses wine freely as an illustration of the abundant life and provision which flows from His heart. Come and receive My abundant life! It is like milk; it is like wine.

I wonder what we are to understand from this?

Wine is desirable; it looks inviting, rich and satisfying. It makes the heart glad. There is also an abundance of it. It was a daily part of the life of the Jewish people. Perhaps drawing all this together gives us a hint at why God used it for this purpose. He is our deepest daily need. He is most desirable and beautiful to see, taste, and experience. He certainly gladdens the heart with His grace and covenant love. And we can never exhaust His offering of Himself for our every need and delight.

Early in his writings Isaiah brings God's love song of Israel to the people. The nation is pictured as a choice vineyard, prepared to produce a good harvest. Sadly, the harvest was of injustice, bloodshed, and distress. The people that God chose to demonstrate His glory, love, provision and wonder to the idolatrous nations have collapsed into the same state. Those who are His "garden of delight" have degenerated into a mirror image of their neighbours (Isa.5:1-7).

The vine and wine are powerful illustrations of God's people throughout the Bible. Jesus speaks of Himself as the Vine:

Jn.15:1

I am the vine, My Father is the gardener.

Jn.15:5

I am the vine, you are the branches.

By remaining in Him, we produce much fruit. The fruit of the Spirit is love, joy, peace, patience, kindness, goodness, faithfulness, gentleness, and self control. This is the wine of heaven. This is what we drink as well as produce. We cannot but be such people as we remain joined to Jesus, taking our life from Him. It is the Father who has the responsibility to tend us as is needed to produce the best harvest - fruit that will remain.

As we have already acknowledged, God is good all the time. He is always working for our good in everything. We submit to His pruning on this basis, knowing that the testing of our faith develops perseverance, which leads to maturity, and completeness (James 1:2-4). God is intent on producing His Son in us, that we may reflect His glory, being changed from one degree of glory to another (2 Cor.3:18). All this fruit is the wine of heaven. Every expression of Jesus that is manifested in our life, words and actions is the flowing wine of heaven.

We are in Christ and He promised to never leave us or forsake us. He is constantly with us. Yet He speaks of us remaining in Him. I believe this is outworked when we choose to submit to His ways for us, to keep Him as our first love. I believe it speaks of us choosing to turn from everything that is not His best for us. It may be fine for someone else, but I am His child and He relates to me, to you, as an individual child, being nurtured and doted on by this amazing Father. I see 'remaining in Him' as choosing to agree with His decisions, choosing to seek Him and His way through every experience of every day. On the occasions that we mess up, we come quickly in repentance, confess and receive that forgiveness and cleansing that only He can give. It is about seeking His heart and mind about the issues of life, the decisions we make - a way of letting the Holy Spirit prompt and direct our path. Jesus spoke of His sheep following Him as He calls them by name.

In Nehemiah's day, when the nation was gathered to hear the reading of the Law, they became so grieved in their spirits at the failings of their ancestors and the state that Israel had fallen into, that they gave way to wailing and weeping. Deep sorrow fell upon them. Nehemiah stands and shouts out to them, "Stop crying! Don't be so sad. This is a great day, a sacred day. Go home and celebrate; eat and drink; give to those without enough. The joy of the Lord is your strength."

Why?

Because they now understood the word of God which had been brought to them, and knowing the truth set them free. The nation now had the spiritual tools to become again the people God longed for them to rise up into.

What has happened here?

A day has dawned - a day of celebration of the good words of God, in His revelation and direction. The words and will of God are not heavy weight, as some would believe. His word is life to us. His will is food - good, pleasing and perfect. His joy is our strength to walk in His ways, to pick up whatever comes our way in His joy, thereby completing our joy also. Taking up the life of remaining in Jesus is a cause for celebration. It should never be seen as a burden, never to be understood as a raw deal.

To take up the cross of daily self crucifixion and following His good, pleasing and perfect will is a sacred celebration of life in all its fullness.

Jesus loved celebrations.

Remember the wedding at Cana?

They ran out of wine. Some may say "and a good job too!" but not Jesus. He comes to the rescue of the host's honour and reputation. He produces something like a hundred and twenty gallons of the best wine ever tasted - and for people who have already been celebrating for some time! Jesus seems unconcerned at the amount of wine already consumed. What He is doing is another example of 'kingdom' life. He is offering all the guests a choice. They can overindulge and suffer the consequences, or they can exercise a measure of control which will honour their host, themselves and all those around them. He honours us with choice. Jesus is always offering us choices. Notice also He made the best wine ever. He is only into doing the best things. He never does half-good things. But every good and perfect gift comes down from the Father. There is no fear in love. His love casts out all fear and assures us of the very best from His hand.

Although Jesus produced a large amount of the best wine ever tasted, He does not advocate a careless attitude to alcohol, or anything else, for that matter. The generation we live in has a mindset that being drunk equals having a good time. A weekend spent in an alcoholic haze means a 'good' weekend. Medical and police statistics prove the lie to that attitude. Lovers and followers of Jesus never have a need or excuse for getting drunk. Jesus is the answer to every need we can ever have. The bottom of a bottle holds no answers. The problem is still there when the hangover has gone.

Eph.5:18

Do not get drunk on wine which leads to debauchery. Instead, be filled with the Spirit.

Paul is here telling us that being filled with the Holy Spirit, keeping filled up with Him, is far better than being full of wine. On the day of Pentecost the disciples were accused of being drunk when the overflow of the Holy Spirit upon and out of them was witnessed. So overwhelmed were they by the power and anointing of the Spirit that their behaviour caused some to declare that they were drunk!

Tell me, when was the last time that comment was made about you or the times when you have met with other believers?

Here are a few things to think through about drunkenness:

- People walk differently - they stagger, they change direction, they are unsteady on their feet.
- They talk differently - their speech is usually slurred, often loud and sometimes incoherent.
- People behave differently - "I didn't know what I was doing" is a frequent comment when people have shamed or embarrassed themselves. Quiet people often become very loud, shy ones often very demonstrative. Loud ones sometimes become quiet and still.
- People's attitudes change - sometimes they are everybody's friend, generous-hearted, other times very aggressive and threatening.
- They have a smell about them - it is obvious even from a few feet away that substantial quantities of alcohol have been consumed. There is an aroma saying 'drunk'.
- People 'sleep it off' as a cure for their time with the drink.

Now, how does Paul's comparison work out here - "Don't get drunk on wine; instead get full of the Spirit"?

When you are full of the Spirit, you walk differently.

Col.2:6 (NKJV)
As you therefore have received Christ Jesus the Lord, so walk in Him.

Col.3:5-8
Put to death, therefore, whatever belongs to your earthly nature: sexual immorality; impurity; lust, evil desires and greed, which is idolatry ... you used to walk in these ways.

John speaks of us walking in the light. Because of the Holy Spirit, we now "speak the truth in love". We are told:

Col.4:6

Let your conversation (speech) be always full of grace, seasoned with salt, so that you may know how to answer everyone.

There are many exhortations like this, also many reminding us of how our speech used to be (before Jesus made us new) "arrogant, lying, deceitful, filthy, coarse" - but not anymore. Now we teach and admonish one another with all wisdom. We sing psalms, hymns and spiritual songs with gratitude in our hearts to God (Col.3:16). Our attitudes reflect the presence of the Spirit in us.

Phil.2:5

Your attitude should be the same as that of Christ Jesus.

Paul also tells us to set our hearts on things above, since we have been raised with Christ. This is where Christ is seated at the Father's right hand. Our minds are to be set on things above rather than on the things of this earth. We are transformed by the renewing of our minds. The spiritual person makes judgments about all things, but the person without the Spirit cannot; such things are only spiritually discerned by those who have the Spirit.

Thus, with a changed heart and mind, and with a Spirit-led attitude, our behaviour also changes, because as a man thinks in his heart, so is he. Throughout the scriptures we are encouraged to live for - and as – Christ:

Gal.2:20

...since it is no longer I that live but Christ that lives in me so the life I now live, I live by the faith of Jesus.

Thus, as we turn from idolatry, we get rid of all malice and deceit. We humble ourselves, put on love, and obey the truth, all in the Spirit. In other words, we behave as those who are the sons and daughters of God.

Next we see that there is an aroma surrounding the Spirit-filled child of God.

2 Cor.2:14-16

Thanks be to God, who always leads us in triumphal procession in Christ and through us spreads everywhere the fragrance of the knowledge of Him. For we are to God the aroma of Christ among those who are being saved and those who are perishing. To the one we are the smell of death, to the other, the fragrance of life.

We carry the smell of life and death upon us. It has nothing to do with your favourite cologne. It is the aroma of heaven. In our beings we witness to the truth and reality of God. This speaks death to those who reject Him, and to those who embrace Him the sweet aroma of life. Jesus gave His life as a "fragrant offering and sacrifice to God" (Eph.5:2). His sacrifice was the sweetest aroma to the Father who was pleased to accept this offering that we may be restored to Him. Often in the OT we read how pleased God was with the sacrifices. Isaiah uses this when he speaks of how "it pleased the Lord to bruise Him and cause Him grief. When He makes His soul an offering for sin, He will see His seed. He will prolong His days, and the pleasure of the Lord will prosper in His hand" (Isa.53:10). Daily, as we lay down our lives in submission as living sacrifices, we present to the Father a pleasing aroma.

As the drunk 'sleeps off' the effects of his indulgence, so the child of God rests in Him.

Heb.4:9-10

There remains then a Sabbath rest for the people of God; for anyone who enters God's rest also rests from his own work.

Matt.11:28-29

"Come to Me," said Jesus, "and I will give you rest ... you will find rest for your souls."

Ps.23:1-2

The Lord is my shepherd; He makes me lie down in green pastures.

Ps.46:10

Be still and know that I am God.

Living in the Spirit is living in rest. When there is fear, tension, stress, striving, we have taken our eyes off the face of the Saviour. Obviously the more wine we drink, the drunker we become! So in the Spirit, the more we receive of Him, the more we hunger and thirst, the more we will live in 'Holy Spirit drunkenness'.

The 'banqueting house' of Solomon's Song means a 'house of wine'. This amazing place Jesus leads us to is a house of wine that we may drink continually of His abundance. Jesus is not a supply of austerity. He is not a provider of sombreness. He does not offer rigidity, coldness, legalistic religion. He offers us a constant supply of celebration. He provides us with pleasures forevermore. In His presence is fullness of joy - joy unspeakable and full of glory.

How can we contain ourselves with this most amazing, incredible, revolutionary, mind-blowing truth that God, in Jesus, has reconciled us to Himself, adopted us into His family, put His Spirit in us, and brought us into a very real intimate relationship where we cry, "Abba Father", where every promise proves to be true and all the glory of His everlasting Kingdom is our inheritance?

Truly this is a banqueting house of wine - the substance that gladdens our heart, that we offer in worship, that attracts our eye and stimulates our desire, that causes us to act, think, speak, feel as He is.

1 Jn.4:17 (Amplified)

In this (union and communion with Him) love is brought to completion and attains perfection with us, that we may have confidence for the day of judgment (with assurance and boldness to face Him), because as he is, so are we in the world.

The wine of Christ-life makes us like Him. In the heart and eyes of the Father we are already perfect. He is working in us to bring us to this realisation that we may experience increasing Christ-likeness day by day. Enoch is an example. Walking with His God, "he was no more, because God took him away" (Gen.5:24).

This has nothing to do with following religious laws and calendars, rituals and rites. This is a heart relationship. It is a passionate love affair where everything springs from and is for love. This is the wine of the kingdom. This is the wine we drink when we remember Jesus together - the wine of His life, of His blood poured out in willing, loving sacrifice that we may drink of Him forever.

Jesus spoke of putting new wine in old skins. He told us:

Lk.5:37-38

If he does, the new wine will burst the wineskins, the wine will run out and the wineskin will be ruined. No, new wine must be poured into new wineskins. And, no one after drinking old wine wants the new, for, he says, the old is better.

What are we to make of these words?

We have many hymns and songs which cry to God to change us:

- Spirit of the Living God, fall afresh on me.
- Take my life and let it be, consecrated Lord to Thee.
- Break me, melt me, mould me, fill me.
- Change my heart O God.
- You are the Potter, I am the clay

...and so on.

What are we seeking?

A fresh touch from God: fresh insight and understanding, fresh anointing and transformation, fresh love and passion, fresh cleansing and empowering, fresh taste of His goodness and love. Through the Holy Spirit we have a constant deep satisfaction in Jesus that is ever crying out for more. A strange anomaly - satisfied, yet hungering for more!

Matt.5:6

Blessed are those who hunger and thirst for righteousness, for they will be filled.

This is the new wine Jesus speaks about - new experiences of God (we all want them), knowing God more perfectly, bringing fresh awareness of the vastness of His being. God is a God of new things. He is unchangeable: the same yesterday, today and forever. Yet he is always making new. I am a new creation in Christ, sealed in the new covenant.

We have a new name, new home, new heart, new hope; our God is making new.

Isa.42:8-9

I am the Lord, that is My name. I will not give My glory to another or My praise to idols. See, the former things have taken place, and new things I declare; before they spring into being I announce them to you.

Isa.43:19

Forget the former things. Do not dwell on the past. See I am doing a new thing. Now it springs up, do you not perceive it?

How we all love those words in Lamentations:

Ch.3:22-23

Because of the Lord's great love we are not consumed, for His compassions never fail. They are new every morning; great is Your faithfulness.

If we are not drinking the new wine, we are missing the very essence of living in God. God is always making us new as we agree with Him. As with the 'manna', yesterday's food is no good for today - daily fresh mercy, daily fresh grace. In God's economy permanent change is here to stay. There is no standing still, no treading water. If we are not moving on in God, we are falling back.

I remember hearing someone who, when giving notices about the activities during the week at church, said on a regular basis, "The service next week will be as usual." Sadly, this was prophetically true! Every week, service by service, the same format, same ritual, same prayers and responses. The only 'new thing' were the words of the sermon. There is still a guaranteed predictability about so much of what we call worship. So many programmes are timed to the minute.

- Where is the 'new thing'?
- Where is the change, the surprise of God, the moving on, the following?
- Where is the 'new every morning'?

Even among charismatic fellowships I find a predictability growing. I find a fresh form of ritual sameness. I have been as guilty as the next man at times. I am praying right now, "Lord, keep me from becoming stale. Keep me from monotony, from sameness. Keep me from dwelling on the 'good old days'."

Isa.43:19

Forget the former things; do not dwell on the past.

I have many precious memories of former days - days in which I saw God in a new way, days when God did things I had not experienced before. I treasure those memories. They are a testimony to Father's faithfulness. But I cannot pray for those days to come back. This is a new day, a day for new things. I must not look back longingly into history. I can use it to stir up faith for the challenges of today. I don't want to be fossilised like Lot's wife! We cannot afford to become trapped in yesterday's blessings. God said to Abram:

Gen.12:1

Leave your country, your people and your father's household and go to the land I will show you.

To follow God there always has to be a leaving. Jesus said that those who love family, property, profession, or anything else for that matter, more than loving Him, are not fit for His kingdom (Matt.10:37). Our roots are exclusively in Jesus. He is the vine; we are the branches. "Leave your country (leave your traditions, your heritage, dogmas, your comfort zone, familiar ways, securities) and follow Me!" is the command of Jesus. The new wine must only be poured into new skins. The person I was last month is not fitted for today's new wine. God can only reveal the new wine of last month if that is where I still am. I have to be a new container, freed from yesterday's limitations to receive the new wine. God loves us too much to destroy us with wine we cannot yet contain.

- Do you really want to know that you are fitted to carry today's revelation?

- Do you want to be allowed into a deeper, closer consciousness of the Father?

We have to be constantly made new in our understanding. It is in the battlefield of the mind that all this work takes place. At the new birth, God has given us "everything we need for life and godliness through our knowledge of Him who called us by His own glory and godliness" (2 Pet.1:3). As our minds get renewed in truth, we embrace this amazing life in God. The new wine is the daily filling of the Holy Spirit into daily renewed minds and clean hearts.

Luke adds this comment:

Luke 5:36b (The Message)
No one who has ever tasted fine aged wine prefers un-aged wine.

Old wine used to be new! It is new wine that has been allowed to mature. Once it has matured, it is recognised as of greater worth than the new with greater taste. It is so important that we mature in God - mature in anointing, gifting, relationship. Chasing the 'new' all the time does not allow the wine to mature. Chasing the latest idea or way of doing things does not necessarily mean we are growing up in God. Good new wine needs time to mature. We need to allow the revelations of His truth that come newly to us to take root and grow - to grow in the disciplines of the Holy Spirit, maturing in prayer life, bible study, worship, fellowship, witness, serving. We need to mature in the exercise of spiritual gifts, knowing wisdom, and the anointing of God. Yes, we must embrace fully every new thing that God reveals to us in the most positive way and grow in that truth into the fullest good of it.

In Acts we have the outpouring on the day of Pentecost. The new wine had arrived!

What happened?

The disciples were said to be drunk! This 'drunkenness' displayed itself in the manifestations of the Spirit, which resulted in three thousand being saved through the preaching of the good news. Peter received revelation: "This is what Joel spoke about."

The wine was flowing. Quickly this wine matured into a vintage not seen since in any great measure.

Acts 2:42-47

They devoted themselves to the apostles teaching and to the fellowship, to the breaking of bread and to prayer. Everyone was filled with awe and many wonders and signs were done by the apostles. All the believers were together and had everything in common. Selling their possessions and goods they gave to everyone as he had need. Every day they continued to meet together in the temple courts. They broke bread in their homes and ate together with glad and sincere hearts, praising God and enjoying the favour of all the people. And the Lord added to their number daily those who were being saved.

What a change from the men who went back to their fishing, who doubted the resurrection.

What had happened?

They had drunk of the new wine and it had compelled them into the marketplace of the world to be forever different. These were those who, after drinking the new wine of the Spirit, "turned the world upside down". Let us welcome the renewing work of grace in order that this wineskin which is 'me' may be fitted to receive every drop of this life-changing, world-transforming wine of the Spirit.

I believe that when we know the life of Christ in the Spirit like this, our use of alcohol will never be a problem. I believe, passionately, that the answer to abuse is not non-use but correct use. The 'not yet Christian' who sees us living in abstinence is more likely to have his ideas compounded that we are all boring, legalistic kill-joys. If he sees us enjoying a drink, but not to excess, not falling down and making an exhibition of ourselves, he may well ask, "How come you...?" and a door is opened into his heart and mind. Don't misunderstand me. I am not advocating drinking as a means of evangelism. I am suggesting that enjoying the good things of life under the control of the Spirit witnesses to Jesus. I also believe that we should not live our lives in reaction to the corrupt mind of a society which has turned from God. We are to live in obedience to the Holy Spirit. We keep our eyes fixed on Jesus, walking in the light in Him.

This is not something I would go to war over. It is my personal perspective. I will not scorn a brother who abstains from alcohol. The kingdom of God is not meat and drink, so I am to live in loving fellowship with every other lover and follower of Jesus. I pray the words of Ezekiel will be increasingly revealed to us all.

Ezek.36:26-27

I will give you a new heart (an undivided heart) and put a new spirit in you; I will remove from you your heart of stone and give you a heart of flesh. And I will put My Spirit in you and move you to follow My decrees and be careful to keep My laws.

Bread

How often do we pray, "Give us this day our daily bread"? These words have been a prayer from childhood for so many. It is good to look to God as our source. Everything comes from Him. Every good and perfect gift comes down from heaven to us by the grace of God. We can look to our employment to fill our freezers. We can use our credit cards to buy things we cannot afford. We can trust in these things, or we can look to Father God. Economies fluctuate, industries collapse, and credit catches up with us. There is truly no security in these things. But...

Matt.6:26-27

Look at the birds of the air, they do not sow or reap or store away in barns, and yet your heavenly Father feeds them. Are you not much more valuable than they?

Ps.104:21, 27-28

The lions roar for their prey and seek their food from God... these all look to You to give them their food at the proper time. When You give it to them, they gather it up. When You open Your hand they are satisfied with good things.

How much more positively can God assure us of His faithful promises to care for us?

Yes, we thank Him for our employment - it is His means of providing for our needs. When that is not there for us, His faithfulness does not diminish. He has committed Himself to care for us, and by one means or another that will happen. Our faith is in His faithfulness, His word of truth, His nature and character.

To praise Him today in our plenty is good. To praise Him tomorrow in our need is a greater declaration of trust and adoration, for He changes not. He is the same in our lack as in our plenty. It is good to ask, "Give us today what we need to live." It is good to express trust in Him and His provision. He is our security. It is right to come before Him with our every need. He never tires of us; He is never fed up with our requests. He loves every time we turn to Him. He wants to show us His love, pleasure and grace. The more we come to Him, the less we rely on ourselves. He loves our company. He delights in the times we spend deliberately with Him.

Of course there is more to this than the bread on our table. Jesus said:

Jn.6:48
I am the Bread of Life.

Thus praying, "Give us today our daily bread," takes us to a different place. "Father, I am thankful for the bread on my table. I can never tire of blessing you for this faithfulness, but please give me today all I can take of Jesus. Open the eyes of my heart to know the reality of the fullness of Jesus in me." More than my daily bread, I need Jesus. A full stomach with an empty fearful heart is no joy, no satisfaction. I recall a hymn from my childhood: "I need Thee every hour, most gracious Lord... I need Thee, Oh, I need Thee".

Yes, we are saved, filled with Holy Spirit, enjoying fellowship with the Father. But there is also a place of chosen fellowship, of chosen intimacy, of chosen time together and sharing. In a marriage, from the moment of becoming married we fully belong to each other. We share a precious, fulfilling love, but without that love being fed with increasing expressions of love, of time together, of intimacy, that relationship can quickly grow cold and stale. This often leads to adulterous affairs. That destroys all the beautiful things that *that* love created. If we don't pursue precious times with Jesus, feeding on His love, giving Him love in obedience, this relationship can also grow stale and cold. Idolatry inevitably follows; compromise taints the purity of His love. We lose that joy, dynamism of union, peace, satisfaction. We have to keep alive our relationship by allowing His love to foster love in us and then to respond to that love with joyful submission to His will.

When you pray, "Give us today our daily bread," ask for greater revelation of Jesus. Seek to feed on Him more and more. Yesterday's portion was sufficient for yesterday. Today I long for the fresh bread of today's fellowship and grace. Yesterday's 'manna' has gone putrid. His mercies are new every morning.

Today is an unknown. Yes, we have our routine and expectations, but it is an unknown adventure as we step out in Jesus into what is ahead. There are appointments in the diary, but what they will open up we know not.

How many lives will be changed dramatically by what happens today?

We don't know what is ahead of us. There are thousands of people across the world who, as this day broke, had no idea that when they sleep tonight they will be sleeping with Jesus in their life for the very first time. They got arrested by Love during their regular daily routine and will never be the same again. Yes, today is an unknown, so how much do we need to know the presence and guidance of Love for every step of this day's journey?

I am reminded of Chloe Glassborough, who has told this story often in meetings. She had such a desire to know Jesus in everything of her days that she deliberately invited Him to accompany her through every step of the day. One day, as she alighted from a train journey and was walking along the platform, she suddenly realised something. "Oh! I've left Jesus on the train!" She was still learning about positively knowing Jesus at all times. She had left the train without asking Him to come with her into the next part of her day. It is a humorous tale, yet carries such a profound truth. Jesus promised to be with us all the time.

Why should we not experience the reality of that?

The Psalmist declares that during the desert wanderings, God "satisfied them with the bread of heaven" (Ps.105:40) - bread from heaven for those on earth.

Isaiah asks:

Is.55:2a

Why spend money on what is not bread and your labour on what does not satisfy?

How much of your life is taken up with what does not satisfy, with what is fleeting?

In the West we have become a people driven by consumerism. Shopping malls have become our cathedrals. How often we hear the sort of comment which suggests a new pair of shoes or handbag is the answer to feeling down, neglected, rejected or depressed! How shallow and false this is! Next pay day we are back for more to bolster up our flagging egos.

God says:

Is.55:2b

Listen to Me, and eat what is good and your soul will delight in the richest of fare.

Jesus is the Bread of Life! He makes this boast:

Jn.6:35

He who comes to Me will never go hungry.

Those feelings that are only momentarily satisfied with the new shoes or shirt are fully satisfied in Jesus. He truly is the good news for all people everywhere. He is the good news to you and me. Heidi Baker tells of an experience she had while praying for the children of Mozambique among whom she gives God's love away.

> *There were thousands coming toward me and I was crying, 'No Lord, there are too many.' Then I had a dramatic, clear vision of Jesus. I was with Him and thousands and thousands of children surrounded us. I saw His shining face and His intense, burning eyes of love. I also saw His body. It was bruised and broken, and His side was pierced. He said, 'Look into My eyes. You give them something to eat.' Then he took a piece of His broken body and handed it to me. It became bread in my*

hands and I began to give it to the children. It multiplied in my hands. Then again the Lord said, 'Look into My eyes. You give them something to drink.' He gave me a cup of blood and water, which flowed from His side. I knew it was a cup of bitterness and joy. I drank it and then began to give it to the children to drink. The cup did not go dry. By this point I was crying uncontrollably. I was completely undone by His fiery eyes of love. I realised what it had cost Him to provide such spiritual and physical food for us all. The Lord spoke to my heart and said, 'There will always be enough because I died.' [7]

The rest, as they say, is history as the Bakers have marched across Mozambique bringing the love of Jesus into the lives of countless thousands of men, women and children. They have established several thousand churches. They also speak to thousands every year at conferences. There will always be enough. Such is the magnitude of the Bread of Life.

Whatever is happening in your life, when you ask for daily bread, you are tapping into the inexhaustible, more-than-enough answer to whatever the challenge or desire is. God cannot fail.

Jesus promises us:

Matt.7:7-11

Ask and it will be given you; seek and you will find; knock and the door will be opened to you. For everyone who asks, receives; he who seeks, finds; and to him who knocks the door will be opened. Which of you, if your son asks for bread, will give him a stone? ... if you then, though you are evil, know how to give good gifts to your children, how much more will your Father in heaven give good gifts to those who ask Him?

How much more?

This is where our confidence resides. It is the Father who is so much more than the best of the rest, the best that can ever be. Take your eyes off your circumstances. Look to your source. Look to the God who has promised to supply your every need out of His abundant eternal

[7] There Is Always Enough, Baker. Pg. 49-50, Sovereign World, 2003. ISBN 185240 2873)

riches. It is all about choosing to take hold of Him and "eat the flesh of the Son of Man" (Jn.6:53).

In faith we take into ourselves the life-giving life, power and words of Jesus. Then they become our daily diet. Mentally or emotionally agreeing with the words of Jesus does not make them living in us. It is only in 'eating' them that we are nourished, strengthened and built up. O taste and see that the Lord is good!

I am not talking about transubstantiation. I am encouraging a daily moment-by-moment absorbing of the living bread of the banqueting house. See the banner of love which flutters like a dove above your head, constantly embracing and enveloping you. Jesus is the Bread of Life who always satisfies. Daniel refused the king's food. It violated his relationship with God. He and his friends were healthier than those who had eaten the best of Babylon. God's provision always outstrips the best of the rest. We can trust Him. There are many things in this life which are good, healthy, pleasant, and enjoyable. God has given all things richly to enjoy. Let us keep Him as number one in our affections. Even in the desert places there is bread from heaven. In the upper room, Jesus took some bread, gave thanks, broke it and gave it to His friends. "This is My body given for you; do this in remembrance of Me."

He had already spoken about being the bread of life. The disciples had seen the five thousand fed. Now he leaves them a remembrance event.

"Eat bread together to remember Me. Remind yourselves that I am your 'food'. I am all you could ever need, because I am giving My life for you. Remember me. Remember what My death means for you and all people. Keep this memorial meal because every time you eat bread together you are proclaiming My death until I come back."

In proclaiming His death, we are witnessing to the truth of the gospel in our lives. We are demonstrating that in Him and with Him we are one. We are one body together in Him, one bride, one building and one people, united in Christ in perfect union.

Paul asks:

1 Cor.10:16-17

Is not the bread that we break a participation in the body of Christ? Because there is one loaf, we, who are many are one body, for we all partake of the one loaf.

The moment we are born again, we become one in and with Jesus. We are the "church which is His body". A body is united in itself and functions as a simple unit in cooperation with itself as every part responds to the directions given by the head. Christ is this head of His church. Thus the real unity of the Spirit in which we live is demonstrated every time we share bread together as a people from every tribe, tongue, nation, background, culture, social standing, male or female. We are all reconciled to God in Jesus and to one another through the power of the death and resurrection of Jesus. This 'impossible' unity is a unity in love. It proclaims the power of Jesus' blood to transform sinners to saints. He brings us into resurrection life as the fruit of His suffering, the new creation in Him in the presence of the Father. This is the glorious, enduring, joyful reality of the gospel and every piece of bread we share shouts it out.

What greater feast could there be than to sit together in the truth of His 'love banner' and share this most simple, yet most symbolic, powerful, liberating meal of bread. On the Emmaus Road two disciples - dispirited, hearts crushed, their hopes lying shattered at their feet - see Jesus as He breaks bread with them. Their faith is re-born, hope restored; hearts swell with faith. He is alive! And they rush to declare this greatest good news. Jesus reveals Himself to us as we eat of His life in broken bread. At this place of humility, surrender, and confession, He assures us of His presence and everlasting life. He speaks to our hearts that He is alive. He has triumphed; sin has been defeated, death conquered. A glorious present and a glorious future have been given us. All this as we hold a lump of bread between our fingers.

The early church grasped this. They saw its significance and relevance.

Acts.2:42-47

They devoted themselves to the apostles teaching and to the fellowship, to the breaking of bread and to prayer. Everyone was filled with awe, and many wonders and miraculous signs were done by the apostles. All the believers were together and had everything in common. Selling their possessions and goods, then gave to anyone as he had need. Every day they continued to meet together in the temple courts. They broke bread in their homes and ate together with glad and sincere hearts, praising God and enjoying the favour of all the people. And the Lord added to their number daily those who were being saved.

These disciples, at least three thousand of them, newly born into the church, devoted themselves to the breaking of bread. In their homes, together with glad hearts, they were all together sharing everything, not claiming anything as their own. They were one in heart and mind. Nobody among them was in need. This was the oneness between them. They laid down their lives for one another. They acknowledged that being God's family superseded every natural relationship and condition. Their Christian brothers and sisters became their primary family. As they daily broke bread they had to live in love and unity. They had to live in humility and service. They didn't wait only for collective times to share bread; as they met in each other's homes, they broke bread. There was no 'once a week', 'once a month', 'once a year' practice for them - no ritual here, no specially-trained, special person, licensed to officiate. This was normal everyday people sharing the joy of Jesus with each other. How far we have strayed from the simplicity and beauty of breaking bread together!

Where did our solemnity come from?

I read here in Acts about "glad and sincere hearts, praising God and enjoying favour". I look in vain, generally, to see and share the gladness and praise of the early church. We remember Jesus. We declare His death, the greatest event in history, which gave us everything of God we could contain, and we sit like mourners at a funeral. Jesus is alive! He is to be celebrated! Yes, He died the most horrendous death, suffering more than any other man possibly could embrace, taking into Himself all the sin of all humanity for all time, bearing our sins in His body on the tree. "I'll never know how much it cost to see my sin upon that cross," as the song writer has said, but morosely concentrating on His sufferings does not enhance the resurrection life He has given us. His death gave us life; His poverty, our riches. We don't live at the cross, but *from* the cross, *out of* the cross. Resurrection new life follows Calvary. Lives laid down in joyful surrender are the only response to His sacrifice.

The full worship in every aspect of life is our only choice as we look at that cross and see Love bleeding for us. I have never sat down with my mother and said how sad it makes me to think of what she went through to bring me into this life. I am appalled when I think of the reality of the sin I inherited. Yet that gave Jesus the opportunity to show me how much He loves me by dying for me. I don't believe He wants us to mournfully dwell on what He went through but to joyfully embrace everything of it. That was the goal of His suffering, pleasing the Father in bringing many children as a gift to Him to have them given back as a reward of that suffering. Breaking bread is a testimony to life and the result of suffering and death.

Let's see much more joy in our times of breaking bread. I am sure we will touch something deeper in the Spirit when we do. As the first believers in Jerusalem lived like this, they developed a counter culture. They served each other, sold things to prevent need amongst them, enjoyed such real togetherness and lived in praise and sincerity.

The result?

New believers added daily to their number - evangelism made easy! As Jesus said:

Jn.13:35
This is how people will know you are My disciples, [through the way] you love one another.

Jesus said, "This is My body..." The apostle wrote that God has appointed this same Jesus to be head over everything for the church which is His body (Eph. 1:22-23). We humans have become so intimately joined to Jesus in the Spirit that we have become part of Him. Every time we break bread and share wine, we are also recognising the living body of Christ which is you and me. Our love to Jesus is also love to each other. Our worship of Jesus is also an honouring of one another. Sharing communion, I believe, is a statement that my life is fully surrendered to Jesus, and fully laid down in service to you. It is never an individual activity; it is always a community one. It is not meant to be something private and isolated. We are His body on earth; we give ourselves to each other in love and service. We share Him as we share ourselves with each other.

We need to learn to dwell together in this, to make time for one another, time to share, listen, encourage, pray, rejoice, weep, to be to each other the human expression of Jesus. In this way we proclaim in a very visible way His death, His resurrection, His indwelling Holy Spirit.

Communion is so much more than just taking a piece of bread and a sip of wine. It bears testimony to everything of the Christian faith and gospel. It exposes the heart, the depth of love in us, the essence of who we are in Christ and our devotion to Him, as well as our devotion to one another. It emphasises the covenant of grace since we witness to the return of Jesus. It assures us of Father's faithfulness, of His constant acceptance of us, of our position as sons and daughters of the most High God.

Oil

After the Last Supper, Jesus went to Gethsemene, just outside the city walls of Jerusalem. It was on the east side, across the Kidron valley, at the foot of (or on) the Mount of Olives. It was here that He prayed before the horrors of His sufferings broke upon Him.

He began to be deeply distressed and troubled.

"My soul is overwhelmed with sorrow to the point of death," He said.

Three times it records that He sought His Father in prayer. Mark uses that beautiful, intimate word 'Abba'. Luke adds the strengthening of the angels and shows how deeply Jesus suffered this anguish when His sweat was as blood-drops falling to the ground. This says something of the appalling anguish and pressure on the pure spirit of Jesus, the only sinless one, as He faced the prospect of being "made sin for us", so that in Him we could become the righteousness of God.

Gal.3:13, NKJV

*Christ redeemed us from the curse of the law by becoming a curse for us
(for it is written: "Cursed is everyone who is hung on a tree.")*

Truly He was led like a lamb to the slaughter. Yet, He affirms that
He lays down His life of His own choosing; no one has taken it from Him
(Jn.10:14-18). Still, the appalling horror of what is before Him crushes His
heart and flesh.

The writer of Hebrews says that during the days of Jesus' life on
earth, he offered up prayers and petitions with loud cries and tears to the
One who could save Him from death (Heb.5:7). Jesus desired to be free
from the cup of death, yet even more desired to fulfil the will of the
Father.

Isa.53:10

*[It was the] Lord's will to crush Him and cause Him to suffer, and
though the Lord makes His life a guilt offering, He will see His offspring
and prolong His days, and the will of the Lord will prosper in His hand.*

It was always Jesus' greatest desire to fulfil the will of the Father,
whatever it entailed.

Jn.12:27-28

*Now My heart is troubled, and what shall I say, 'Father save Me from
this hour?' No, it was for this very reason I came to this hour. Father,
glorify Your name.*

Now, He is faced with this unimaginable choice. As Hebrews says:

Heb.10:9-10

*Then He said, "Here I am, I have come to do Your will." ... and by that
will, we have been made holy through the sacrifice of the body of Jesus
Christ once for all.*

How fitting that this took place at Gethsemene. The name means
'oil press'. Jesus went to this favourite frequented place to face the greatest

ordeal of His will. This is the place where the olives were crushed to force the oil from them. This is the place where he chooses to put Himself through the same crushing challenge. Jesus often chose to visit Gethsemane - every time surrounded by the symbolism of what awaited Him, yet it became somewhere precious, somewhere He could relate to. Jesus was crushed, that through His obedience he would become the first of a new creation, bringing many sons to glory. In His embracing of the will of the Father, there is a joy which gilds the horror. It was for the joy set before Him that He endured the cross.

Romans remind us that God's will is good, pleasing and perfect (ch.12:2). As we go through the process of yielding our will to the Father's in any given situation, we find that to be true.

Oil is mentioned more than two hundred times in scripture. Apart from Esther 2:12 where it speaks of the oil of myrrh, every other reference is to olive oil.

It was a common basic ingredient in food in the OT world. One example is found in the story of Elijah and the widow of Zarapheth. She was extremely poor, having only a handful of flour and a little oil, just enough for one last cake before she and her son lay down to die. Her obedience to Elijah's request brought an abundance of flour and oil which sustained her through the famine. Elisha was used to bring a similar miracle to a widow as her supply of oil was multiplied.

Moses testifies of God's faithfulness in His provision for the Israelites:

Deut.32:13

He nourished him with honey from the rock and with oil from the flinty crag.

The manna which sustained the people throughout their desert wanderings had a taste like olive oil (Numbers 11:7-9). This testimony is further borne out by Ezekiel in his lyrical description of Israel as an unfaithful lover.

Ezek.16:13-19

Your food was fine flour, honey and olive oil... the food I provided for you, the fine flour, olive oil and honey I gave you to eat...

Yes, oil was such a basic, vital, daily ingredient in life. Jesus used it as He told the story of the five wise and five foolish virgins. Their oil was for light. This shows us something of the diversity of use that oil was put to. Oil was so vital to life that it is difficult to see how life could go on without it. It punctuates the sacrificial system at every turn. There are numerous references to its use in the daily offerings as well as right across the whole system - in the meal offering, the consecration of the priests and Levites, the purification of lepers, the special offering at the erection of the Tabernacle. Everywhere you look, you see oil as an integral ingredient in the worship life of the nation. It is used in the special, sacred anointing oil as described in Exodus 30:22-33. It is right in there in the preparation of the most sacred oil in the land. The oil is for exclusive use, not an everyday commodity, nor is it to be imitated. It is holy, set apart for its particular purposes which are to set apart everything it anoints for sacred service. It is used to anoint the instruments of worship. It is used to sanctify the Tent of Meeting and the Ark as well as the altars. Once anointed, these utensils and objects are set apart for sacred purposes.

The priests were appointed with this sacred oil, setting Aaron and his sons apart to holy service as God's exclusive servants in the ministry of the Tabernacle. Anointing has always been a major use of oil.

Psalm 23:5b

You anoint my head with oil, my cup overflows.

David was anointed by Samuel to be king. This practice is found frequently in scripture. The use of oil to infer God's favour and setting apart for royal service is seen as part of the culture. It was a sign of kingly office. In fact David is anointed three times in this regard: the initial setting apart by Samuel, then as king of Judah, and finally as king of all Israel and Judah. This anointing is recognised as the individual entering into the office for which they have been anointed; Joash and Jehoahaz are similarly anointed for kingly office.

So, anointing with oil sets apart those who are anointed.

Ps.105:15

Do not touch My anointed, do My prophets no harm.

Isaiah speaks of the Lord's servant in the same way:

Isa.61:1

The Spirit of the Sovereign Lord is upon me because the Lord has anointed me to preach good news to the poor...

Jesus embraced these words for Himself in the synagogue at Nazareth:

Lk.4:17-21

Today this scripture is fulfilled in your hearing.

There is a very real sense in which everyone chosen by God is called 'anointed'. It is said of Cyrus whom God chose and used to return the exiles to Jerusalem. God calls him "My shepherd", and he is referred to as "My anointed" (44:28, 45:1). Habakkuk has the same idea when he says:

Hab.3:13

You came out to deliver Your people, to save Your anointed one.

Being chosen by God carries an anointing. It symbolises belonging to God as His exclusive possession and servant. This is seen also in NT teaching when Paul states:

2 Cor.2:21-22

Now it is God who makes both us and you stand firm in Christ. He anointed us, set His seal of ownership on us, and put His Spirit in our hearts as a deposit, guaranteeing what is to come.

John says:

1 Jn.2:20

You have an anointing from the Holy One and all of you know the truth.

1 Jn.2:27

The anointing you received from Him remains in you.

Jesus is declared to be the 'Anointed One' (Acts.4:26). Everyone is anointed when they belong to God. Oil is also used as remedy for sickness. We are familiar with the story of the Samaritan who used oil along with wine to heal the wounds of the unfortunate who was mugged on the road to Jericho (Lk.10:30-35). Mark tells us that when the twelve were sent out to preach and demonstrate the good news they "anointed many sick people with oil and healed them" (Mk.6:13). James leaves instructions for the whole church:

James.5:14-15

Is anyone of you sick? He should call the elders of the church to pray over him and anoint him with oil in the name of the Lord. And the prayer offered in faith will make the sick man person well.

The incident with the Samaritan shows the natural healing properties of oil and wine. We can see the spiritual significance of the blood of Jesus and the anointing of the Spirit. In the natural, pouring oil on someone's head is not going to heal a wound in their body. We have to recognise the spiritual implications of anointing with oil for healing. It is accompanied with prayer. It is the prayer of faith, coupled with the anointing of the Holy Spirit (the oil) which brings healing. It does not say that prayer without oil is ineffective, but we have modelled for us in the scriptures a process whereby we may press through and touch the reality of the kingdom of heaven and see it come on earth. There is no 'magic' power in the oil. To allow it to take on fetish charms or powers of its own is wrong and dangerous. It is used by God to achieve His purposes.

Oil was used extensively in the burning of the lamps in the Tabernacle and Temple. The Lord said to Moses:

Lev.24:1-4

Command the Israelites to bring you clear oil of pressed olives for the light so that the lamps may be kept burning continuously outside the curtain of the Testimony in the Tent of Meeting. Aaron is to tend the lamps before the Lord from evening to morning, continuously. This is to be a lasting ordinance for the generations to come. The lamps on the pure gold lamp stand before the Lord must be tended continually.

The book of Ezra gives us some idea of the quantity of oil needed for this task. It mentions "100 baths of olive oil" (Ezra.7:22). This is approximately six hundred gallons. It was to be pure virgin olive oil which was used in the temple lamps. No 'second hand chip shop' oil here, only pure, never-before-used oil to represent the purity of God and of worship which He seeks. It is also true that pure olive oil burns without leaving any soot - no residue, nothing to make dirty or to be cleaned up afterwards. Everything was to be burned. This oil is used up rapidly. It is not slow-burning oil. The lamps were to be tended and replenished daily. Remember how the manna was also to be picked up and used daily. Father God tells us that His mercies are new every morning. Oil for the lamps is freshly presented daily. Our life in God happens day by day. Today's grace is for today. Worship we offer today is for today. Worship becomes meaningless if we adopt an attitude which says, "I worshiped You yesterday; it doesn't matter if I don't worship today." Or, "I don't need to today." Worship is the love of God in us oozing out toward Him in gratitude and wonder. We choose to allow His love to ooze out because we can't really do anything else when we consider who He is and all that He has done.

Oil was extensively used for cosmetic purposes. It was used as a soothing balm for the heat of the sun, as is well attested in ancient writings. Jesus alludes to its daily social use when He admonishes the Pharisee who invited Him to dinner yet failed to anoint Him with oil. He also tells the people when fasting to continue using oil so that the fast remains a secret offering before God (Lk.7:46, Matt.6:17). This oil is used to make the face shine (Ps.104:15). We shine with the radiance of Jesus as the Holy Spirit is poured out upon us in fresh daily anointing, which leads us deeper into Jesus. As we gaze upon Him, so we become like Him. Truly those who look to Him are radiant (Ps.34:5). Their faces are never covered with shame. The Hebrew words used here imply being made light and bright.

I am reminded of Paul's words to the believers in Philippi that they "shine like stars in the universe" as they live righteously before God (Phil.2:15). He is echoing Jesus' words when He said the righteous would shine as the sun in the kingdom of the Father (Matt.13:43).

There is much to be gained and enjoyed in welcoming, embracing and walking in Holy Spirit anointing. Not only do the faces of the faithful shine, but in Jesus we see the joy which comes from this anointing.

Lk.10:21

Jesus full of joy through the Holy Spirit...

Heb.1:9

Therefore God, Your God, has set You above Your companions by anointing You with the oil of joy.

Jesus, embracing the words of Isaiah in the synagogue, includes you and me, all believers, in those who will know this oil of gladness, or joy, instead of mourning, praise for despair (Isa.61:1-3, Lk.4:16-21).

The life He has given us is a life of joy and gladness, praise, comfort, beauty. This is the Jesus who knew He was to die for the sins of all humanity. It is a hard truth for us to enter into, but Jesus, in His crushing as in an olive press, knew deep joy in His Spirit in His obedience to the perfect will of the Father. We shy away from the unwelcomed, the unpleasant, the painful. Everything in us has an aversion to that which hurts our bodies, minds, emotions, spirit and heart.

Yet, what is it James says?

James.1:2

Consider it pure joy whenever you face trials of many kinds.

How contrary to the natural this is! His words endorse the truth that in everything God is working for good for those who love Him. Ultimately, everything we go through in life is leading us into Jesus and His perfection. To choose faith in the face of the most indescribable horrors of this life is what the Spirit of God in us desires us to embrace.

Paul, who knew suffering above what most people will, declared that the kingdom of God is righteousness, peace and joy in the Holy Spirit

(Rom.14:17). Peter confirms that this joy is characteristic of the Christian inheritance and lifestyle.

1 Pet.1:8
Though you have not seen Him, you love Him, and even though you do not see Him now, you believe in Him and are filled with an inexpressible and glorious joy.

Jesus expects joy to characterise our lives. He gave His words to the disciples that...

Jn.15:11
...my joy may be in you, and that your joy may be complete.

It is all through the anointing of the Holy Spirit that Jesus' words become real to us:

Jn.15:12
Love each other as I have loved you.

This love, which can only come from the Lord and be lived out in the Spirit, brings our joy to completion, to fullness and overflow! I believe there is a real lack of joy in the experience of so many Christians. It is not dependant on our circumstances. It comes through His truth taking root in us and the Holy Spirit having free flow in, upon and through us. It is what the kingdom of God consists of. If you are a true lover and follower of Jesus, you live in a kingdom of joy. We need to rediscover the reality of Holy Spirit joy. It was for the "joy set before Him" that Jesus endured the cross, scorning its shame, and sat down at the right hand of the throne of God (Heb.12:2).

Joy has a quality of supreme knowing the goodness of God which surpasses and overwhelms the circumstances and situations of life, so that we "count it pure joy" to go through whatever comes in the purpose of Father for us in conforming us to the likeness of Jesus in the reality and experience of resurrection life.

The burial of the dead sees another use of oil. At the meal at Bethany where Jesus was a guest of Simon the leper, a woman entered, pushed through the crowd and fell at Jesus' feet. She broke open a flask of very expensive perfume - oil of spikenard from India, and greatly prized. She poured it on Jesus, anointing Him with its sweet perfume. The whole house was filled with the fragrance. Such extravagance! Jesus stilled the anger of some by stating that she had anointed His body ahead of burial (Mk.14:3-9).

After His crucifixion we see how His body is anointed with oils. On the day of resurrection, His women friends came with "prepared spices and fragrant oils" to anoint His body afresh. This oil was more than the average oily perfumes used at burials. This has so much greater significance. This death was for the salvation of the whole world. This man was not just any man. This was God incarnate, the pure, sinless Lamb of God. This anointing foretold the greatest event in human history: "Christ, the Anointed One" giving up His life in sacrificial atonement for me, for you, for all, knowing the joy set before Him of receiving a name, the name above every name, at which every knee would bow, and every tongue confess He is Lord, to the Father's glory - oil for burial, so beautifully played out in that Jewish home in the hands of a woman.

Now, what does all this mean for us?

I have stated throughout that the banqueting table is ever before us, always within hands' reach. The banner declaring love is always unfurled, declaring the father's heart toward us. The Holy Spirit is the indwelling Lord, revealing the father, leading into truth, pointing to and glorifying the Son.

Oil throughout the scriptures is a symbol of the Spirit of God. In this way he is our food. We 'ingest' Jesus, our daily bread, through the ministry of the Spirit. He opens up the wonders of Jesus that we may embrace all we can and feed on Him moment by moment. We cannot live without Him.

He gives light to our understanding and the direction of our daily living. He reveals the truth of scripture and the heart of the Father that we may walk aright in the light of truth; also in the light of a pure heart as we choose, through Him, to willingly yield to God's will. It is in the Spirit that we worship. Worship, I believe, is the offering of all of life, 24/7. Worship is who I am. As Jesus recognised that He could do nothing of Himself, so we need to acknowledge that only in the Spirit can we offer an acceptable sacrifice of praise, a life of utter devotion to the Father. Such are the worshippers the Father is looking for (Jn.4:23). Driving the car, playing with the children, cleaning the home, busy at work, making love with one's spouse, watching TV, enjoying the company of friends; all this, as well as specific spiritual activities such as prayer, bible study, meeting together - all is worship.

This comes into reality as we recognise and embrace the truth of sacred anointing in the Spirit to belong exclusively to God. It is the anointing of, and in, the Holy Spirit which is the seal of God's ownership. We are now a kingdom of priests - kings and priests in the kingdom of God, a chosen people, a holy nation, a people belonging to God (1 Pet.2:9). We are not our own; we are bought with a price (1 Cor.6:19-20). As such we are aliens in this world. We are those who belong to a different kingdom, a different culture, a different way of living. We are to be marked out as His disciples through our love for one another. The way we live is to be in the light, that God may be glorified through our good works.

We are to be those who do not love this world's systems, thinking, cultures and attitudes. To love this world is to make ourselves enemies of God. This in no way means we are to cut ourselves off from society, but to so live in contrast to it as to be seen to be different - to live in such a way that the difference is noted and the difference brings glory to God. We have been set apart as God's exclusive property. This means He can do just what He wants with us. We have handed over ownership and control to Him.

- Can we complain at His dealings with us?
- On what basis?

We are no longer our own. We have been bought with such a price. We know that he is Father, full of love, compassion, mercy and grace. We know He rejoices over us with singing. Or as the original Hebrew dramatically says, he leaps up and down, twirling round in joy over us (Zeph.3:17). We know His plans for us are to prosper us, to give us hope and a future, never to harm us. We also know that in everything He is always working good toward us (Jer.29:11, Rom.8:28).

In this confidence we can submit ourselves to His loving, gracious dealings, knowing that these present trials are slight in comparison to the glory set before us.

Set apart for His glory we can know the Holy Spirit as God's power for healing in our bodies, minds, emotions and spirits. Through Him the blood of Jesus is applied for our healing so we may declare:

1 Pet.2:24

By His stripes we are healed.

The Psalmist put it this way:

Ps.103:1-3

Praise the Lord, O my soul, all my inmost being praise His holy name. Praise the Lord O my soul and forget not all His benefits; who forgives all your sins and heals all your diseases.

I declare this as truth, as one who has nursed a very severely mentally handicapped daughter for over thirty years. I declare it as one whose wife, at the time of writing, daily struggles with the challenges of MS. I declare it as one who himself is still afflicted with irritating conditions in his body, which have a negative and limiting effect on how he is able to live. I declare God's word to be true irrespective of any situation in which I find myself. I declare as one who has witnessed many healing miracles in other people, one who has healed others in Jesus' name, while still living in the situations just mentioned. I have prayed with many and not seen any tangible change. All that said, I will declare as long as God gives me breath that "by His stripes we are healed".

This subject is far too complex for a few paragraphs here, and Christian bookshops have shelves filled with books about healing. I believe in God as our healer, in this life as well as the next. I believe it because He tells us in the Bible that it is so. I believe it because I see it in His nature and character as revealed in scripture, as well as in what I have seen in my own life. I believe it because I see it constantly in the ministry of Jesus who showed us what the Kingdom of God looks like. I believe He is happy for us to come to Him with our needs for healing as the multitudes did to Jesus.

His banner of love and banquet provision is ever before us. His grace is sufficient, more than sufficient, in truth, for every need we have - even when we don't see the healing we so desperately look for. I believe it and declare it because God says it is so. Standing in faith brings us His pleasure and gives Him pleasure. His pleasure is a light in the gloom that often seems to surround our days. Standing in faith causes us to be as light, or as Paul puts it:

Phil.2:14-16

Do everything without complaining or arguing, so that you may become blameless and pure, children of God without fault in a crooked and deprived generation in which you shine like stars in the universe as you hold out the word of life.

It is only in the Spirit that the beauty of the character of Jesus is seen in us. Our appearance and demeanour show the grace of His beauty. Such beauty cannot be purchased at a cosmetic counter. The oil of the Spirit will cause us to shine with the joy and graciousness of Jesus. It won't happen through knowledge or disciplines. It won't happen by effort. It will only happen as we choose to yield to the Holy Spirit and let Him lead us into more of knowing Jesus. This is God's cosmetic work on and in us.

I have already stated that I believe there is a real lack of joy in our Christian communities.

Are we too held in our culture? Are we too concerned about how others may see us? Or of appearing superficial? Are we afraid of actually living a victorious, fulfilling life in Jesus?

I have heard so many testimonies over the years which suggest that once one has become a follower of Jesus, all the fun goes out of life! Joy is not only what the kingdom of God consists of; it is also fruit of the Spirit. This tells us that joy is the natural outcome of being joined to Jesus in the vine, as John points out. It just happens as we are living in the Spirit. So, I suggest where we have a lack of joy, we have a blockage which is stopping the flow of Christ-life into us. I am not talking of walking around with a silly grin on your face all day. I am speaking of that consciousness that whatever is happening we are secure in the love of Father God, that ultimately He will fulfil His purposes in our life and we will reign with Him forever. This is a deep-seated anchor in our souls, something solid that undergirds everything else, just like the everlasting arms which forever hold us close in His bosom. We don't have to freak out when things go wrong, when challenges seem overwhelming. We have a joy which rises above what Paul calls "our light and momentary trouble" (2 Cor.4:17).

Our reading through what he experienced in following Jesus places these words into a very real context. Jesus knew the joy of doing the Father's will even though it led Him to the cross - joy, the life of living in the Spirit of God. For every experience we have of God, for every time of euphoric mountaintop wonder, for every moment of deep intimate worship, when we draw near to kiss His feet, there is always more.

Everything of God is beyond measure, inexhaustible. We can never overindulge in the myriad of delights which are ours in Christ - an unfurled banner ever declaring love, a never empty table furnished with every delight, every wonderful gift of grace, furnished with deeply nourishing sweetmeats of the treasures of His heart.

All is presented for our enjoyment, enriching, transforming, restoring and conforming to the likeness of the whole beauty which is beyond description - Jesus. The realisation that we have been crucified with Christ and that 'I' am now dead is the opening to the riches of the banqueting house. In every situation, in every circumstance, every trial and every success, through every tear and all the laughter, choosing to live dead to self and alive in Christ makes us the radiance of His glory and the exact representation of His being. This is the goal of the Father's heart: you and I being completely whole, at one with Him, taking on the divine nature, being His glory on earth and the marvel of the angels in heaven. The table provides everything to accomplish this goal, everything for us to live in the good of being His children.

When we share the beautiful love feast of bread and wine, I believe we represent and demonstrate all I have written in this book. Christ is *All and In All*. He is the *Sufficiency of All Things*. He is the *Only Answer* to all the deepest yearnings of the human heart! All is *about Him, through Him and for Him*!

He is the *Banner of Love* constantly unfurled over us! He is the *Banqueting House* and *Table* from whom we receive absolutely everything needful and desired! He is the *Lover Above All Lovers* who consumes the heart with *His Pure and Perfect Love*. He is the *Bridegroom* who brings His spotless Bride into the fullness of who He is - *all* symbolised in a *Glass of Wine* and a *Loaf of Bread*...

From the Publisher

Titles in the **Timeless Teaching** series:

1.	What do These Stones Mean?	*Joyce Sibthorpe*
2.	Motherhood	*Diana Jeffery*
3.	A Walk with Wisdom	*Luke Jeffery*
4.	Four Mountains to Climb Before you Die	*Mark Jeffery*
5.	Can You Hear God?	*Joyce Sibthorpe*
6.	The Christian Guide to Jobs and Careers	*Charles Humphries*
7.	Alive for a Purpose	*Kofi Owusu*
8.	Equipped to Heal	*Dr. Ian Andrews*
9.	Diagnosing Ills and Ailments of Relationships	*Adedeji Majekodunmi*
10.	Pursuing Holiness	*Sam Masamba*
11.	Single without Sinking	*Shade Vaughan*
12.	Redeeming a Nation	*Philip Quenby*
13.	Calling Things that Are Not as though They Were	*Barb Witt*
14.	Jesus: Uncovering the Facts	*Michael Shaw*
15.	Feasting on the Father	*William L Smith*

Books available from the publisher:
www.onwardsandupwards.org